HANDLING SIN:
CONFESSION IN THE MIDDLE AGES

This volume prints papers delivered at a conference held by the University of York's Centre for Medieval Studies at King's Manor, York, on March 9, 1996, under the title 'Confession in Medieval Culture and Society', together with a further invited paper by Rob Meens and an edition by Michael Haren. It concludes with the second of the Annual Quodlibet Lectures on medieval theology, which was delivered by John Baldwin on June 5, 1996.

Following Peter Biller's introduction which sketches medieval confession and its modern study, Rob Meens re-examines the frequency and character of early medieval penance, in the light of the general debate among modern scholars, including Alexander Murray, about the gap between the Carolingian ideal of penance and what was realised in penitential practice. Here Alexander Murray himself takes further his use of *exempla* to listen in on thirteenth-century confession, concentrating on the confessor acting in obedience to the 1215 canon *Omnis utriusque sexus* as counsellor to troubled persons. Jacqueline Murray develops further our knowledge of medieval sexuality in her sharp delineation of the males who wrote *summae* and manuals for confessors, the ways in which these males' texts constructed woman as sexual, and the broader significance of this in medieval ideas of sexuality and gender. Lesley Smith continues her work towards the rehabilitation of William of Auvergne, bishop of Paris, by examining his remarkable writing on penance. She suggests literate lay people as William's intended audience and reminds us that he was an intimate of the king of France, Louis IX, and the confessor of Louis' mother. In his two contributions Michael Haren investigates the particular world of the author of the mid fourteenth century *Memoriale presbiterorum*. He traces and discusses the growth of estates interrogatories, and goes some way to remedying the lack of editions of England's fourteenth-century pastoral manuals by editing and translating a large proportion of the *Memoriale*'s interrogatories. Then Peter Biller investigates the use of confessors' manuals for demographic history, suggesting that the manuals' shifting concerns reflected chronological and regional patterns in people's attempts to avoid offspring.

In his 'Quodlibet Lecture' John Baldwin traces the appearance in French romances of the themes of a penitent's contrition of the heart and confession of the mouth, the priest's job in listening to the penitent and enquiring after circumstances, and the priest's application of the spiritual medicine of *conseil* and penance. This analysis brilliantly juxtaposes vernacular literature and the writings of Paris theologians, and examines the movement of the views of these theologians into the literature and thought-world of French nobles.

YORK MEDIEVAL PRESS

York Medieval Press is published by the University of York's Centre for Medieval Studies in association with Boydell and Brewer Ltd. Our objective is the promotion of innovative scholarship and fresh criticism on medieval culture. We have a special commitment to interdisciplinary study, in line with the Centre's belief that the future of Medieval Studies lies in those areas in which its major constituent disciplines at once inform and challenge each other.

All inquiries of an editorial kind, including suggestions for monographs and essay collections, should be addressed to: The Secretary, University of York, Centre for Medieval Studies, The King's Manor, York YO1 2EP (E-mail: LAH1@unix.york.ac.uk).

Previous publication in York Studies in Medieval Theology:

Medieval Theology and the Natural Body, ed. Peter Biller and A. J. Minnis (1997)

Previous publications of The Centre for Medieval Studies:

Latin and Vernacular: Studies in Late-Medieval Texts and Manuscripts, ed. A. J. Minnis (1989) [Proceedings of the 1987 York Manuscripts Conference]

Regionalism in Late-Medieval Manuscripts and Texts: Essays celebrating the publication of 'A Linguistic Atlas of Late Mediaeval English', ed. Felicity Riddy (1991) [Proceedings of the 1989 York Manuscripts Conference]

Late-Medieval Religious Texts and their Transmission: Essays in Honour of A. I. Doyle, ed. A. J. Minnis (1994) [Proceedings of the 1991 York Manuscripts Conference]

York Studies in Medieval Theology II

HANDLING SIN:
CONFESSION
IN THE MIDDLE AGES

Edited by
PETER BILLER and A. J. MINNIS

THE UNIVERSITY *of York*

YORK MEDIEVAL PRESS

First published 1998

Transferred to digital printing

A York Medieval Press publication
in association with The Boydell Press
an imprint of Boydell & Brewer Ltd
PO Box 9, Woodbridge, Suffolk IP12 3DF, UK
and of Boydell & Brewer Inc.
668 Mt Hope Avenue, Rochester, NY 14620, USA
website: www.boydellandbrewer.com
and with the
Centre for Medieval Studies, University of York

ISBN 978-0-9529734-1-6

A CiP catalogue record for this book is available
from the British Library

This publication is printed on acid-free paper

CONTENTS

ABBREVIATIONS

AESC	*Annales. Économies. Sociétés. Civilisations* (Paris, 1929–)
AMN	Analecta Mediaevalia Namurcensia (Louvain, etc., 1950–)
L'Aveu	*L'Aveu. Antiquité et moyen-âge. Actes de la table ronde organisée par l'École française de Rome avec le concours du CNRS et de l'Université de Trieste, Rome 28–30 Mars 1984*, Collection de l'École Française de Rome 88 (Rome, 1986)
Avril, 'Pouvoirs du prêtre'	J. Avril, 'À propos du "proprius sacerdos": Quelques reflexions sur les pouvoirs du prêtre de paroisse', in *Proceedings of the Fifth International Congress of Medieval Canon Law. Salamanca, 21–25 September 1976* (Rome, 1980), pp. 471–6
Avril, 'Pratique'	J. Avril, 'Remarques sur un aspect de la vie paroissale: La pratique de la confession et de la communion du Xe au XIVe siècle', in *L'encadrement religieux des fidèles au Moyen-Age et jusqu'au Concile de Trente. La paroisse – le clergé – la pastorale – la dévotion. Actes du 109e congrès national des sociétés savantes, Dijon, 1984. Section d'histoire médiévale et de philologie* I (Paris 1985), pp. 345–63
Baldwin, *Peter the Chanter*	J. W. Baldwin, *Masters, Princes and Merchants. The Social Views of Peter the Chanter & His Circle*, 2 vols. (Princeton, N.J., 1970)
Bériou, 'Latran'	N. Bériou, 'Autour de Latran IV (1215): La Naissance de la confession moderne et sa diffusion', *Pratiques de la confession*, pp. 73–92
Biller, 'Pastoral geography'	P. Biller, 'Marriage Patterns and Women's Lives: A Sketch of a Pastoral Geography', in *Woman is a Worthy Wight. Women in English Society c.1200–1500*, ed. P. J. P. Goldberg (Stroud, 1992), pp. 60–107
Bossy, 'Arithmetic'	J. Bossy, 'Moral Arithmetic: Seven Sins into Ten Commandments', in *Conscience and Casuistry in Early Modern Europe*, ed. E. Leites (Cambridge, 1988), pp. 214–34
Bossy, 'Social'	J. Bossy, 'The Social History of Confession in the Age of Reformation', *TRHS* 5th ser. 25 (1975), 21–38
Boyle, '*Oculus*'	L. E. Boyle, 'The *Oculus sacerdotis* and some other works of William of Pagula', *TRHS* 5th ser. 5

	(1955), 81–110, reprinted in Boyle, *Pastoral Care*, IV
Boyle, *Pastoral Care*	L. E. Boyle, *Pastoral Care, Clerical Education and Canon Law, 1200–1400* (London, 1981) [Reprinted articles, designated by Roman numeral (indicating order of appearance) and title, and separately paginated]
Boyle, 'Study'	L. E. Boyle, 'A Study of the Works attributed to William of Pagula, with special reference to the *Oculus sacerdotis* and *Summa summarum*' (unpublished D.Phil. thesis, Oxford, 1956)
Boyle, 'Summae confessorum'	L. E. Boyle, '*Summae confessorum*', in *Les genres littéraires dans les sources théologiques et philosophiques médiévales. Définition, critique et exploitation*, Université Catholique de Louvain, Publications de l'Institut d'Études Médiévales ser. 2/5 (Louvain, 1982), pp. 227–37
Caesar, *Dialogus*	Caesar of Heisterbach, *Dialogus miraculorum*, ed. J. Strange, 2 vols. (Cologne, Bonn, Brussels, 1851)
CaF	Cahiers de Fanjeaux (Toulouse, 1966–)
CCCM	Corpus Christianorum, Continuatio Medievalis (Turnhout, 1966–)
CCSL	Corpus Christianorum, Series Latina (Turnhout, 1953–)
CH	*Church History* (New York, Chicago, 1932–)
Chanter, *Summa*	Peter the Chanter, *Summa de sacramentis et animae consiliis*, I, II, III(1), III(2a), III(2b), ed. J.-A. Dugauquier, AMN 4, 7, 11, 16, 21 (1954–67)
Chanter, *Verbum*	Peter the Chanter, *Verbum abbreviatum* (short version), *PL* 205, 1–554
Chobham, *Summa*	Thomas of Chobham, *Summa confessorum*, ed. F. Broomfield, AMN 25 (1968)
COD	*Conciliorum oecumenicorum decreta*, ed. J. Alberigo et al. (Basle, Freiburg, Rome, 1972)
Councils & Synods	*Councils and Synods with other Documents Relating to the English Church II. AD 1205–1313*, ed. F. M. Powicke and C. R. Cheney, 2 vols. (Oxford, 1964)
Courson, *Summa*, ed. Kennedy	V. L. Kennedy, 'Robert Courson on Penance', *MS* 7 (1945), 291–336
Cum ad sacerdotem	*Summa 'Cum ad sacerdotem'*, ed. J. Goering and P. J. Payer, in 'The "*Summa Penitentie fratrum predicatorum*": A Thirteenth-Century Confessional Formulary', *MS* 55 (1993), 1–50
DA	*Deutsches Archiv für die Erforschung des Mittelalters*
de Jong, 'Boetedoening'	M. de Jong, 'De boetedoening van Iso's ouders. Kanttekeningen bij een verhaal uit Ekkehards *Casus Sancti Galli*', in *Ad Fontes: opstellen aangeboden aan prof. dr. C. van de Kieft ter gelegenheid van zijn afscheid als hoogleraar aan de*

	Universiteit van Amsterdam (Amsterdam, 1984), pp. 111–139
de Jong, 'Public'	M. de Jong, 'What was Public about Public Penance? *Paenitentia publica* and Justice in the Carolingian World', in *La Giustizia nell'alto medioevo II (secoli IX–XI)*, SSSpoleto 44 (1997) pp. 863–902
EHR	*English Historical Review* (London, 1886–)
Faire croire	*Faire croire. Modalités de la diffusion et de la réception des messages religieux du XIIe au XVe siècle*, Collection de l'école française de Rome 51 (Rome, 1981)
Flamborough, *Liber*	Robert of Flamborough, *Liber poenitentialis*, ed. J. J. F. Firth, Studies and Texts 18 (Toronto, 1971)
Friedberg	*Corpus iuris canonici*, ed. E. Friedberg, 2 vols. (Leipzig, 1879)
FS	*Franciscan Studies* (New York, 1924–)
Grosseteste, *De modo*	J. Goering and F. A. C. Mantello, 'The Early Penitential Writings of Robert Grosseteste', *Recherches de théologie ancienne et médiévale* 54 (1987), 52–112 (text on pp. 80–111)
Grosseteste, *Deus est*	S. Wenzel, 'Robert Grosseteste's Treatise on Confession, "*Deus est*" ', *FS* 30 (1970), 218–93
Haren, 'Social Ideas'	M. J. Haren, 'Social Ideas in the Pastoral Literature of Fourteenth-Century England', in *Religious Belief and Ecclesiastical Careers in Late-Medieval England. Proceedings of the Conference held at Strawberry Hill, Easter 1989*, ed. C. Harper-Bill, Studies in the History of Medieval Religion 3 (Woodbridge, 1991), pp. 43–57
Haren, 'A Study'	M. J. Haren, 'A Study of the *Memoriale Presbiterorum*, A Fourteenth-Century Confessional Manual for Parish Priests', 2 vols. (unpublished D.Phil. thesis, Oxford, 1975)
JEH	*Journal of Ecclesiastical History* (London, 1950–)
JMRS	*Journal of Medieval and Renaissance Studies* (1971–)
JTS	*Journal of Theological Studies* (London, 1899–)
Kerff, 'Libri'	F. Kerff, 'Libri paenitentiales und kirchliche Strafgerichtsbarkeit bis zum Decretum Gratiani. Ein Diskussionsvorschlag', *ZRG KAbt* 75 (1989), 23–57
Kerff, 'Mittelalterliche'	F. Kerff, 'Mittelalterliche Quellen und mittelalterliche Wirklichkeit. Zu den Konsequenzen einer jüngst erschienenen Edition für unser Bild kirchlicher Reformbemühungen', *Rheinische Vierteljahrsblätter* 51 (1987), 275–86
Kottje, *Bußbücher*	R. Kottje, *Die Bußbücher Halitgars von Cambrai und des Hrabanus Maurus. Ihre Überlieferung und ihre Quellen*, Beiträge zur Geschichte und

	Quellenkunde des Mittelalters 8 (Berlin, New York, 1980)
Kottje, 'Bußpraxis'	R. Kottje, 'Bußpraxis und Bußritus', *Segni e riti nella chiesa altomedievale occidentale*, SSSpoleto 33 (1987), pp. 369–95
Mahadevan, 'Überlieferung'	L. Mahadevan, 'Überlieferung und Verbreitung des Bussbuchs "Capitula Iudiciorum" ', *ZRG KAbt* 72 (1986), 17–75
Mansi	J. D. Mansi, *Sacrorum conciliorum nova et amplissima collectio*, 31 vols. (Florence, Venice, 1757–98)
Meens, 'Fragmente'	R. Meens, 'Fragmente der Capitula episcoporum Ruotgers von Trier und des Scarapsus Pirminii', *DA* 48 (1992), 167–74
Meens, 'Kanonisches Recht'	R. Meens, 'Kanonisches Recht in Salzburg am Ende des 8. Jahrhunderts. Das Zeugnis des *Paenitentiale Vindobonense B*', *ZRG KAbt* 82 (1996), 13–34
Meens, *Tripartite*	R. Meens, *Het tripartite boeteboek. Overlevering en betekenis van vroegmiddeleeuwse biechtvoorschriften (met editie en vertaling van vier tripartita)* (Hilversum, 1994)
Meens, 'Volkscultuur'	R. Meens, 'Religieuze volkscultuur in de elfde eeuw. Een handboek voor de zielzorg als spiegel van religieus gedrag', *Volkskundig Bulletin* 21 (1995), 1–26
MGH Cap. Ep.	*Monumenta Germaniae Historica, Capitula Episcoporum* (Hannover, 1984–)
Michaud-Quantin, *Sommes*	P. Michaud-Quantin, *Sommes de casuistique et manuels de confession au moyen âge (XII–XVI siècles)*, AMN 13 (1962)
MS	*Mediaeval Studies* (Toronto, 1939–)
Murray, 'Confession'	A. Murray, 'Confession as a Historical Source in the Thirteenth Century', in *The Writing of History in the Middle Ages*, ed. R. H. C. Davis and J. M. Wallace-Hadrill (Oxford, 1981), pp. 275–322
Murray, '1215'	A. Murray, 'Confession before 1215', *TRHS* 6th ser. 3 (1993), 51–81
Pantin, *English Church*	W. A. Pantin, *The English Church in the Fourteenth Century* (Cambridge, 1955)
Peter, *Summa*	Peter of Poitiers, [*Summa de confessione*] *Compilatio praesens*, ed. J. Longère, CCCM 51 (1980)
PL	*Patrologia Latina*, ed. J.-P. Migne, 217 vols. (Paris, 1841–64)
Poschmann, *Kirchenbuße*	B. Poschmann, *Die abendländische Kirchenbuße im frühen Mittelalter*, Breslauer Studien zur historischen Theologie 16 (Breslau, 1930)
Pratiques de la confession	Groupe de la Bussière [= M. Sot *et al.*], *Pratiques de*

	la confession, des Pères du désert à Vatican II. *Quinze études d'histoire* (Paris, 1983)
Rusconi, 'Prédication'	'De la prédication à la confession: transmission et contrôle de comportement au XIIIe siècle', *Faire croire*, pp. 75–85
SCH	Studies in Church History (London, 1964–)
Serlo, *Summa*	J. Goering, 'The *Summa de penitentia of Magister Serlo*', *MS* 38 (1976), 1–53
SOPMA	T. Kaeppeli and E. Panella, *Scriptores Ordinis Praedicatorum medii aevi*, 4 vols. (Rome, 1970–93)
SSSpoleto	Settimane di Studio sull'alto medioveo, 1952– , Centro Italiano di studi sull alto medioevo (Spoleto, 1954–)
Stavensby, *Tractatus*	Alexander of Stavensby, *Quidam tractatus de confessionibus*, in *Councils & Synods*, I, 220–26
Tentler, *Sin*	T. N. Tentler, *Sin and Confession on the Eve of the Reformation* (Princeton, N.J., 1977)
Thacker, 'Monks'	A. Thacker, 'Monks, Preaching and Pastoral Care in Early Anglo-Saxon England', in *Pastoral Care Before the Parish*, ed. J. Blair and R. Sharpe (Leicester, London etc., 1992), pp. 137–70
Trois sommes	*Trois sommes de pénitence de la première moitié du XIIIe siècle*, ed. J. P. Renard, 2 vols., Lex Spiritus Vitae 6 (Louvain, 1989)
TRHS	*Transactions of the Royal Historical Society* (London, 1871–)
ZKG	*Zeitschrift für Kirchengeschichte* (Gotha and Stuttgart, 1878–)
ZRG *Kabt*	*Zeitschrift der Savigny-Stiftung für Rechtsgeschichte* (Weimar) *Kanonistische Abteilung* (1911–)

Handling Sin:
Confession in the Middle Ages

Confession in the Middle Ages: Introduction

Peter Biller

This volume prints papers delivered at a conference held by the University of York's Centre for Medieval Studies at King's Manor, York, on March 9, 1996, under the title 'Confession in Medieval Culture and Society', together with a further invited paper by Rob Meens and an edition by Michael Haren. It concludes with the second of the Annual Quodlibet Lectures on medieval theology, which was delivered by John Baldwin on June 5, 1996.

1. Confession in the Rhineland around 1200

Several thirteenth-century collections of *exempla* provide us with windows through which we seem to glimpse individual and ordinary lay women and women, engaged in all sorts of acts of piety: we seem to see something of their 'lived religion'.[1] One is Thomas of Cantimpré's *Bonum universale de apibus*,[2] which includes many stories about people in northern France and the Low countries, and another is Stephen of Bourbon's *Tractatus de variis materiis predicabilibus*,[3] whose stories are set in central and southern France. Let us begin with a story which comes from a third collection, the *Dialogue of Miracles*, which was written some time around 1223 by Caesar, a monk in the Rhineland Cistercian monastery of Heisterbach.[4]

---

[1] The phrase is borrowed from the title of a volume edited by Jean Delumeau, *Religion vécue du peuple chrétien*, 2 vols. (Toulouse, 1979). The use here and later in this chapter of the phrases 'lived religion' and 'lived confession' is intended to evoke the historiographical revolution which has brought *lay* people and their piety, devotion and 'religious' *experience* into the foreground. On this revolution, which was pioneered by French historians in the 1970s, see P. Biller, 'Popular Religion in the Middle Ages', in *Companion to Historiography*, ed. M. Bentley (London, 1997), pp. 221–46 (pp. 225–7).

[2] On the work, see *SOPMA* IV, 352–5, and for its confession stories see Murray, 'Confession'.

[3] On the work, see *SOPMA* III, 354–5, and on the use of its stories for the devotion and piety of the laity, including confession, see P. Biller, 'The Common Woman in the Western Church in the Thirteenth and Early Fourteenth Centuries', in *Women in the Church*, ed. W. Sheils and D. Wood, SCH 27 (1990), 127–57 (at pp. 135–6, n. 39), and Biller, 'Popular Religion', pp. 232–3.

[4] On *exempla* dealing with confession, see J. Berlioz, 'Les ordalies dans les *exempla* de la

The *Dialogue* has a pedagogic form, with a conversation between a monk who teaches, illustrating his lessons with stories, and a novice who listens, putting further questions and asking for more. Confession crops up throughout the *Dialogue*'s twelve parts, but of course mainly in part three which is devoted to confession. This contains fifty-three chapters in which points about confession are put over, and illustrated by anecdotes. The sources of these stories? Most come from monks living at Heisterbach itself or other houses, but some come from ecclesiastical dignitaries of Cologne, Soest and Bonn, parish priests, and, in one instance, a parishioner – people who 'told me this' (or some similar formula), as Caesar claimed in virtually every story. Although the majority of stories concern the sins and confessions of the religious, a substantial minority feature lay people confessing in these Rhineland cities and villages, in the decade or so before Caesar wrote. Hermann, the dean of Bonn, was the source of several stories, three from his time as parish priest at St Martin's in Cologne. Here is one of them.

When Hermann, the dean in Bonn, was parish priest at St Martin's in Cologne, a certain woman came to him at the time of Lent to confess her sins. On her knees in front of him, she began to enumerate whatever good thing she remembered doing. Along with the Gospel Pharisee, she said, 'Lord, I am in the habit of fasting on bread and water during the year on so many Fridays, giving my alms, going to church', and much more in this vein. The parish priest said to her, 'Lady, for what purpose have you come? Surely you don't want to receive penance for these works? Why aren't you telling [me] your sins?' She replied, 'In myself I'm conscious of nothing wrong.' The parish priest said, 'What is your job?' The woman replied, 'I usually sell iron.' To this he said, 'Are you sometimes in the habit of mixing smaller pieces of iron in larger bundles, in order to sell the whole lot together in this way?' To her saying 'I do' he replied, 'Look, this is a mortal sin, because it's fraud.' And he added, 'Are you sometimes in the habit of lying, swearing, perjuring, cursing your rivals, and being jealous of those who sell more?' She replied, 'In such things I often overstep the mark.' The parish priest said, 'And all of these things are mortal sins, and unless you'll have done suitable penance, you'll go to hell at your leisure.' Frightened by his words, she admitted that she had sinned, and she learnt [from him] what she ought to confess in future. (Hermannus Decanus Bonnensis, quando plebanus fuit apud sanctum Martinum in Colonia, venit ad eum mulier quaedam tempore quadragesimali peccata sua confiteri. Flectens coram eo genua, quicquid se boni meminerat commisisse, coepit enumerare, et cum Pharisaeo evangelico iustificare se, dicens: Domine, tot sextis feriis soleo per annum in pane et aqua ieiunare, eleemosynas meas dare, ecclesiam

confession (XIIIe–XIVe siècles)', in *L'Aveu*, pp. 315–40 (p. 319 on Caesar of Heisterbach), and J. Berlioz and C. Ribaucourt, 'Images de la confession dans la prédication au début du XIVe siècle. L'exemple de *l'Alphabetum narrationum* d'Arnold de Liège', in *Pratiques de la confession*, pp. 95–115. For earlier use of Caesar's *exempla*, see Biller, 'Common Woman', pp. 133–7.

frequentare, et multa in hunc modum. Cui plebanus dixit: Ad quid, domina, venistis? Numquid pro istis operibus vultis suscipere poenitentiam? Quare non dicitis peccata vestra? Respondente illa: Nihil mihi conscius sum; ait plebanus: Cuius estis officii? Respondit mulier: Ferrum vendere soleo. Ad quod ille: Soletis aliquando minores ferri particulas in ligaturis maioribus intermiscere, ut sic totum simul vendatis? Dicente illa, soleo; respondit: Ecce hoc mortale peccatum est, quia dolum. Et adiecit: Soletis aliquando mentiri, iurare, periurare, aemulis vestris maledicere, aliis plus vendentibus invidere? Respondit illa, quia in talibus saepe excedo. Plebanus dixit: Et ista omnia peccata sunt mortalia, et nisi poenitentiam egeritis condignam, ocius ibitis in gehenna. Territa illa in verbis eius, peccasse se recognovit, et quid de cetero confiteri deberet, didicit.)⁵

Normally the *Dialogue's* stories about ordinary lay people start with Lent, and they often evoke a particular setting and an atmosphere of throng and bustle.

A certain priest was sitting in his Church during Lent, and hearing the confessions of those committed to his care [his parishioners], [and] some were coming and others were going. (Sacerdos quidam cum tempore quadragesimali in ecclesia sua sederet, et sibi commissorum confessiones audiret, aliis recedentibus atque aliis accedentibus.)⁶

In these Rhineland churches, over three hundred years before the confession box was invented,⁷ people can see each other while confession is going on.

At one time during Lent, while the aforesaid dean of Bonn [Herman] was sitting in St Martin's church, where he was parish priest, and hearing hearing the confession of some little old woman, he saw two of his parishioners sitting opposite him, some distance away, in the window-recesses, spending their time in chat. (Supradictus Decanus Bonnensis [Hermann], cum tempore quodam Quadragesimae sedens in ecclesia sancti Martini, in qua erat plebanus, audiret confessionem cuiusdam vetulae, vidit eminus contra se duos ex parochianos suis in fenestra sedere, et fabulis vacare.)⁸

The stories sometimes tell us by implication what is the norm when recounting the exception, an abuse. One was recounted to Caesar by a parish priest, and concerned his predecessor, who used to gather together all his parishioners during Lent and lead them in German in a general confession – he

---

5 Translated from Caesar, *Dialogus*, III.xlvi, I, 165.
6 *Dialogus*, III.xxvi, I, 143
7 On the invention of the confessional-box, see Bossy, 'Social', pp. 29–33, and J. A. Bossy, *Christianity in the West, 1400–1700* (Oxford, 1985), pp. 134–5.
8 Caesar, *Dialogus*, III.lii, I, 169.

did not hear individual confessions.[9] Another was told by a parishioner, about another parish priest in the province:

> When people came to him for confession during Lent he would say, 'Whatever penance was imposed on you by my predecessor, I impose the same on you now', and to others, 'This year do whatever [penance] I imposed on you last year.' (In Quadragesima venientibus sibi ad confessionem dicere consuevit: Qualis poenitentia iniuncta fuit vobis ab antecessore meo, talem vobis iniungo. Aliis dicbat: Quod vobis iniunxi anno praeterito, hoc et isto anno servetis.)[10]

These two underline the norm, one of individual confessions by parishioners during Lent and their parish priest's careful modulation of penance according to sin and sinner – where the sinner would be well-known to him, and sometimes also the sin. When Hermann looked across the Church at St Martin's to two of his parishioners, he knew he was looking at one who was a money-lender and another who was publicly known to be a murderer.[11] Hermann recounted how once a woman 'came during the Lenten period . . . confessing to me some quite tiny and everyday sins, but keeping totally quiet about [her] adultery (tempore . . . Quadragesimae venit . . . peccata quaedam minima ac quotidiana mihi confitens, adulteriumque omnino subticens)', though Hermann knew about the serious sin through someone else's confession.[12] Occasionally the women and men who confessed are identified; for example, two Cologne merchants, or (as already mentioned) a moneylender and a woman who sold iron. But usually the person is simply one among all the parishioners. They are all coming to confession during Lent, not just the pious, and their coming is a matter of custom and ingrained habit. The sexual sinner who came to Herman and confessed tiny sins 'came during Lent more out of custom than any contrition (magis ex consuetudine quam ex aliqua contritione)'. All the stories reflect something deeply ingrained and customary.

The last story cited here is set on a road between a nearby parish and the town of Soest. Two men from the parish are travelling together along the road to Soest, where they are going to market, and, when the baggage belonging to one of them falls into the mud, its owner starts to swear about his parish priest, who is responsible for all this hard work. A conversation starts. The man had been told he must pay his parish priest eighteen pence to say masses, after confessing to having sex during Lent. The other man had had a similar experience at the hands of the parish priest, Hegennaird, with one exception. When confessing he had admitted the opposite – *not* having sex with his wife during Lent. The dreadful Hegennaird had upbraided him:

9   *Dialogus*, III.xlv, I, 164.
10 *Dialogus*, III.xliv, I, 163.
11 *Dialogus*, III.lii, I, 169.
12 *Dialogus*, III.xxxi, I, 148.

'You have done very badly, keeping yourself from your wife for such a long time. She could have conceived a child with you, but with your continence you've shut off that possibility.' As is usual with simple people, the man was terrified. When he asked for advice about this crime, the confessor replied, 'You give me eighteen pence, and I'll placate God on your behalf with the same number of masses.' (Valde male fecisti, tempore tanto ab uxore tua te cohibendo. Prolem illa poterat de te concepisse. Territus homo, sicut mos est simplicibus, cum ab eo consilium quaerereret pro tali delicto, respondit confessor: Tu mihi dabis decem et octo denarios, et ego totidem missis Deum pro te placabo.)

After this roadside conversation, the two men went to Soest, and laid a complaint with the Dean and canons of St Patroclus; the great stir which this caused is the last we hear of this story.[13] While Caesar's conscious goal in telling this story, the abuse, may be of little general use to the historian, the casual assumptions of the story are. These assumptions are of a system, and a system which stretches far. Here, in this instance, confession is in a village, and it is stretching far into the lives of some 'simple' men and their wives, bringing under its purview intimate areas of their sexual relations with their wives, and stimulating everyday roadside conversation. Confession is part of, and penetrates deeply into, the lives of ordinary people.

This introduction does not investigate Caesar's shaping of his material, his construction of confession, and how the *Dialogue*'s audience read these *exempla*. It takes these stories, with deliberate simplicity, as a few rare colourful snapshots of the Church's penitential system at work: in one region of Latin Christendom, and at one time, the beginning of the thirteenth century. They constitute a prelude to the more panoramic view of the next section, which concentrates on the principal surviving textual traces of medieval confession: church legislation, and the many works, extant in enormous numbers of manuscripts, which told a priest how to hear confession and impose penance.

2. 1215 and Later: Legislation and Confessors' Literature

The annual confession practised at St Martin's in Cologne when Hermann was parish priest was prescribed for the whole of the church at the great fourth Lateran Council of 1215, in the canon *Omnis utriusque sexus*.[14] For the lay person confession was to be annual and to their own parish priest. The parish priest tending spiritual ills when hearing confession and imposing penance was compared to a physician tending wounds. He was required to enquire into circumstances of sin and sinner in order to provide right counsel and remedy;

13 *Dialogus*, III.xl, I, 160.
14 See the discussions of *Omnis utriusque sexus* by Bériou, 'Latran', and by Murray and Baldwin in chapters 3 and 9 below, pp. 63, 66, 67, 69, 81, 191, 198, 200–1, 202–4.

this part of the canon is quoted in chapter three below.[15] The analogy of the physician of the body was ancient. It had been applied to Christ by the early fathers of the Church,[16] and the image of doctor and medicine was commonplace in the early medieval penitentials.[17] The canon touches on several features of our Rhineland picture: on the crowds at annual Lenten confession, on enquiry after the 'job' of selling iron, which was one of the 'circumstances' of a sinner, and on Hermann's energetic attention to spiritual 'wounds'. And where the canon's general provisions do this we are reminded of one elementary point, that this great text, *Omnis utriusque sexus*, was not legislating in a vacuum. Rather it was making something uniform out of the norms and practices of various regions, and universalising this for the Church as a whole.[18]

Omnis utriusque sexus has a dense *pre*-history, on the one hand in these varying practices of different dioceses and regions of Latin Christendom, and on the other hand in twelfth-century intellectual developments in the schools of northern France. Theological attention had been paid, in particular by Peter Abelard and Peter Lombard, to the relative importance of various parts of penance; and an interior and subjective matter, inner contrition, had emerged as the act of primary importance.[19] Following this, in later twelfth-century Paris, a circle of reforming theologians had paid extraordinary attention to the 'circumstances' of sin and sinner, thereby intellectually preparing the ground for the penitential (and other) provisions of the fourth Lateran Council of 1215. To these we return below.

The later story: in the years shortly after 1215 the regional legislation of the provinces and dioceses of different parts of Latin Christendom dealt with confession, applying locally the new theology and the provisions of the Fourth Lateran Council; this process can be seen easily in the English and French legislation. Parish priests were required to keep copies of the synodal statutes of their diocese, and they were thus given some instruction through the statutes' succinct provisions about confession, which included the stipulations of *Omnis utriusque sexus* or in some cases similar provisions taken from Paris or

---

[15] See p. 66.

[16] See for example R. Arbesmann, 'The Concept of "Christus medicus" in St Augustine', *Traditio* 10 (1954), 1–28.

[17] J. T. McNeill, 'Medicine for Sin as Prescribed in the Penitentials', *Church History* 1 (1932), 14–26. Nicole Bériou discusses medicine as an analogy for penance in thirteenth-century theology in her 'La confession dans les écrits théologiques et pastoraux du XIIIe siècle: médication de l'âme ou démarche judiciaire?', in *L'Aveu*, pp. 261–82.

[18] Its *immediate* legislative roots were the statutes issued by Eudes de Sully for Paris and Stephen Langton for Canterbury; Bériou, 'Latran', p. 75; see the Paris statutes, nos. 26–38, in *Les statuts de Paris et le synodal de l'Ouest (XIIIe siècle)*, ed. O. Pontal (Paris, 1971), pp. 62–6, and the Canterbury Statutes, nos. 40–4, in *Councils & Synods*, I, 32.

[19] Baldwin, *Peter the Chanter*, I, 50.

Canterbury statutes.[20] In later synodal legislation, the points about confession became longer,[21] and soon, in some regions by the second quarter of the thirteenth century, an obvious further educational opportunity was being taken. Short instructional tracts on confession, intended for the ordinary parish priest, were being included in such statutes, and thus getting into the parish priest's hand via his copy of the statutes.[22] For a while the provisions for confession and penance specified in local legislation went on developing. For example, there would be increasing length and detail in their lists of those complex and grave sins which could not be handled by the parish priest but had to be remitted to the expert of the diocese, the episcopal penitentiary. In much of the Church, from Salisbury to Liège, and from Tournai to Würzburg, such local legislation had its heyday between the fourth Lateran Council and the 1320s or 1330s, by which time – in England, at least – it was beginning to tail off.[23]

Another category of texts worked side by side with such copies of legislation in supplying priests with instruction. These were monographic confessors' *summae* and manuals, in a line which can be taken to start with those written by Alain de Lille[24] around 1200, Robert of Flamborough (between 1208 and 1213),[25] and Peter of Poitiers[26] and Thomas of Chobham[27] around or just after 1216. (The vexed question of the degree of discontinuity between these and early penitential books is not discussed here.)[28] This genre was then widened and enriched in the following decades through the most fundamental pastoral development of the central Middle Ages, the rise of the mendicant Orders, in particular the Dominican, and their rapid spread through the cities and towns of Latin Christendom. The Rhineland, for

---

[20] See n. 18 above. Some later thirteenth-century legislation follows these more closely than the Lateran Council.

[21] See the comments on this development in Languedocian statutes by R. Foreville, 'Les statuts synodaux et le renouveau pastoral du XIIIe siècle dans le midi de la France', in *Le Credo, la morale et l'inquisition*, Cahiers de Fanjeaux 6 (Toulouse, 1971), pp. 119–50 (pp. 145–7).

[22] For example, in England, *Councils & Synods*, I, 220–6; France, Pontal, *Statuts de Paris*, pp. 190–226; see discussion of similar material in Spain in P. Linehan, *The Spanish Church in the Thirteenth Century* (Cambridge, 1971), pp. 71–7. On further measures ensuring these texts got through to the parish priest, see C. R. Cheney, *English Synodalia of the Thirteenth Century*, 2nd edn (revised edn, Oxford, 1968), pp. 42–3, and J. Goering and D. S. Taylor, 'The *Summulae* of Bishops Walter de Cantilupe (1240) and Peter Quinel (1287)', *Speculum* 67 (1992), 576–94 (pp. 577–9).

[23] Pantin, *English Church*, pp. 194–5; Cheney, *Synodalia*, p. 36.

[24] Michaud-Quantin, *Sommes*, pp. 16–19; Baldwin, *Peter the Chanter*, I, 43; Alain de Lille, *Liber poenitentialis*, ed. J. Longère, 2 vols., AMN 17–18 (1965).

[25] Michaud-Quantin, *Sommes*, pp. 21–4; Baldwin, *Peter the Chanter*, I, 32–3; ed. Flamborough, *Liber*.

[26] Baldwin, *Peter the Chanter*, I, 33–4; ed. Peter, *Summa*.

[27] Michaud-Quantin, *Sommes*, pp. 21–4; Baldwin, *Peter the Chanter*, I, 34–6; ed. Chobham, *Summa*.

[28] For an exposition of discontinuity, see Michaud-Quantin, *Sommes*, pp. 15–16.

example, was being taken over just before Caesar wrote his *Dialogue*. The first
Dominican house was set up in Cologne around 1220, while other cities
rapidly followed suit, acquiring their own houses: Trier by 1225, Worms in
1226, Koblenz by 1230, Soest in 1241,[29] and so on. Now, the professional
activity of the vast majority of the friars, the 'fratres communes' (common
brothers), was preaching and hearing confession.[30] They needed specialised
works of instruction. By around 1221 Paul of Hungary had produced the
earliest penitential work written by a Dominican for Dominicans.[31] From this
time on, works on confession by seculars were accompanied by an
ever-growing stream of works written by mendicants.

Among the seculars the genre was intertwined with the development of the
general priests' manual, which naturally always had a large section on
confession. Two of the most notable and widespread examples were written in
the early fourteenth century, in England William of Pagula's *Oculus
sacerdotis*,[32] and in Spain Guido of Monte Roterio's *Manipulus curatorum*.[33] So
ubiquitous that it is even named on a brass in a church in Buckinghamshire, the
Oculus could be said almost to have 'won a place for itself as a regular item of
church furniture'.[34] The further development of the instructional treatises for
priests and confessors has a history continuing into the sixteenth century,[35]
and one conjecture is that this specialist literature came to supersede the short
provisions or tracts of copies of synodal literature and to take a larger place[36]
on the bookshelf of the later medieval parish priest. A century after Caesar, not
only mendicants in Rhineland cities but also secular clergy would have been
using the works on confession written around 1300 by the Dominican John of
Freiburg,[37] one of which was adapted to local, German conditions.[38]

These works faced in one direction, towards their use by a parish priest or
friar, and towards the layperson, confessing sins in a church and talking with

---

29 A convenient table and map of expansion in the German province is provided in
    Albertus Magnus and the Sciences. Commemorative Essays 1980, ed. J. A. Weisheipl,
    Studies and Texts 49 (Toronto, 1990), pp. 48–51.
30 L. E. Boyle, 'Notes on the Education of the fratres communes in the Dominican Order
    in the Thirteenth Century', in Boyle, *Pastoral Care* VI.
31 Boyle, p. 252; Michaud-Quantin, *Sommes*, pp. 24–6.
32 Boyle, '*Oculus*'.
33 Written in 1333, it was printed in Albi *c.* 1475. See H. S. Otero, 'Guido de Monte
    Roterio y el "Manipulus curatorum" ', in *Proceedings of the Fifth International Congress
    of Medieval Canon Law* (Vatican, 1980), pp. 259–65. Otero states that there are over 180
    manuscripts extant. See also P. Michaud-Quantin, 'Gui de Montrocher', *Dictionnaire
    de Spiritualité* 6 (Paris, 1965), cols. 1303–4.
34 Boyle, '*Oculus*', p. 94.
35 See Michaud-Quantin, *Sommes*.
36 Earlier synodal legislation was not, however, displaced from the shelf, for copies
    continued to be made: Cheney, *English Synodalia*, p. 36.
37 Michaud-Quantin, *Sommes*, pp. 43–50; L. E. Boyle, 'The *Summa confessorum* of John of
    Freiburg and the Popularisation of the Moral Teaching of St Thomas and Some of his
    Contemporaries', in Boyle, *Pastoral Care* III.
38 See below, chapter 8, p.173.

the confessor. Their contents also point towards debate, writing and teaching in the schools: the law schools of Bologna from the time of Gratian (*c.* 1140) onwards; the theological schools of northern France, especially Paris; and from the 1220s the overlapping higher centres of study of the mendicant Orders. The writings of Paris academic theologians between the 1170s and the second decade of the thirteenth century show several of them, in particular Peter the Chanter and Robert of Courson, spending most of their time raising and investigating problematic questions of conscience.[39] Their discussions brought together earlier theological tradition, canon law in Gratian's *Decretum* and later canon law collections and commentaries from Bologna and elsewhere, and the contemporary world. These theologians were observing contemporary sins with great acuteness and a desire for reform which was to be achieved partly through legislation – some of their concerns were to be taken up in the Lateran Council of 1215. In modern language, they were intellectuals taking a reformist view of contemporary political, economic and social problems. Their cases – for they discussed particular cases, not grand themes – were large in number. They ranged, for example, from the way French nobles manipulated the Church's rules of prohibited degrees of marriage to secure easy divorce, to the dilemma of a royal servant (and later a Thomas More or Clive Ponting) when faced with the choice between right-doing and his duty of obedience to the king; and from complex devices which concealed the extension of credit, to rather simple methods of defrauding when selling something. Hermann's questioning of the woman in St Martin's in Cologne about her deceit when selling iron had been anticipated by Peter the Chanter in the theological schools of Paris, when he discussed the penance a parish priest should impose on a butcher who sold tainted meat, and 'how far the responsibility of the original seller extended in subsequent resales of defective goods'.[40]

Subsequently Paris theology saw a considerable swing towards the discussion of very abstract theology and philosophy, as Aristotle and the Arabs came to dominate. This fact (and nearly exclusive modern preoccupation with it) can overshadow the pastoral and penitential-case tradition, which continued, albeit now as a smaller part of the scene. William of Auxerre continued to raise matters of conscience.[41] The bachelor's hurdle from the 1220s onwards, 'reading' the *Four Books of the Sentences* of Peter Lombard, gave an opportunity at a late stage to ventilate pastoral matters, when the lecturer came in the fourth book to the sacraments of baptism, penance and marriage. And there was the quodlibet, the discussion of 'what-you-will', a genre which emerged in Paris around 1230, which achieved its classic form by

---

[39] The following recapitulates Baldwin, *Peter the Chanter.*
[40] Baldwin, *Peter the Chanter*, I, 265.
[41] Especially in the later part of the third book of his *Summa aurea*, ed. J. Ribailler, 5 vols. In 7 parts, Spicilegium Bonaventurianum, 16–20 (Grottaferrata, 1982–87), 18b; William is used in the penitential *Summula Conradi* of *c.* 1226–29, *Trois Sommes*, I, 71.

around 1250, and flourished up to the 1320s. In the (still mainly unprinted) manuscripts of quodlibets, the questions raised and answered were principally abstract. However, some dealt with ecclesiastical problems. Alongside these, a substantial minority tackled concrete moral problems (in which marriage and moneylending predominate).[42] The administration of confession and penance also featured, in questions which addressed such things as secrecy of confession, sins a penitent had forgotten, and confession to someone who was not one's parish priest.[43] Quodlibets reflected the interests of masters and audience, and here they were ventilating matters which bore directly on the future pastoral activities of the mendicant friars, priests, and prelates-to-be who were in the audience.

There was a direct flow outwards, from these academic moral theological debates into the works of instruction.[44] The first large example is the production of several works of instruction for the confessor in Paris in the late twelfth and early thirteenth centuries, including those (already noted) by Robert of Flamborough, Peter of Poitiers and Thomas of Chobham. These works included many reminiscences of the questions raised in Paris.[45] Thomas's treatise continued to spread Parisian moral theology, both through its massive diffusion (it is still extant in over 100 manuscripts)[46] and also via later works, such as William of Pagula's *Oculus sacerdotis*, which copied and adapted parts of it.[47] A second example lies in the concrete cases-of-conscience quodlibets of later thirteenth-century Paris, especially those of St Thomas Aquinas, which the German Dominican expert on confession, John of Freiburg, copied and adapted into his *Summa confessorum* in 1298. Paris moral theology was then further diffused, directly through the large numbers of copies of the *Summa confessorum* and indirectly through the various works which plundered it for their quotations of Paris theologians.[48]

I moved away from the scene of one confession in St Martin's in Cologne, to take a more general view of the Church's discussion, legislation and provision

---

42 On Paris quodlibets airing questions of trade and money, see now O. Langholm, *Economics in the Medieval Schools. Wealth, Exchange, Money and Usury according to the Paris Theological Tradition, 1200–1350*, Studien zur Geistesgeschichte des Mittelalters 29 (Leiden, New York and Cologne, 1992), pp. 249–98.

43 L. E. Boyle, 'The Quodlibets of St. Thomas and Pastoral Care', in Boyle, *Pastoral Care* II, pp. 242–51. The tracing of the theme is not encouraged by the indices of the standard list, P. Glorieux, *La littérature quodlibétique de 1260 à 1320*, 2 vols. (Paris, 1925–35), although they do provide useful entries for confession ('Confessio sacramentalis', 'Confessor', etc.), and concrete pastoral themes such as contract of sale ('Contractus venditionis'), lending and usury ('Mutuum', 'Usura'), marriage and related matters ('Matrimonium', 'Copula conjugalis', 'Parentes', 'Uxor', etc.), and professions, such as that of the physician ('Medicus'). The lists of questions have to be read through.

44 In addition to the following examples, see n. 41 above.

45 Baldwin, *Peter the Chanter*, I, 32–6.

46 Chobham, *Summa*, pp. lxxiv–lxxvi.

47 Boyle, 'Oculus', p. 86.

48 Boyle, 'The *Summa confessorum* of John of Freiburg'.

of instructional literature. Intense development in every area of confession and penance in the decades around 1200, the evolution of specialist texts and the system which they underpinned and articulated, and the establishment of something whose shape and outlines remain roughly similar for the rest of the Middle Ages: these dominate the panorama. I am now selecting just three particular themes for closer examination: first, one salient feature of the confession in St Martin's, the fact that the penitent was a woman; secondly, that Hermann asked her what her job was; and, thirdly, the competition which may have been provided, not only outside this Cologne church but outside the Church, by other penitential systems in the Rhineland.

3. The Penitent's Gender[49]

'Circumstances' of sin and penitent fill the thirteenth- and fourteenth-century works of instruction for the confessor. As regards the penitent, this was his instruction: 'enquire who the penitent is, what sort of job he has, and frame your question accordingly'. One 'circumstance' of the penitent was sex, and many of those confessing to the male who was a parish priest were like the person confessing to Hermann, female. How many? One mid thirteenth century German Franciscan was starkly clear about the differences between women's piety and men's. 'You women go more readily to church than men do, speak your prayers more readily than men, go to sermons more readily than men.'[50] Given this, we can conjecture that women may also have been readier to confess than men; certainly many appear in *exempla* about confession.

The two sorts of texts which we have been examining, *exempla* and instructional writings, present this theme of women confessing in different ways. The danger of confession becoming the occasion of sexual entanglement is reflected in warnings which are commonplace in the instructional literature: the priest was to avoid looking at the woman and to hear confession in a place where both can be seen. Even with modest and chaste confessors and penitents, the difference of gender could still make things awkward. It might induce considerable shame and embarrassment which went beyond, and were different from, the shame which the penitent appropriately felt about the sins she had committed. Raymond of Peñafort tackled this problem, writing in his *Summa de poenitentia* that, when a confessor was confronted with a woman penitent, 'he should persuade her not to be ashamed to confess, for she is

---

[49] The theme of female religious confessing their sins to abbesses is excluded from this discussion, which concentrates on the ordinary lay penitent.

[50] Quoted in Biller, 'Common Woman', p. 140, where the plausibility of this generalisation is discussed.

confessing not to a man but to God (suadeat ei quod non verecundetur confiteri, quia non homini confitetur, sed Deo)'.[51]

Much of a confessor's *summa* or manual would consist of interrogations under the seven deadly sins, the ten commandments, and, increasingly from the mid thirteenth century (as we shall see), interrogations according to rank or job. Usually the questions to be put to a penitent did not suggest that this penitent was or could be a woman, and interrogations according to estate or profession only occasionally envisaged a category of women. Here religious women could form a group for a special interrogatory; one example is a list of questions to be put in confession to an abbess.[52] When ordinary women did form a group for a special interrogatory, as they did in the *Memoriale presbiterorum*, they entered as 'married women, and also widows and other sexually exerienced women'.[53]

Ususually, then, in these interrogations about sin, a male penitent was either assumed or stood in for both sexes. I say 'assumed', because Latin, with only the occasional denotation of gender through *ipse/ipsa* or *ille/illa*, did not compel the author to indicate gender quite as often as the vernacular would have done. 'Ask the same question' of a woman may have been implied, but it was not usually spelled out.[54] On a wide range of sins, therefore, women had virtually no explicit presence in these works of instruction. On the other hand, a woman did become present in these texts when they specified questions to be put under 'Lechery' or the sixth commandment, where a woman entered as a man's temptress or partner in sexual sin. Silence on woman under most other sins only serves to emphasise these texts' confinement of women to sexual matters.[55] Caesar's *exemplum* showed the meeting of one confessor and one woman penitent. A male, seated and vested with authority, is haranguing a woman who is on her knees. So, *this* scene is gendered. But the man is also doing something else. He obeys the injunction to ask about one circumstance of the penitent, his 'job' (*officium*) – by writing 'his' I am trying to imitate in

---

51 Raymond of Peñafort, *Summa de poenitentia et matrimonio*, III.xxxiv.30 (Rome, 1603), p. 465b. On Raymond's work, see n. 68 below.

52 John of Freiburg, *Confessionale*, in Oxford, Bodleian Library, MS Laud Misc. 278, f. 360va: De abbatissa. De hiis inquirere poteris ab abbatissis (On the abbess. You will be able to enquire about these things from abbesses).

53 See chapter 7 below, p. 157. Women formed a group in Johannes de Deo's *Liber poenitentiarius* (Vatican, MS Vat. Reg. Lat. 177, fs. 1v and 7v), and brief questions were provided for women in Henry of Susa's *Summa aurea*, V, *De poenitentiis et remissionibus*, art. 50 (Venice, 1537), col. 1812, where the groups listed are secular princes, knights, burgesses and merchants, peasants and, finally, women. Women are together with men in the category of 'the married' in an interrogatory in John of Freiburg's *Confessionale*; see chapter 8 below, pp. 169 and 174.

54 See Haren's comment on the questions in the *Memoriale presbiterorum*, chapter 7 below, p. 145, n. 2 of the English translation.

55 See J. Murray, 'The Absent Penitent: The Cure of Women's Souls and Confessors' Manuals in Thirteenth-Century England', in *Women, the Book and the Godly*, ed. L. Smith and J. H. M. Taylor (Cambridge, 1995), pp. 13–25, and chapter 4 below.

English a manual's gender-slant – and the further specification of questions about a merchant's fraud in selling. He is following, therefore, what is only hinted at in the instructional text: 'ask these questions also of a woman'. So, he asks a woman about her job. She sells iron. So, he asks her about sins usually incurred in the selling of iron, including slipping smaller bits of iron into bundles which purport to contain larger pieces. Hermann was not just a puppet pulled by the strings of an instructional text, for he could interpret that text as he read it, seeing what it did not spell out, and he could also have supplemented the text from his own experience. As an educated and alert Rhinelander he could have used his knowledge of things in his world, which are now usually examined by economic and social historians – the jobs in which women were occupied in Rhineland cities and towns. Evidence from later medieval Cologne and other later medieval and early modern German cities suggests that urban women were engaged mainly in petty trading and second-hand retailing;[56] given that patterns of women's work changed very slowly, this is likely also to have been the picture in Cologne around 1200.

If we are shown here a perceptible gap between instructional manual and *exemplum*, we are also gently reminded of another difference, between on the one hand predominant focus on sexuality and gender in modern books and articles on medieval confession, and on the other hand the overriding preoccupations of the literature of medieval confession. Certainly, the surviving medieval evidence about confession contains a great deal on sexual sins, but *less* than there is after the penitential developments which occurred around 1400, some of which are associated with the work of Jean Gerson.[57] Before 1400 there was an overriding preoccupation with what affected one's neighbour, and therefore with such sins as stealing and lending money at interest, and with how restitution should be effected.[58] With sexual sins, there was perhaps more concern with sins that clearly affected others, such as adultery, with its effect on the stability of a marriage tie and the transmission of property to a legitimate heir, and less concern with self-affecting sins such as masturbation.[59]

---

[56] On women trading in metals in later medieval Cologne, see E. Ennen, *Frauen im Mittelalter* (Munich, 1985), p. 161. Earlier study of medieval women's urban work (and in particular in Cologne) concentrated on high status jobs, while more recent study of medieval cities and towns has emphasised women's domination of the areas mentioned here.

[57] I am here following the account of Gerson and the changes which begin around 1400, which is given by Bossy in his three discussions of confession: 'Social'; *Christianity in the West*, chapter 3, particularly pp. 48–9; 'Arithmetic', pp. 222–5.

[58] Bossy, 'Social', pp. 24–5.

[59] Bossy, 'Social', pp. 35–8; Bossy, *Christianity in the West*, pp. 37–8, 48.

4. The Penitent's Job

'What is your job?' 'I sell iron.' What was present textually in the works of
instruction for confessors, concern with the jobs followed by penitents, was
translated into the reality of dialogue with the penitent. 'You are a doctor, then.
Have you been negligent in administering medicine to your patients? Have
you overcharged?'[60]

From one point of view what we can see, in the confessional emphasis on
theft and restitution and on the ways in which people can harm others while
exercising their professions, is the pre-Gerson Church's preoccupation with
social peace. From another point of view what we can see, in the increasing
numbers of professions as well as ranks which came to be listed in confessors'
literature, and the increasingly detailed questions of the interrogatories which
were provided for each group, is a response to the proliferation of specialised
occupations and professions which accompanied the urban expansion of the
thirteenth century and later. And if one's first reaction to these lists of
questions is their negative character – they list *sins* – it takes only a moment's
reflection to see them in reverse, as providing developing professions with an
ethic.[61] 'Confessors' manuals . . . were one of the principal tools in the
formation of professional consciousness in medieval men from the thirteenth
century on', providing a 'justification for . . . new socioprofessional status'.[62]
When one fourteenth-century Dominican, Guy of Toulouse, made extracts on
matters concerning merchants from John of Freiburg's *Summa confessorum*, he
chose a title with echoes of rules for the religious, 'Rule of Merchants', *Regula
mercatorum*.[63]

> Many say and claim that they are experienced in the medicinal or
> surgical art, without ever having heard [= studied] it in the schools and
> come to understand it. And there are others who have heard it well, and
> are experienced in this art, but nevertheless act negligently when
> administering medicines to the ill. (Multi dicunt et pretendunt se peritos
> in arte medicinali vel cirurgicali, qui tamen in scolis illam artem
> nunquam audierunt vel intellexerunt. Et alii sunt qui bene audierunt et
> experti sunt in arte illa, negligenter tamen agunt in ministrando infirmis
> medicinas.)[64]

So begins the *Memoriale presbiterorum*'s account of penances to be
administered to doctors for various sorts of malpractice, other kinds of which

---

[60] See below and n. 64.
[61] J. Le Goff, 'Trades and Professions as Represented in Medieval Confessors'
Manuals', reprinted in his *Time, Work and Culture in the Middle Ages*, English
translation (Chicago and London, 1980), pp. 107–21.
[62] Le Goff, pp. 112 and 121.
[63] Michaud-Quantin, *Sommes*, p. 48; SOPMA II, 74–5.
[64] Cambridge, Corpus Christi College, MS 148, f. 68vb.

(such as overcharging) the work goes on to detail. When this list of sins committed by doctors is turned around it becomes a code of what a doctor should do: for example, administer medicines carefully. Such penitential codes supplemented the deontological provisions of learned medical texts, and their evolution can be seen as one aspect of the 'professionalising' of doctors in the fourteenth century.[65]

From yet another point of view, what we are looking at, in manuals' concern with the 'circumstances' of the sinner, i.e. her or his rank, estate or occupation,[66] is one of the roots of later medieval estates satire.[67] In Raymond of Peñafort's *Summa de poenitentia*, one section deals with 'How interrogations should be done (Qualiter faciendae sint interrogationes)'. After going through various categories of the religious and the clergy, noting typical sins about which the confessor should enquire, Raymond procedes to several categories of lay people.

> Item, with princes [ask] about [the mal-administration] of justice; with knights, [ask] about pillage; with merchants, and officials, [and those] practising the mechanical arts, [ask] about perjury, lying, theft, fraud, and suchlike; with burgesses and citizens generally, [ask] about usuries and securities; with peasants, [ask] about envy, theft – especially about tithes, first-fruits, dues and taxes. (Item, circa principes, de iustitia; circa milites, de rapina; circa mercatores necnon et officiales, [et] artes mechanicas exercentes, de periurio, mendacio, furto, dolo et similibus; circa burgenses et cives communiter, de usuris et pignoribus; circa rusticos, de invidia, furto, maxime circa decimas, primitias, tributa, et census.)[68]

Coming in a text which was both influential and early (it was written 1224–26), these brief words were both elementary and fundamental. In the mid thirteenth century works written by two Bolognese canonists, Johannes de Deo[69] and Henry of Susa (Hostiensis),[70] listed many more groups and many more questions to be put to each of them. Their treatises, in turn, influenced the elaborate interrogatories for various ranks, estates and professions which were provided in the Dominican John of Freiburg's *Confessionale* (written around

---

[65] See the medieval deontological articles reprinted in D. W. Amundsen, *Medicine, Society and Faith in the Ancient and Medieval Worlds* (Baltimore and London, 1996), in particular chapter 9, 'Casuistry and Professional Obligations: The Regulation of Physicians by the Court of Conscience in the Late Middle Ages'.

[66] For the following, see Haren, 'Social Ideas'.

[67] J. Mann, *Chaucer and Medieval Estates Satire. The Literature of Classes and the General Prologue to the Canterbury Tales* (Cambridge, 1973).

[68] Raymond, *Summa de poenitentia*, III.xxxiv.33, p. 467a–b; see Haren, 'Social Ideas', p. 46. On Raymond's work, see Michaud-Quantin, *Sommes*, pp. 34–42, and *SOPMA* III, 285.

[69] See Haren, 'Social Ideas', p. 47; Michaud-Quantin, pp. 26–7.

[70] See Haren, 'Social Ideas', pp. 47, 50–1, and chapters 6–7 below, pp. 110–11, 114–15, and 124.

1300 and one of the most popular of all medieval confessors' manuals),[71] the *De planctu ecclesie* written in 1332 by another expert in confession, the papal penitentiary Alvarus Pelagius,[72] and in England a manual of the 1340s, William Doune's *Memoriale presbiterorum*.[73]

There are several assumptions in these lists of sins, always implicit and sometimes spelled out. In the case of necessarily illicit or dubious professions, such as those of people who fight for hire, beggars, and prostitutes, the sins are those which are implicated in the job itself. In the case of other professions, the sins are those which the job's exercise provides the opportunity to commit – which, therefore, *may* be committed. But *may* shades into *often*, and this leads to the notion of 'the sins which are more frequently committed' by a particular group.[74] Now, in practice this meant lists of sins which provided sharp moral profiles of particular groups, outstanding examples of which are the secular interrogatories of the *Memoriale presbiterorum*. 'Ascribing patterns of behaviour to social groups' slightly misleads through semantic-conceptual anachronism, but it roughly describes what these interrogatories can do by around 1300. Penitential 'circumstance' has helped stimulate a sort of moral 'sociography'. Perhaps less significant, but still striking, is that these lists have now become the umbrella for much miscellaneous 'social' comment, as, for example, when Alvarus Pelagius uses a vast list of the sins of one estate, women, as an excuse to comment on Florentine mothers spoiling their children.[75]

5. Penitential systems compared: the Church, Waldensians and Cathars[76]

By the 1140s or earlier Caesar of Heisterbach's familiar Cologne and Bonn had been evangelised by the missionaries of one competing faith, Catharism. The Cathars did not resist pressure for as long in this part of Germany as they did in

---

[71] Haren, 'Social Ideas', p. 49; Michaud-Quantin, *Sommes*, p. 50; chapter 8 below, pp. 169 and 171–3.

[72] Haren, 'Social Ideas', p. 49; N. Iung, *Un franciscain, théologien du pouvoir pontifical au XIVe siècle. Alvaro Pelayo, évèque et pénitencier de Jean XXII* (Paris, 1931), pp. 23 and 52–5.

[73] Haren, 'A Study'; Haren, 'Social Ideas', pp. 49–51; chapter 7 below.

[74] Chapter 8 below, pp. 172–3.

[75] Alvarus Pelagius, *De planctu ecclesie*, II.xlv (Venice, 1560): 'Nimis delicate nutriunt filios, quos carnaliter diligunt, sicut domine Florentine' ('Like Florentine ladies they [= some women] bring up their children, whom they love physically [rather than spiritually], with excessive indulgence').

[76] This section's account of Waldensian confession and penance is based on P. Biller, 'Multum ieiunantes et se castigantes: medieval Waldensian Asceticism', in *Monks, Hermits and the Ascetic Tradition*, ed. W. J. Sheils, SCH 22 (1985), 215–28. Its discussion of confession among the Cathars rests upon A. Borst, *Die Katharer*, Schriften der Monumenta Germaniae Historica 12 (Stuttgart, 1953), J. Duvernoy, *La religion des*

Languedoc and southern Italy, where they took stronger root. Another clandestine movement which was present in Germany before 1218, and also spread into Rhineland cities, was a proscribed religious Order, the Order of Waldensian friars.[77] This lasted longer in German-speaking areas, not being effectively picked off by inquisitors until the 1390s. There was some sort of confession among both Cathars and Waldensians, and this prompts an obvious enquiry. How is 'lived confession' illuminated by comparison of the three penitential systems of the Church, the Waldensians and the Cathars?

The paucity of evidence about the clandestine movements means that the following cannot focus on the Rhineland, and has to draw upon evidence from any region from which it is forthcoming. I am looking first at the Waldensians and 'lived confession' among them, beginning with a background sketch. The Waldensian movement originated in the 1170s, and was rooted in enthusiasm for literal imitation of the life of the apostles and obedience to the evangelical precepts of poverty and preaching. In other words, they were part of the religious movement which also produced the Franciscan and Dominican Orders, and the forms of life and activity of the male branches of the Waldensian, Franciscan and Dominican religious Orders had many similarities. All three lived off alms, and, like Franciscans and Dominicans, Waldensian friars preached and heard confessions. However, after their lapse into disobedience and heresy and their subsequent persecution, the Waldensian friars did these things clandestinely. They preached to, and heard the confessions of, lay followers who shared their beliefs and put them up in their houses while they were visiting; in public the lay followers behaved like lay Catholics, getting baptised, marrying and hearing mass in their local Church.

So, Waldensian friars heard confessions, and they enjoined penances. What little survives of their penitential system suggests broad similarity to the Church's system. Like Dominican and Franciscan friars, Waldensians carried little vade-mecum books in their pockets, and surviving late alpine-dialect books used by the Waldensian friars even contain a comparable Latin instruction manual for the confessor, which is entitled *De imposicione penitentie*. In depositions in front of inquisitors, the lay followers recall confessing their sins to the Waldensian friars, who imposed penances on them. The penances usually consisted of saying the *Our Father* a certain number of times and

---

Cathares (Toulouse, 1976), the comments of Cathar followers in Languedoc which are preserved in depositions in front of inquisitors, and a description written by a former Cathar turned Dominican, cited in n. 79 below.

77 See Biller, 'Waldensian Asceticism', pp. 217–19, on the Waldensians forming an Order – in *their* eyes although not, of course, the Church's. Like Dominicans and Franciscans, they were known among themselves as *fratres*. Translating this word as 'friars' helps to remove the veil which has been cast over the generic similarity of the Waldensians, Franciscans and Dominicans by the hostilities both of the medieval period and of the later centuries of Protestant and Catholic polemical historiography.

engaging in some fasting. Penitential prayers did not, however, include the *Hail Mary*, which was precluded by Waldensian objection to the invocation of Mary or the saints. When we gain brief glimpses of wealthy merchants and citizens who are Waldensian followers in a later medieval city (in Fribourg around 1400),[78] their heavy involvement in alms and the local hospital suggests their performance of penitential 'satisfaction' in doing good works in a style which is similar to that of Catholics of the same milieu. One Waldensian letter, which survives in one of the late alpine-dialect Waldensian books, suggests a combination of penance and maintaining social peace in rural communities which parallels the Church's practice in rural parishes. The letter shows Waldensian friars attending to loans, the restoration of animals, marriages, the settling of quarrels, and the appointment of arbitrators between disputing parties.

There are, nevertheless, some special emphases. One is general penitential rigour. Late-medieval followers commented upon Waldensian Brothers imposing heavier penances than were imposed in the Church, and there is a hint of greater severity in penance imposed for sexual sins. Since the evidence is slight, let us also look at the emphasis on certain sorts of sin in Waldensian preaching. Detectable already among early Waldensians, in reports in depositions of what Waldensian friars said to their followers, was a particular concern with sins of the tongue, such as lying or swearing, and detectable in the late alpine-dialect books was preoccupation with the dangers of going out to drink in pubs or to dances. The tone which is apparent here needs to be put alongside the hostile comment of Catholic writers, who accused the Waldensians of pride. This charge rested in part on the moral-theological commonplaces which ordered sins under one or other of the seven deadly sins, among them heresy as a sub-species of pride. But it also rested on a Waldensian sense of moral superiority which these Catholic commentators saw and disliked.

Postponing for a moment the conclusions to be drawn from this, I turn now to the Cathars. In its parts and the naming of these parts, Catharism can be compared to the Catholic Church. It had bishops, deans, dioceses, and houses in which men or women lived a conventual life of regular prayer and abstinence, and followers called (by both Cathars and inquisitors) 'believers'. A Cathar 'sacrament' called the *consolamentum* produced a divide between those who had received it, who were called the 'Good Men' or the 'Good Women' or 'Perfects', and those who had not, the 'believers'. With rough approximation, the 'Good Men' who were bishops or deans or itinerant preachers can be seen as the Cathar Church's 'clergy', the 'Good Men and Women' as its 'religious', and the 'believers' as its 'laity'. While 'believers' were the Cathars' 'laity' in some senses, in that they provided material support for the Perfects, venerated them and attended their sermons, in one crucial

---

[78] P. Biller, '*Curate infirmos*: the medieval waldensian practice of medicine', in *The Church and Healing*, ed. W. J. Sheils, SCH 19 (1982), 55–77 (pp. 69–70).

sense they were not. For the 'believers', unlike Catholic laity, were not *theologically* members of the Cathar Church until they received the *consolamentum*. Hence there was no reason for a penitential and moral system to extend over them, and (with minor exceptions which will be noted in a moment) the Cathar 'Good Men' did not provide their followers with one.

One former Perfect who became a Dominican, Rainier Sacconi, wrote a brilliant hostile account of Cathars in which the most telling part is a sustained account of the contrast between penance and confession among the Cathars and in the Catholic Church.[79] Among the Cathar 'clergy' and 'religious' there were two occasions when sins were confessed. First, during the rite of reception of the *consolamentum*, there was a public and general confession of sins, which were absolved through the receiving of the *consolamentum*.[80] Secondly, there was a monthly gathering where one person, speaking for all the others, made a general public confession of sins.[81] There was no individual confession of one's particular sins. Cathar Perfects prayed, fasted, and abstained, but this had nothing to do with works of satisfaction in remission of sins. For the *consolamentum* had wiped out both guilt and punishment. There was, then, among the Cathars no penance, no restitution of ill-gotten gains, no such things as works of satisfaction, and hence, for example, no impulse to almsgiving.

When we turn to the many hundreds of Cathar depositions to look at the 'lived confession', we find broad confirmation of Sacconi's account. There are some traces of the monthly rite of general confession among the Perfects. The fasts and abstinences of the Perfects mark them apart, as does their avoidance of sex and (in the case of the males) abhorrence of the slightest touch of a female: a matter of purity, not repentance. When we turn away from the Perfects themselves to look at them living and working among their followers, we see no penitential system at all. The instruction given to followers was doctrinal rather than moral; followers were given dogmas, such as 'the devil created this world', not moral injunctions such as 'do not lie' or 'do not steal'. There is a great contrast with deposition glimpses of the Waldensian friars. Their followers remember the Waldensians exhorting them morally much more than instructing them doctrinally; telling them what to do or not to do more than what to believe or not to believe.

There is one interesting qualification[82] which needs to be noted. The Cathar

---

[79] Rainier Sacconi, *Summa de Catharis*, ed. F. Sanjek, *Archivum Fratrum Praedicatorum* 44 (1974), 31–60. See the sections entitled *De manus impositione* (On the imposition of hands [= the *consolamentum*]), *De falsa penitentia Catharorum* (On the false penance of the Cathars), *De confessione Catharorum* (On the confession of the Cathars), *De confessione venialium* (On the confession of venial [sins]), and *De satisfactione et penitentia Catharorum* (On the satisfaction and penance of the Cathars), pp. 43–7.

[80] Duvernoy, *Religion*, pp. 152–3, 156, 158.

[81] Borst, *Katharer*, pp. 199–200; Duvernoy, *Religion*, pp. 203–8.

[82] Minor qualifications to the picture given here are noted in Duvernoy, *Religion*, pp. 258–60.

perfects lived among noble families many of whose members supported them in faith while continuing to live, marry, dispute and fight in the world. To whom could these nobles turn when they fell out among themselves? They revered the 'Good Men' for their austerity and possession of the truth, and, unsurprisingly, turned to them for help. These 'Good Men', therefore, were drawn into establishing 'peace' and 'concord' and dispelling 'discordia' (*pax, concordia, discordia*) between disputing parties.[83] In one instance the language of the deposition suggests formal arbitration: a Cathar bishop and others 'tractaverunt de pace inter dictos homines . . . et tunc dictae partes compromiserunt in manu dicti Bertrandi Martini Episcopi haereticorum (discussed the question of peace between the said men . . . and then the said parties [to the dispute], [with their hands] in the hand of the said Bertrand Martin, bishop of the heretics, promised mutually to abide by the decision)'.[84] But acting to preserve social peace did not spring from the penitential concerns of Catharism. Rather it was pressure in these communities which occasionally brought the Cathar 'Good Man' into a role comparable to that played by a parish priest when he settled disputes at the beginning of Lent, and that played formally and in public by a mendicant friar in an Italian city when invested with powers to make peace between the city's feuding families and parties.

The comparison can be turned in two directions. First, it can be used as a help in trying to get to grips with the 'lived religion' of this heretical religious Order and this heretical Church. Set alongside the Church, Waldensian confession shows Waldensianism as (a) in general, medieval Catholic in nature, while being also (b) infused with (in modern terms) a strain of stern, pleasure-hating, morally-smug evangelicalism. Set alongside the Church and Waldensian moral rigorism, Cathar lack of concern with the moral behaviour of their followers is breath-taking. This void, together with the nature of Cathar concern with the sins of their Perfects (a matter of their spiritual and ritual apartness from this world), reminds us of the logic of the Cathar position. In an utterly evil world, in which a few good spirits were hidden in evil flesh, the only path was separation from and rejection of the world and the flesh; the only exit was through the reception of the *consolamentum*, which would enable one to fly off to the world of the good creator when one's evil fleshly envelope died; and the only necessity, after its reception, was rejection of those things which might contaminate during the wait for death. There was no point in grappling *with* this world, given that it was not morally mixed, but rather utterly and totally evil. This is not making the polemicist's point – Cathar proneness to evil acts[85] – but a subtler and different point about these

---

83 The key-words are those used by the deponents, translated, of course, from Occitan into Latin. Among the depositions in Paris, Bibliothèque Nationale, MS Collection Doat 22, there are examples on ff. 73v, 84r, 121r, 161r–v, 167r–v, 206r–v, and 221r–v.

84 MS Doat 22, f. 121r. See Toulouse, Bibliothèque Municipale, MS 609, f. 19v, for an example in a different milieu, where Cathars 'made peace' ('fecerunt pacem') between a butcher from Mas-Saintes-Puelles and another man.

85 Most medieval polemicists tried to blacken the name of Cathars with moral slurs,

pure spirits: their lack of interest in trying to improve this world, and the lack of connection in their eyes between moral behaviour and salvation.

Secondly, one can turn away from these heretical minorities and look again at the vast apparatus of the Church's system of confession and penance, this time using heretical penitential systems to throw light on the Church's. In the annual confession of ordinary people in the pre-Gerson Church, as it can be seen through *exempla* and confessors' manuals, parish priests try to get their ordinary sinning Catholic parishioners to confess and repent. Some depressions, some inner agonies or some doubts of faith may be receiving counselling,[86] but much of the time confessors were concentrating on grainier sins which hurt or upset neighbours or members of one's family – stealing animals, drunken fighting after coming back from the pub, infidelity to a spouse, sharp-practice in a shop. So much of the medieval Church *was* this system of confession and penance, with all its ramifications; the whole apparatus, for example, of medieval charities and charitable institutions rested on founders' and donors' concern with remission of the sins they had committed alongside, of course, obedience to the evangelical precept of charity.[87] The Cathar example does something both elementary and fundamental, illuminating the Church's penitential system by contrast. It shows the Church's pastors getting their hands dirty. That is to say, it shows the Church turned towards and implicated in a flawed world, grappling with the sins of ordinary people, trying to get them to improve and get on with each other better, and to do this in order to acquire salvation. At the same time a much smaller distance, that which lay between the Waldensian penitential system and the Church's, locates the Church's penitential system as relatively moderate and tolerant.

>

6. Modern Scholarship

The statements that I have been making above about, for example, the history of confessor' literature, John of Freiburg, Peter the Chanter and Gerson, recapitulate and depend on fundamental studies which have been published by Pierre Michaud-Quantin, Leonard Boyle, John Baldwin and John Bossy respectively. Other parts of my account are inspired by and summarise the studies of Billy Pantin,[88] Alexander Murray, Jacqueline Murray, Michael Haren, and many other scholars. The sketch is personal, and thus only one of many possible views of the subject. But it deliberately follows the work of

and this trait can also be found in some modern Catholic historians – see Duvernoy, *Religion*, pp. 254–8 – and this has obstructed serious discussion of the role of penance among the Cathars.

[86] Murray, 'Confession', pp. 296–302.

[87] J. Imbert, *Les hopitaux en droit canonique* (Paris, 1947), p. 36 and n. 3.

[88] W. A. Pantin.

those scholars who have made and shaped the subject in recent decades in order to parade the results of their labours.

Let me now look at the subject from another angle, seeing how these scholars have constructed the modern building, 'medieval confession', beginning with the more technical scholarship which provides its foundations. Pierre Michaud-Quantin's magisterial survey of works of instruction for confessors written between the twelfth and the sixteenth centuries was fundamental,[89] as was also Leonard Boyle's account of the varying forms of this literary genre;[90] to Boyle's other studies I shall return. The other foundation stones have been editions of texts, and accompanying studies of manuscripts, authorship, sources and influence. Salient here are the many editions of texts written between the late twelfth and the mid thirteenth centuries: Jean-Albert Dugauquier's edition of Peter the Chanter's *Summa de animae consiliis*;[91] Jean Longère's editions of Alain de Lille's *Liber poenitentialis*[92] and Peter of Poitiers' *Compilatio praesens*;[93] J. J. Francis Firth's edition of Robert of Flamborough's *Liber poenitentialis*;[94] F. Broomfield's edition of Thomas of Chobham's work (known with some anachronism as his *Summa confessorum*);[95] Jean Pierre Renard's edition of three little penitential *summae*;[96] and several editions from the current master in this field, Joseph Goering,[97] from whom further important editions are to be expected.[98]

With the vast *summae* of cases of the later Middle Ages, incunabula and early printings of a high proportion of the important works had always assisted modern scholarship. But they have also in part held it back, by discouraging modern editions – who would ever try to edit these vast works? What is blocked is the further illumination which modern technical editions would bring. A more serious defect has been lack of access to the extraordinarily rich pastoral treatises of fourteenth-century England, nearly all of which have never been printed. They were outlined by Billy Pantin in his account of the fourteenth-century Church,[99] and Pantin was also the doctoral

[89] Michaud-Quantin, *Sommes*.
[90] Boyle, '*Summae confessorum*'.
[91] Peter the Chanter, *Summa*.
[92] See n. 24 above.
[93] Peter, *Summa*.
[94] Flamborough, *Liber*.
[95] Chobham, *Summa*. On the title *Summa confessorum*, which was first used by John of Freiburg for the work he wrote in 1298, see Boyle, '*Summae confessorum*'.
[96] *Trois sommes*.
[97] They include *Cum ad sacerdotem*; Grosseteste, *De modo*; Serlo, *Summa*; J. Goering and F. A. C. Mantello, 'The *Perambulavit Judas . . . (speculum confessionis)* attributed to Robert Grosseteste', *Revue Bénédictine* 96 (1986), 125–68.
[98] Editions in progress include (together with H. Pryce), Cadogon of Bangor, *De modo confitendi*; (together with G. Silano), John of Kent, *Summa de penitentia*; Pseudo-Prepositinus [= Richard II of St Victor], *Summa de penitentia iniungenda*; *Speculum Iuniorum*. I am grateful to Professor Goering for communicating this list.
[99] Pantin, *English Church*, pp. 189–219.

supervisor of Leonard Boyle during his research on the most important of these texts, William of Pagula's *Oculus sacerdotis*. Although Boyle's thesis supplied the material for the essay with which he won the Royal Historical Society's Alexander Prize,[100] the thesis itself remained unpublished. Two decades later Pantin supervised Michael Haren's research on another work from fourteenth-century England, the *Memoriale presbiterorum*.[101] This treatise is largely outside the main English tradition, which mainly adapted and reworked the *Oculus sacerdotis*, and it survives in only a few manuscripts. It is, nevertheless, of great interest because of its remarkable estates interrogatories. Haren's thesis, a study and edition of the text,[102] like Boyle's remained unpublished. Decades later this is at last being remedied. Boyle and Goering are editing Boyle's thesis,[103] and Haren's is appearing in the Oxford historical monograph series.[104] The lack of an edition of the *Oculus* remains the biggest problem. Among the texts from the tradition which it initiated and inspired, only its 'second edition', John de Burgo's *Pupilla oculi*, is accessible, and only through its sixteenth-century printings.[105]

Built upon these foundation stones of surveys, technical literature and editions is a floor which consists of those scholarly works which study penitential literature and the workings of confession and penance within the terms of the medieval Church's pastoral experts. There is less (or less obvious) grinding of interpretative axes than in those works which comprise another floor, higher up in the building. On this floor very remarkable scholarship has illuminated the contribution of theology in the schools. John Baldwin examined the case-questions raised by Peter the Chanter and Robert de Courson in Paris in the late twelfth and early thirteenth centuries, which are preserved both in the works which they wrote and in the confessors' instruction works, written in Paris at this time, which contained reminiscences of these discussions. With painstaking brilliance he showed these figures on the one hand acutely observing 'social' matters (by which Baldwin meant such concrete things in their world as kingship, government, court life, war, taxation, administration of justice, trade, provision of credit, and regulation of marriage), and on the other hand analysing the licitness or otherwise of a multitude of particular possible actions in these areas.[106]

A passionate concern to demonstrate the connection between the theology of the schools and practical pastoral education has been at the heart of the many fundamental articles written by Leonard Boyle.[107] He drew attention to

---

[100] Boyle, '*Oculus*'.
[101] Haren, 'Social Ideas', p. 50.
[102] Haren, 'A Study'.
[103] Information from Josph Goering.
[104] See below chapter 6, p. 109, n. 4.
[105] See M. W. Bloomfield *et al.*, *Incipits of Latin Works on the Virtues and Vices, 1100–1500 A.D.* (Cambridge, Mass., 1979), no. 2441, p. 216.
[106] Baldwin, *Peter the Chanter*.
[107] Boyle, *Pastoral Care*.

the confessors' problems which were debated in theological quodlibets at universities, and the flow of such discussions into John of Freiburg's *Summa confessorum*. Boyle's larger aim is exemplified in his revolutionary account of St Thomas's *Summa theologiae*.[108] Here he showed that it was a pedagogic work for *beginners*, those Dominican 'common brothers' who would spend their lives preaching and hearing confessions; that much of its concrete pastoral part was an adaptation of parts of Raymond of Peñafort's *Summa de poenitentia*; and that it was *this* pastoral part (rather than the more speculative theology in which St Thomas tried to package it) that later medieval Dominican convents particularly wanted. In doing these things Boyle was not just humorously overturning modern scholars' solemn use of the *Summa* as 'thirteenth-century scholastic thought'. He was concerned with the conscious subordination of *all* Dominican intellectual work to a pastoral end.[109] The penetration and deep conviction of this modern Dominican have produced work from which much flows. After Boyle it has been much easier to discern the continuing place of concrete pastoral concerns in university theology. After Boyle the interconnections of areas of study and action in the penitential system, from the theology faculty to individual confession in the parish church, have been easier to envisage; and the connections of texts, from compilations of canon law to that briefest of pastoral aids, the manual scrawled on the few leaves of a little pamphlet, have been more readily apparent.

Many scholars on this floor, such as Nicole Bériou, Roberto Rusconi, and Joseph Avril,[110] have studied other particular parts of the penitential system, using either (or both) the instructional literature and diocesan legislation to study such themes as the norm of annual confession, the norm of confession to one's parish priest, confession as a means of instruction, and so on. To be singled out among them is one scholar who has managed to break the seal of secrecy of medieval confessions: Alexander Murray has made remarkable and pioneering use of thirteenth-century *exempla* in order to eavesdrop on conversations which took place in some individual confessions.[111] Murray has also turned his attention to the thought-world of mid thirteenth century pastoral experts. He sketched the interests which one group of pastoral professionals took in ethics, knowledge and sin, and suggested their milieu as the intelligible context and stimulus for Robert Grosseteste's translation into

---

[108] L. E. Boyle, *The Setting of the 'Summa theologiae' of Saint Thomas*, The Étienne Gilson Series 5 (Toronto, 1982).

[109] Most passionately expressed in his 'The Summa for Confessors as a Genre, and its Religious Intent', in *The Pursuit of Holiness in Late Medieval and Renaissance Religion*, ed. C. Trinkaus and H. O. Oberman, Studies in Medieval and Reformation Thought 10 (Leiden, 1974), pp. 126–30.

[110] Bériou, 'Latran', and the article cited in n. 17 above; Rusconi, 'Prédication', and 'Ordinate confiteri. La confessione dei peccati nelle "summae de casibus" e nei manuali per i confessori (metà XII–inizi XIV secolo)', in *L'Aveu*, pp. 297–313; Avril, 'Pouvoirs du prêtre' and 'Pratique'.

[111] Murray, 'Confession'; see also works by Berlioz which use *exempla* to study confession, cited in n. 4 above.

Latin of Aristotle's *Nicomachean Ethics*. This work supplied a need which was being felt by these men for moderation and experience in ethics.[112]

These scholars have usually been specialists, concentrating on the elucidation of *one* part of the medieval Church's penitential system. Syntheses and overall general accounts have been lacking. Most have also paid more attention to the Church and its clergy (the Church legislating about confession and the clergy being instructed in its administration) than to the laity. In other words, their work has been mainly rooted in a historiographically older world in which *ecclesiastical* history predominated. Less of their work has been influenced by the newer genre of *religious history*, whose most salient feature was that it brought into the centre of the stage lay people and their 'lived religion'.[113] It has been left to an early modernist, John Bossy, to broad-brush a fresco of the 'lived religion' of confession and penance in medieval Christianity. This he did in the chapter headed 'Sin and Penance' in his general account of later medieval and early modern Christianity,[114] which is a solitary masterpiece.

John Bossy belongs mainly to a higher floor of the building we are examining. There is no clear line, rather a continuum, between the two groups of historians, for those on the ground floor are not without their own overall concerns. In surveying fourteenth-century pastoral literature of instruction for parish priests,[115] for example, the Catholic Billy Pantin was also supporting his proposition that the medieval Church should be seen more positively, viewed as developing forwards from the reforms of 1215, rather than negatively, seen backwards from the Reformation and later medieval 'abuses'. And past Dominican education emerges as as a pastorally practical system when its history is written by the Dominican Leonard Boyle. But the historians on the higher floor have broader interpretative schemas, and they are often using medieval confession in order to write the history of something else.

Located on this higher floor is Jacques Le Goff, who took earlier observations by Marie-Dominique Chenu and Pierre Michaud-Quantin and developed them further, looking to the interrogatories of confessors' literature for a reaction to, and in some sense a validation of, the increasing professional specialisation of thirteenth-century cities and towns.[116] There is also Thomas Tentler, who imported modern sociology in his attempt to see medieval confession as a system of 'social control'.[117]

---

[112] Pp. 317–21.

[113] See n. 1 above.

[114] J. A. Bossy, *Christianity in the West, 1400–1700* (Oxford, 1985). In a book which begins with St Anselm, the title's '1400' is misleadingly late.

[115] Pantin, *English Church*, p. 2.

[116] M.-D. Chenu, *La théologie au douzième siècle* (Paris, 1957), pp. 238–44; P. Michaud-Quantin, 'Les categories sociales dans le vocabulaire des canonistes et moralistes au XIIIe siècle', in his *Études sur le vocabulaire philosophique du moyen âge* (Rome, 1970), pp. 163–86 (especially p. 180); Le Goff, cited in n. 61 above.

[117] T. N. Tentler, 'The Summa for Confessors as an Instrument of Social Control', in

Sex, gender and sexuality in varying ways have been at the centre of some other scholars' attention. It is an old tradition in German scholarship, which stretches back to 1956, in Josef Ziegler's study of marriage in penitential *summae*, and even further back to 1932, in Peter Browe's study of medieval sexual taboos, which was based partly on penitential literature.[118] Some scholars use confessors' literature to explore such themes as (to use the title of a book by Pierre Payer) *The Bridling of Desire* in the Middle Ages.[119] One group has tried to place confessors' literature at the service of the history of population and the family. Its pioneers were John T. Noonan[120] and Jean-Louis Flandrin.[121] I have tried to find traces of the divide between northwestern and southern European marriage-patterns in contrasts between the penitential literature of these two regions.[122] Another group consists of scholars whose subject is the medieval construction of sexuality, alongside the overlapping but distinct genres of history of women and history of gender. Among these, Jacqueline Murray has been combining her acute historiographical grasp of these modern approaches[123] with her deep knowledge of the confessors' literature of the first half of the thirteenth century, in order to investigate medieval penitential contribution to the construction of sexuality.[124]

I turn now to an historian who has illuminated medieval confession while looking back upon it from the Reformation and Counter-reformation, John Bossy. The 'social' already concerned him in the first of his three accounts of confession ('The Social History of Confession on the Eve of the Reformation'),[125] and it is important to be clear about, and not to confuse, the

---

Pursuit of Holiness, ed. Trinkaus and Oberman, pp. 103–26; see the riposte by Leonard Boyle (cited in n. 101 above) and Tentler's response, both printed in the same volume, pp. 126–37, and Tentler's later monographic account, Tentler, *Sin*. Tentler's work was the point of departure for H. Martin, 'Confession et contrôle sociale à la fin du moyen âge', in *Pratiques de la confession*, pp. 117–36.

[118] P. Browe, *Beiträge zur Sexualethik des Mittelalters* (Breslau, 1932); J. G. Ziegler, *Die Ehelehre der Pönitentialsummen von 1200–1350. Eine Untersuchung zur Geschichte der Moral- und Pastoraltheologie* (Regensburg, 1956).

[119] P. J. Payer, *The Bridling of Desire. Views of Sex in the Later Middle Ages* (Toronto, Buffalo and London, 1993). Much of Payer's work has been on sex in the penitentials; see his 'Early Medieval Regulations concerning Marital Sexual Relations', *Journal of Medieval History* 6 (1980), 353–76, and *Sex and the Penitentials: The Development of a Sexual Code, 550–1150* (Toronto, 1984).

[120] J. T. Noonan, *Contraception. A History of its Treatment by the Catholic Theologians and Canonists* (Cambridge, Mass., 1966), chapter 5, pp. 152–70 (on the penitentials) and pp. 258–74 (later medieval penance). See chapter 8 below, pp. 165–6 and 185 n. 78.

[121] J.-L. Flandrin, 'Contraception, mariage et relations amoureuses dans l'Occident chrétien', reprinted in his *Le sexe et l'occident. Évolution des attitudes et des comportements* (Paris, 1981), pp. 109–26.

[122] Biller, 'Pastoral Geography'.

[123] See her survey, J. Murray, 'Introduction', in *Desire and Discipline. Sex and Sexuality in the Premodern West*, ed. J. Murray and K. Eisenbichler (Toronto, Buffalo and London, 1996), pp. ix–xxviii.

[124] See n. 55 above.

[125] Bossy, 'Social'.

various meanings with which the word is being charged by Bossy and other modern students of confession. In the case of the sub-title of John Baldwin's book, *The Social Views of Peter the Chanter and his Circle*, we have seen that 'social' is a fairly neutral word of convenience, denoting thought which is not about abstract otherworldly things, but rather about concrete matters in a human community, such as money or marriage laws. By contrast, 'social' in Thomas Tentler's 'social control' is a self-conscious import from sociology. It needs to be capitalised, to be written as 'Social', in order to signal its modern abstract-conceptual nature. For Bossy the word has had even more importance, albeit negatively. By the time he came to write the second and third of his accounts of medieval confession,[126] he was attacking the long semantic-conceptual development which had led up to the possibility, by the time of Durkheim, of equating the abstractions 'Religion' and 'Society'.[127] To historians he was advocating a semantic-conceptual spring-cleaning, which cleared out of historians' cupboards various modern words (or older words in modern meanings) which they used when describing the past. Such a word as 'social', according to Bossy, should not be used in a sense other than the the sense it generally held in the past period about which the historian is writing. In the Middle Ages 'social' meant only a relation, one between a few companions (Latin *socii*), friends, kin, or a married couple (between whom there was *societas*), and it was remote from the modern capitalised and abstract 'Society' or 'Social control'. Bossy criticised, therefore, those historians who import a sociological 'Social'. Positively, however, Bossy put forward an intricate relation between the sacrament of confession (as also the sacrament of marriage) and the 'social' in the Middle Ages. Just as Bossy's treatment of the sacrament of marriage and the 'social' in the Middle Ages would discuss marriage establishing a relationship and peace between families and kin not previously related, so his treatment of confession and penance would deal with their role in the restoration of social peace, the bringing about of concord between angrily quarreling neighbours and feuding families.[128]

In many and complex ways – and not just interiorisation – confession began to change with the turn of 1400. Bossy's thesis acquired its most elegant form in the last of his three accounts of medieval and early modern confession, 'Moral Arithmetic'.[129] Here he established and pondered the move from overwhelming emphasis on Seven (the Deadly Sins) in the period up to 1400, to emphasis on Ten (the Commandments) thereafter. His reflections pointed to the dominance of sinners in relation to their neighbours in the Seven Deadly

---

126 Bossy, *Christianity in the West*, chapter 3, and Bossy, 'Arithmetic'.
127 The attack was launched at the inaugural lecture Bossy delivered in the University of York, February 11, 1981, which was printed in revised form as 'Some Elementary Forms of Durkheim', *Past and Present* 95 (1982), 3–18.
128 This part of Bossy's thesis is commented upon by H. Martin, 'Confession et contrôle sociale', in *L'Aveu*, pp. 118–19.
129 Bossy, 'Arithmetic'.

Sins, a horizontal relation; and the greater presence of sinners in relation to God or parents in the Ten Commandments, a vertical relation.

The whole of this introduction has, so far, assumed that the period around the Fourth Lateran Council of 1215 was a watershed – or, as Nicole Bériou, put it, 'un tournant', a historical turning-point.[130] The twelfth century provided a prelude. Its theological interiorisation of confession and penance was (so it has been claimed) connected with a broader and deeper shift in the concept of the individual; Colin Morris entitled his account of this 'the discovery of the individual'.[131] There followed the legislation of 1215, and the further legislation and production of pastoral literature which were sketched earlier. The period thereafter, up to the reformations of the sixteenth century, was a connected whole, containing development within broad continuity. In what follows, I am calling this notion of a central medieval penitential revolution '1215 and All That'. Now, as we have just seen, Bossy does not see it this way. For him the deep sea-change starts occurring around 1400. He does not believe in '1215 and All That', and he is not alone in this view. Recently there was the posthumous publication of a book written by an American historian, Mary Mansfield, who died tragically young after writing a thesis on public humiliation in the penance of northern France in the thirteenth century.[132] She also queried '1215 and All That', for she found that public humiliation still persisted and remained important in her period. This called into question the interiorisation of confession and primacy of private penance in the system that was supposed to have been established by '1215 and All That'. And it showed the need for re-examination of the fundamental discontinuity which has been argued or assumed to exist between the penitential systems of the 'Dark Ages' and the period after 1215. My use of the outmoded term 'Dark Ages' is explained below.

Here I come to the final part in this survey, which has not so far turned towards the penitential system of this earlier period and its literature of instruction, those 'penitential books' which originated in sixth-century Irish monastic circles and flourished in the Carolingian era. This period has its own modern scholarly construction, with its surveyors (especially Cyrille Vogel[133] and Allen Frantzen[134]) and its editors and students of the penitentials (many German scholars, together with Allen Frantzen on Anglo-Saxon penitentials[135] and Rob Meens on the 'tripartite' penitential). There is convenient access to

---

[130] Bériou, 'Latran', pp. 74–6.

[131] C. Morris, *The Discovery of the Individual, 1050–1200* (New York, 1972); pp. 70–5 discuss confession.

[132] M. C. Mansfield, *The Humiliation of Sinners. Public Penance in Thirteenth-Century France* (Ithaca and London, 1995).

[133] C. Vogel, Les *'Libri paenitentiales'*, Typologie des Sources du Moyen Âge Occidental 27 (Turnhout, 1978); see this work's bibliography at pp. 18–27 and 113–15, which includes on pp. 26–7 a list of Vogel's earlier studies.

[134] A. J. Frantzen, *Mise à jour du fascicle no. 27. C. Vogel, Les 'Libri paenitentiales'* (Turnhout, 1985).

[135] A. J. Frantzen, *The Literature of Penance in Anglo-Saxon England* (New Brunswick,

this building through Rob Meens' footnotes in chapter 2 of this volume and Alexander Murray's recent survey of confession before 1215.[136]

Here I shall not attempt further description of it, and I am confining myself to one general point. In practice the two modern scholarly worlds of 'Dark Age' penance and '1215 and All That' live and work independently, and tend not to communicate much with each other. Further, the later historians tend to assume (as historians usually do about the preceding period), that the earlier period is dark, and that their own period has shown remarkable progression from it. The contrast of the richness of the material from the period around the 1215 Council (think only of Thomas of Chobham and Caesar of Heisterbach) and the poverty of early medieval evidence encourages this. Further influence comes from two ancient prejudices which still lurk in the background, one about the 'darkness' of the early Middle Ages and the other about the 'barbarism' or 'primitiveness' apparently revealed by the bizarre contents of the penitentials.[137]

7. *Handling Sin*

A rare and important exception to the separateness between these two scholarly worlds came in 1993. While Alexander Murray had hitherto concentrated on confession after 1215, he then turned to look at the earlier scholarly world and the early penitential system. In an important and powerful article he surveyed both of these, and he argued that there was a large gap between the ideal of the penitentials, which were very thinly diffused in early medieval Europe, and what was realised in penitential practice.[138] The agenda for discussion was thereby set. Rob Meens pursues the theme further in chapter 2 of this volume, in which he examines the frequency and character of early medieval penance in the light of Murray's claim.

The other chapters in *Handling Sin* are similarly set on the various levels of the building sketched in the previous section. In the case of chapter 9 this is a happy accident, for a York Quodlibet lecture has no necessary thematic connection with the volume in which it is printed. Published *honoris causa* at the end of this book, John Baldwin's lecture should be read, chronologically speaking, as the volume's second chapter. Baldwin has been looking for the lay voice and lay religion (in which confession and penance predominate) in vernacular romances of around 1200. He juxtaposes this vernacular literature and the writings of Paris theologians, and examines the carrying-over of the

N.J., 1983). The text was revised and the bibliography updated in the French translation, *La littérature de la pénitence dans l'Angleterre Anglo-Saxonne*, Studia Friburgensia, new series 75 (Fribourg, 1991).

[136] Murray, '1215'.

[137] Prejudice against the penitentials is discussed in Frantzen, *Literature of Penance in Anglo-Saxon England*, pp. 1–3.

[138] Murray, '1215'.

views of these theologians into the literature and thought-world of French nobles. He traces the appearance in the vernacular, then, of the themes of a penitent's contrition of the heart and confession of the mouth, the priest's job in listening to the penitent and enquiring after circumstances, and the priest's application of the spiritual medicine of *conseil* and penance. Baldwin thus manages to draw near to the 'lived confession' of the French nobles who constituted the audience of this literature. Alexander Murray takes even further his use of *exempla* to listen in on thirteenth-century confession, here concentrating on the confessor acting in obedience to the 1215 canon *Omnis utriusque sexus* as counsellor to troubled persons. This figure who, as we have seen, provides *conseil* in Baldwin's terms, also features in Lesley Smith's chapter as psychiatric counsellor.

Jacqueline Murray develops further our knowledge of medieval sexuality in her sharp delineation of the males who wrote *summae* and manuals for confessors, the ways in which these males' texts constructed woman as sexual, and the broader significance of this in medieval ideas of sexuality and gender. In her chosen period, the first half of the thirteenth century, there were two figures, two men who knew each other, who were of towering importance in many areas, including penance. Both were bishops, Robert Grosseteste of Lincoln, William of Auvergne of Paris. Both were important in both secular and ecclesiastical politics, and in the universities of Oxford and Paris. Both were writers of extraordinary power and originality (and in William's case vividness of imagery). And both were passionately concerned with the cure of souls. However, whereas Grosseteste has attracted much modern attention, William of Auvergne has been ignored. Lesley Smith is remedying this, and here in *Handling Sin* she examines the remarkable work on penance which William wrote. She suggests literate lay people as William's intended audience and reminds us that William was an intimate of the king of France, Louis IX, and the confessor of Louis' mother. Jacques Le Goff's magisterial account of 'La religion de Saint Louis' in his recent biography of the king has now acquired the supplement of Smith's chapter.[139]

In his two chapters Michael Haren investigates the particular world of the author of the mid fourteenth century *Memoriale presbiterorum*, carrying forward earlier accounts of fourteenth-century English pastoral literature. He traces and discusses the growth of estates interrogatories. And he goes some way to remedying the lack of editions of England's fourteenth-century pastoral manuals, as alluded to above, by editing and translating (in chapter 7) a large proportion of the *Memoriale*'s interrogatories. Finally, concluding the pre-Quodlibet section of the volume, I continue the efforts of historical demographers and historians of the family to appropriate this material to our use. I suggest that around 1300 confessors' literature was showing a growing capacity to react to, and generalise about, people who were committing one particular sin, trying to avoid offspring; that some of this literature reflects the

---

[139] J. Le Goff, *Saint Louis* (Paris, 1996), 'La religion de Saint Louis', pp. 744–80.

'medicalisation' which was affecting some parts of Europe around 1300; and that both around 1300 and in the tenth century confessors' literature bore the mark of pastoral experts who were reacting to a demographic reality during periods of overpopulation, namely *more* women and men trying to avoid having children.

The editors of this volume are grateful to all those who took part in the original conference, and in particular to John Bossy for his contribution in discussing public and private confession and penance; to the contributers for their patient responses to the editors; and to Pru Harrison for her invaluable help in the final preparation of the text of the volume.

The Frequency and Nature of Early Medieval Penance[1]

Rob Meens

Our views of early medieval penance still rely greatly on the studies of Bernhard Poschmann, Josef Andreas Jungmann and Cyrille Vogel.[2] Though much was done subsequently on several important texts and their manuscript tradition, it did not alter the general picture painted by these three scholars,[3] and it is only recently that some of their basic assumptions have come to be scrutinised. Alexander Murray has reconsidered the problem of the frequency of penance before the twelfth century and Franz Kerff has questioned the purpose of penitential handbooks, while Mayke de Jong has voiced reservations about the validity of the traditional distinction between public and private penance.[4] Although these recent opinions sometimes also need criticism in the light of the extant manuscript evidence, it is now time to modify the traditional views propounded by Poschmann, Jungmann and Vogel.

Historians tend to look for origins: but working from a retrospective view has its own particular pitfall, the danger of treating a topic in an evolutionary way. An example is one scholar, who recently studied early medieval sermons

---

[1] I want to thank Mayke de Jong who read an earlier draft of this paper. I also profited a lot from the contributions of Ludger Körntgen, Nicole Zeddies and Sarah Hamilton to my session 'Confession before 1215' at the International Medieval Congress at the University of Leeds, 1996.

[2] Poschmann, *Kirchenbuße*; J. A. Jungmann, *Die lateinischen Bußriten in ihrer geschichtlichen Entwicklung* (Innsbruck, 1932); C. Vogel, *Les 'Libri Paenitentiales'*, Typologie des sources du moyen âge occidental 27 (Turnhout, 1978). For the influence of these scholars, see Kottje, 'Bußpraxis'.

[3] Most of this work has been initiated by Raymund Kottje in a research project that should result in a critical edition of all the continental penitentials of the early Middle Ages; see R. Kottje, 'Erfassung und Untersuchung der frühmittelalterlichen kontinentalen Bußbücher. Probleme, Aufgaben eines Forschungsprojektes an der Universität Bonn', *Studi Medievali* 26 (1985), 941–50. Alongside several studies illuminating the textual transmission of several penitentials (see note 32 below), the first volume of these new editions has now been published as *Paenitentialia minora Franciae et Italiae saeculi VIII–IX*, ed. R. Kottje, aided by L. Körntgen and U. Spengler-Reffgen, CCSL 156 (1994).

[4] Murray, '1215'; Kerff, 'Mittelalterliche Quellen' and 'Libri paenitentiales'; de Jong, 'Public'.

without citing one single sermon from this period,[5] basing his (interesting) argument on later medieval sermons and related material, informed by modern anthropological theories of oral communication. Illustrative is the following: 'We have evidence from as late as the thirteenth century that people could go for a year or two without hearing a sermon. One can imagine how rarely Anglo-Saxon peasants who lived outside the immediate pale of a city or monastery heard preaching.'[6] Alexander Murray has also ridden out on a quest, looking for the origin of the practice of regular lay confession, which was, he argues, well in place by the twelfth century, some time before the Fourth Lateran Council (1215) enjoined annual confession on all adults. Similar decrees would have been issued in Carolingian times, but Murray rightly questions the effectiveness of such decrees.[7] While it can be shown that in proclaiming the famous decree *Omnis utriusque sexus* the Fourth Lateran Council was merely bolstering an existing institution, the canons of Carolingian church councils would have been mostly ineffective. Like so many of the famous Carolingian reforms, they had only partial success.[8] Murray might be right in assuming that a distinction between ideal and reality was a peculiarity of Carolingian culture, maybe more than he knows. The Carolingian bishops, however, were not trying to establish a system of regular lay confession, as Murray seems to suggest, but rather, as I will argue here, to control an extremely diverse existing practice of penance which seemed to elude their grasp.[9]

It has been argued by Poschmann, Kottje and others that in the Carolingian period the practice of penance and confession was well established in the Latin church.[10] These scholars came to this conclusion on the basis of three main arguments. The first is the regular injunctions of Carolingian rulers and bishops that priests possess penitential handbooks and that people regularly confess their sins. Secondly, the existing handbooks for confessors, the so-called penitentials, provide ample evidence that such a practice in fact existed. Lastly, evidence about parish priests' possession of books indicates

---

5   R. Emmet McLaughlin, 'The Word Eclipsed? Preaching in the Early Middle Ages', *Traditio* 46 (1991), 77–122.

6   Emmet McLaughlin, 'The Word Eclipsed?', p. 106.

7   Murray, '1215'.

8   R. Kottje, 'Einheit und Vielfalt des kirchlichen Lebens in der Karolingerzeit', *ZKG* 60 (1965), 323–42; R. McKitterick, 'Unity and Diversity in the Carolingian Church', in *Unity and Diversity in the Church*, ed. R. Swanson, SCH 32 (1995), pp. 59–82.

9   Murray, '1215', p. 58: 'The doctrine of repeatable confession, then, with its internal, moral, contritional character, was formulated by the leading Carolingian reformers. The same in principle goes for lay practice of it. Some dozen conciliar or episcopal enactments survive from between the eighth century and the tenth, enjoining regular penance and confession on the laity with a periodicity of once, twice or even three times a year.' Murray relies here on Avril, 'Pouvoirs du prêtre'.

10 Poschmann, *Kirchenbuße*; Kottje, 'Bußpraxis'.

that priests generally owned these handbooks. These three arguments Murray tries to undermine, because 'the sources may say the opposite of what they seem'.[11]

Penance and Carolingian Legislation

As to the injunctions in capitularies and episcopal statutes to confess one's sins regularly, suspicion is indeed warranted. The digging of a canal between the Rhine and the Danube was not the only Carolingian ideal not to be realised (although we should not forget that this canal has only recently come into being; after all Napoleon also failed in this respect).[12] But did Carolingian bishops really decree that all Christians confess their sins once a year to their local priest? The two texts cited by Joseph Avril which unequivocally decreed such a thing are now both considered to be forgeries fabricated by a seventeenth-century lawyer from Arras, Claude Despretz.[13] Haito of Basle only decreed that parishioners confess their sins to their own priest or bishop before leaving on a pilgrimage.[14] Ruotger of Trier was worried that some people did not confess at all, and he urged his fellow priests to take care to ensure that people confessed their sins, especially those with possessions in more than one parish who lived now here and now there, for it was often unknown to whom these people had confessed.[15] It was not the frequency of lay confession that worried the Frankish episcopacy, but the way it was done. Councils worried whether priests heard confession and administered penances according to the rules laid down in a penitential. They also worried about the type of penitential priests used. Their main concern was the uniformity of penitential practice, not its frequency.

Confession was apparently closely linked to receiving communion. This is made explicit in a text reflecting the popular dissemination of the decisions of a Bavarian council held somewhere around the year 800. This gathering decided that Christians had to prepare themselves for receiving communion by sexual abstinence as well as by confession and penance. They had to receive communion once every third or fourth Sunday at the very least and not, as many apparently did, only once a year. After all the Greeks, Romans and even the Franks communicated every Sunday.[16] The *Scarapsus Pirminii*, a

---

11 Murray, '1215', p. 58; cf. p. 60: '*Libri paenitentiales* . . . are another kind of document to be read between the lines, and if they are, illustrate precisely . . . the opposite of what they seem to illustrate.'
12 Murray, '1215', p. 58, compares this Carolingian ideal to reality.
13 See *Capitula Episcoporum III*, ed. R. Pokorny, MGH *Cap. Ep.* III, 375–6; the texts are known as Ps.-Hubertus and Ps.-Sonnatius, and they are cited as Carolingian texts in Avril, 'Pouvoirs du prêtre', p. 474, notes 22 and 24.
14 Haito of Basle, *Capitula Episcoporum* c. 18, ed. P. Brommer, MGH *Cap. Ep.* I, 216.
15 Ruotger of Trier, c. 26, ed. P. Brommer, MGH *Cap. Ep.* I, 70.
16 *Capitula Bavarica*, c. 6, ed. Pokorny, MGH *Cap. Ep.* III, 196. Pokorny dates this text, which was formerly known as the *Concilium Baiuwaricum*, to the beginning of the

catechetical text attributed to Pirmin of Reichenau, proclaims that all mortal
sinners should confess before approaching the body and blood of the Lord.[17]
Theodulf of Orléans, stressing the importance of approaching the altar in a
pure state, linked confession to Lent as a period of preparation for
approaching the altar and receiving communion.[18] Confession is also linked to
Lent by several other episcopal capitularies, those proclaimed by Radulf of
Bourges and Ruotger of Trier as well as some anonymous ones.[19] One of the
sermons attributed to Boniface deplores the habit of some who approach the
altar and dare to take communion without having confessed their sins.[20]
Liturgical *ordines* from the ninth century also link confession to the beginning
of Lent.[21]

The requirement that Christians receive communion three times a year
seems to have been a minimum demand in Carolingian times. Injunctions
demanding that Christians receive communion more than three times a year
imply that believers in general kept to the obligation of going to Mass at Easter,
Pentecost and Christmas. The close connection between receiving communion
and confessing your sins might point to a regular practice existing in some
regions of confessing your sins at least as a preparation for these three major
festivals.[22] Jonas of Orléans deplored the fact that people only went to Mass
and received communion three times a year, which shows that this minimum
usage was in fact well established by that time around the city of Orléans.[23]

ninth century. This dating is corroborated by the fact that the text alludes to a canon
from the penitential of Theodore of Canterbury, which was known in Bavaria
directly, as well as indirectly via the *Excarpsus Cummeani*, at the end of the eighth
century; see Meens, 'Kanonisches Recht', pp. 19–21.

[17] C. 25, ed. G. Jecker, *Die Heimat des hl. Pirmin, des Apostels der Alemannen*, Beiträge zur
Geschichte des alten Mönchtums und des Benediktinerordens 13 (Münster, 1927), p.
58; for the date and authorship of this text, see Meens, 'Fragmente'.

[18] Capit. I, c. 36; Cap. II, c. 10, 4, ed. Brommer, *MGH Cap. Ep.* I, 133–4 and 173. R.
Pokorny has expressed his doubts about the authenticity of Theodulf's second
capitulary, and he proposes a date around the middle of the ninth century; *MGH
Cap. Ep.* III, 91, n. 70.

[19] Radulf of Bourges, c. 32; Ruotger, c. 27, ed. Brommer, *MGH Cap. Ep.* I, 258–9 and 70;
Capitula Helmstadensia, c. 11 (*MGH Cap. Ep.* III, 186); *Capitula Neustrica* IV, c. 3 (*MGH
Cap. Ep.* III, 71).

[20] Sermo 11; *PL* 89, 1043.

[21] See the so-called *ordo* of St Gatien, ed. E. Martène, *De antiquis ritibus libri III*, 2nd edn
(Antwerp, 1736–38), p. 778: 'in quadragesima, sicut constitutum est, confessus non
fui, neque paenitentiam de praeteritis criminibus egi'. This *ordo* is still extant in two
manuscripts, Paris, Bibliothèque Nationale, MS n.a.l. 1589 (s.IX ex.) and Tours,
Bibliothèque municipale 184 (s.X in.), identified by A.-G. Martimort, *La
documentation liturgique de Dom. Edmont Martène: Étude codicologique*, Studi e Testi 279
(Vatican, 1978), pp. 330–1. See also the *ordo* included in Ps.-Alcuin, *Liber de divinis
officiis*; *PL* 101, 1192: 'Imprimis praemonere debet sacerdos omnes christianos ex
sacris Scripturarum testimoniis, quatenus in capite ieiunii, hoc est, hodie ad veram
confessionem veramque poenitentiam festinantius accedant'.

[22] See Avril, 'Pratique', pp. 349–50.

[23] Jonas of Orléans, *De institutione laicali* II.18; *PL* 106, 202.

The Manuscript Evidence

The bulk of the evidence, however, is constituted by the still extant manuscripts containing penitential texts. Murray estimates that some three hundred manuscripts, written in the Carolingian realms between roughly 800 and 1000, contain penitential texts.[24] Even allowing for massive losses, this would account for less than one manuscript per two thousand square miles of Europe. Regardless of the accuracy of the calculation itself, it runs into problems when set beside the number of sacramentaries from this period. In his study of early medieval liturgical manuscripts Klaus Gamber listed almost a thousand manuscripts. He included all sorts of liturgical books, such as lectionaries, antiphonaries, pontificals and, for the earlier period, even psalters and evangelaries.[25] Sacramentaries, therefore, have not come down to us in significantly greater numbers than penitential texts. But, such liturgical books were indispensable tools for a priest, and *all* ninth-century inventories of priest's posessions list a sacramentary among his assets.[26] We also have to reckon with less risk of loss in the case of sacramentaries, because these were generally more precious and held to be of more intrinsic value than penitentials. The latter often remained unbound and thus ran a higher risk of wear and tear. For the earlier insular penitentials the case is even worse. While it can be established that a considerable amount of Irish and Anglo-Saxon penitentials were used on the continent, where they were incorporated in newly composed works, they are only known from continental manuscripts. Kottje has argued that one reason for this apparent loss of manuscripts was that these insular compositions were written in an insular script, which made these manuscripts hard to read and useless once this script had become obsolete.[27] The council of Paris of 829, moreover, called upon priests and bishops to find anonymous penitentials and to burn them. We do not know how many of these works were indeed burned, but this decision certainly did not favour the preservation of manuscripts containing these works.

Instead of looking at absolute numbers, it is more fruitful to consider the distribution of penitential manuscripts at certain centres for which there is reliable evidence. If we adopt this strategy it is obvious that such texts were

---

[24] Murray, '1215', p. 60. L. Körntgen, in his article 'Bußbücher', *Lexikon für Theologie und Kirche*, vol. 2, 3rd edn (1994), 822–4, speaks of some 400 manuscripts.

[25] K. Gamber, *Codices Liturgici Latini Antiquiores*, 2nd edn, 2 vols. (Freiburg, 1968), I, 21.

[26] C. Hammer jr., 'Country Churches, Clerical Inventories and the Carolingian Renaissance in Bavaria', *CH* 49 (1980), 5–19, and J.-P. Devroey, *Le polyptyque et les listes de cens de l'abbaye de Saint-Remi de Reims (IXe–XIe siècles)*, Travaux de l'Académie Nationale de Reims 163 (1984).

[27] R. Kottje, 'Überlieferung und Rezeption der irischen Bußbücher auf dem Kontinent', in: *Die Iren und Europa im früheren Mittelalter*, 2 vols., ed. H. Löwe (Stuttgart, 1982), I, 511–24.

eagerly read and copied at centres like St Gall, Lorsch, Rheims and Salzburg.[28] One may wonder whether these copies were meant to be used in a priestly pastoral setting or rather in an episcopal juridical one. It has recently been argued by Franz Kerff that penitentials were mainly intended to be used in the episcopal setting of the itinerant synodal inquisitions. In his view the penances prescribed in these texts were more of an amercement, with all the financial connotations attached to the word, than a real penance of which the first aim should be to cure the sinner. Penitentials were no separate genre for the use of the priest-confessor, but rather should be seen as specific collections of canon law.[29] This particular use of penitentials is suggested by an analysis of the texts themselves as well as of the manuscript context.

It should be said, however, that Kerff based his verdict on an analysis of only a limited and specific group of manuscripts, that is, those manuscripts containing the penitential that Bishop Halitgar of Cambrai wrote at the request of Archbishop Ebo of Reims. Written as a consequence of the Carolingian reform councils, this penitential naturally reflects an episcopal bias. Moreover, it tries to merge the insular tradition of penitentials with the mediterranean, 'canonical' tradition of canon law, in that it adopts canons from late antique councils dealing with so-called canonical, that is episcopal penance. We do not know, however, how these late antique canons were interpreted and used in Carolingian times. At any rate it does not seem plausible to view such texts as a self-evident reflection of ninth-century practice, as Kerff seems to do.[30] Further, Halitgar's penitential played a specific role in the discussion among Frankish bishops concerning the deposition and reinstallation of Archbishop Ebo after his role in the coup against Louis the Pious of the year 833: a good reason for its having many bishops as readers.[31]

Kerff asked for a thorough investigation of the manuscripts containing penitentials in order to evaluate the intended audience for these books. His own conclusions were based on only a small sample of the available material. A closer look at a larger body of texts, however, reveals that while some manuscripts can indeed be identified as having been intended for an episcopal

---

[28] See for St Gall: R. Kottje, 'Kirchenrechtliche Interessen im Bodenseeraum vom 9. bis 12. Jahrhundert', in *Kirchenrechtliche Texte im Bodenseegebiet. Mittelalterliche Überlieferung in Konstanz, auf der Reichenau und in St. Gallen*, ed. J. Autenrieth and R. Kottje, Vorträge und Forschungen, Sonderband 18 (Sigmaringen, 1975), pp. 23–41; for Lorsch: R. Haggenmüller, 'Frühmittelalterliche Bußbücher – Paenitentialien – und das Kloster Lorsch', *Geschichtsblätter Kreis Bergstraße* 25 (1992), 125–54; for Rheims: Kottje, *Bußbücher*, p. 85; for Salzburg: Meens, 'Kanonisches Recht'.

[29] Kerff, 'Mittelalterliche Quellen' and 'Libri Paenitentiales'; Kerff's view is approved of by Murray, '1215', p. 61.

[30] See 'Libri paenitentiales', p. 29, where Kerff cites Halitgar's penitential concerning the right of a bishop the reconcile penitents, only in a case of emergency to be assumed by a priest. Halitgar's text, however, is a canon from the third council of Carthage, taken from the *Collectio Dacheriana* (Kottje, *Bußbücher*, p. 182), and is therefore taken from the context of late antique canonical penance.

[31] Kottje, *Bußbücher*, pp. 86–90.

audience, the majority seems to have been used by simple priests in the daily work of pastoral care. The following conclusions are based on a sample of 106 manuscripts containing one or more of the so-called tripartite penitentials, by which I understand penitentials drawing upon three traditions: Irish, Anglo-Saxon and Frankish. Among these works I count the *Excarpsus Cummeani*, the *Paenitentiale Remense*, the *Paenitentiale Vallicellianum I*, the *Paenitentiale Merseburgense A*, the *Paenitentiale Capitula Iudicorum*, the *Paenitentiale Parisiense compositum*, the *Paenitentiale Sangallense tripartitum*, the *Paenitentiale Vindobonense B*, and the *P. Ps.-Romanum* that was incorporated as book VI in the penitential of Halitgar of Cambrai. Since all of these texts have recently been studied in depth, we can rely on recent and reliable descriptions of the manuscripts containing these works.[32]

Fourteen of these manuscripts probably were meant to be used by a bishop, and thirteen of these contain Halitgar's penitential. Apart from Halitgar's work only one other manuscript, with the *Excarpsus Cummeani*, has been assigned to an episcopal milieu. This is the manuscript Stuttgart, Württembergische Landesbibliothek, Cod. HB VI 113, written at the end of the eighth century in Rhaetia, which contains not only the *Excarpsus*, but also two collections of canon law, Ps.-Jerome's *De vita clericorum* and Gennadius of Marseille's *Liber sive definitio ecclesiasticorum dogmatum*. It was considered a part of an episcopal library on the basis of its contents, though no text specifically points to a bishop as possessor of the manuscript.[33] There is more reason to assume that a manuscript was intended for use by a bishop when it combines both penitentials and collections of canon and of secular law, as for example the manuscript Münster, Staatsarchiv, MS 5201, written in the first half of the tenth century in Corvey. This manuscript contains laws of the Saxons, the Franks and the Thuringians, the so-called *Capitula Angilramni*, a collection of canons from mainly ninth-century East Frankish church councils (Mainz 813, 847 and 852, Worms 868), the penitential written by Hrabanus Maurus for Heribald of Auxerre, parts of Halitgar's penitential (but without the practical sixth book) and the so-called mixed version of the penitential attributed to Bede and Egbert.[34] A number of manuscripts with Halitgar's penitential include a combination of texts dealing with the topic of the

---

[32] For a full presentation of the evidence, which can only be adduced here in its essentials, see Meens, *Tripartite*, pp. 220–66, and for a discussion of the notion of the 'tripartite penitentials', *ibidem*, pp. 308–11. The recent studies are F. B. Asbach, *Das Poenitentiale Remense und der sogen. Excarpsus Cummeani: Überlieferung, Quellen und Entwicklung zweier kontinentaler Bußbücher aus der 1. Hälfte des 8. Jahrhunderts* (Regensburg, 1975); R. Kottje, *Bussbücher*; G. Hägele, *Das Paenitentiale Vallicellianum I. Ein oberitalienischer Zweig der frühmittelalterlichen kontinentalen Bußbücher. Überlieferung, Verbreitung und Quellen*, Quellen und Forschungen zum Recht im Mittelalter 3 (Sigmaringen, 1984); Mahadevan, 'Überlieferung'; Meens, *Tripartite*.

[33] See J. Autenrieth, *Die Handschriften der ehemaligen königlichen Hofbibliothek* (Wiesbaden 1963), III, 114: 'Für die Zugehörigkeit zu einer Dombibliothek spricht der Inhalt'.

[34] See Kottje, *Bußbücher*, pp. 45–6 and H. Mordek, *Bibliotheca capitularium regum*

restoration of lapsed clerics, which apparently reflects the problems which arose from the deposition and reinstallation of Ebo of Rheims. These manuscripts were probably also intended for an episcopal audience.

Twenty-two items of our sample can be characterized as canon law manuscripts. Most likely several of the latter were also meant for an episcopal audience, though we should not forget that simple priests were also required to know their canon law. The manuscript Copenhagen, Ny. Kgl. S. 58, for example, written in an uncial hand in the first half of the eighth century, possibly in Septimania, was characterized by Allen Frantzen as a fine example of the genre of penitential handbooks that were 'floating through the ranks of the clergy'.[35] It contains material from canon law, decretals, the *Epitome Hispana* and excerpts from the *Collectio Hibernensis*, the *Libellus Responsionum* written by Gregory the Great to Augustine of Canterbury, and the *Excarpsus Cummeani*. Such a collection of texts could very well be of use for a priest, as Frantzen suggests, maybe in a missionary context. Another manuscript with the *Excarpsus*, Munich, Bayerische Staatsbibliothek, Clm 6243, looks more like a manuscript meant for an episcopal audience. Apart from the *Excarpsus*, it contains two unique collections of canon law, the so-called first and second collection of Freising, canons from the synods of Rome (595), Verneuil (755) and Ascheim (755–60), a letter of Pope Hormisdas, a list of metropolitan sees and their suffragans and a list of names, probably for liturgical commemoration.[36] The older part of this manuscript, written at the end of the eighth century near Lake Konstanz, was already attested very soon after its completion in the episcopal see of Salzburg where it was used in the composition of the *Paenitentiale Vindobonense B*, and possibly for the canon law collection of Diessen.[37] Perhaps it was there that the later part, written around 800 in Freising, was added.

Another category of manuscripts seems to have been intended for service in a pastoral setting. Thirty-two of these can be identified in our sample. These were probably composed for parish priests, as for example the manuscript Paris, Bibliothèque Nationale, MS Lat. 1207 (I), written in the second half of the eleventh century, in northern France, probably in the archdiocese of Trier. It contains the *Paenitentiale Parisiense compositum*, fragments from the episcopal capitulary of Ruotger of Trier concerning baptism and burial, a sermon on the last judgment (*de die iudicii*) attributed to Augustine, and the first two chapters of the little compendium of Christian dogma, the history of salvation and Christian ethics known as the *Scarapsus Pirminii*, here attributed to Augustine. The manuscripts may originally have included the whole *Scarapsus*, since it

---

Francorum manuscripta. Überlieferung und Traditionszusammenhang der fränkischen Herrschererlasse (München, 1995), pp. 378–86.

[35] A. Frantzen, 'The Significance of the Frankish Penitentials', *JEH* 30 (1979), 409–21 (p. 412).

[36] Asbach, *Poenitentiale Remense*, pp. 24–5.

[37] See Meens, 'Kanonisches Recht', p. 17.

breaks off right after chapter two.[38] A rich manuscript now in the Bibliothèque municipale at Sélestat, written in the later part of the ninth century, maybe in Mainz, has recently been characterized as a well designed handbook for a Carolingian cleric in the form of a thick paperback.[39] It contains two sets of episcopal capitularies, an exposition of the Mass, exorcisms, benedictions, prayers for baptismal rites, and excerpts from Isidore of Seville's *Etymologies* concerning clerical grades and three penitentials including the *Excarpsus Cummeani*.[40] Because of the inclusion of episcopal capitularies, Kerff sees this manuscript as designed for use in synodal inquisition under the authority of the bishop.[41] Yet episcopal capitularies were written for parish priests, so the characterization of this manuscript as a codex compiled for pastoral purposes seems more plausible.[42]

Another group of manuscripts also appears to have been intended for use in a pastoral setting. These are the liturgical manuscripts which also include a penitential. In our group we find four such manuscripts. One, recently edited, sacramentary, written in France around the year 800, contains the *Excarpsus Cummeani*, as well as the Hieronymian martyrology and exorcism formulas.[43] The liturgical material in a manuscript written in the first half of the eleventh century, probably for the church of S. Lorenzo in Rome, reflects a liturgical setting that is, towards the end, more geared to a penitential context. Apart from the *Paenitentiale Vallicellianum I*, this manuscript, Rome, Biblioteca Vallicelliana, E 15, contains *missae sanctorum*, a *missa super penitentem*, a *caput ad reconciliandum penitentem* and a burial Mass.[44]

Nineteen manuscripts of our group originally contained only penitentials. Some of these consisted of just one penitential, while others presented a whole group of these texts to their readers. Seven manuscripts containing only Halitgar's penitential, written in the north-eastern part of France soon after the text was finished, still exist.[45] This phenomenon has been attributed to the

---

[38] See Meens, 'Fragmente' and 'Volkscultuur'.

[39] H. Mordek, 'Karolingische Bischofskapitel in der Humanistenbibliothek zu Schlettstadt', *Zeitschrift für die Geschichte des Oberrheins* 134 (1986), 413–21 (p. 417).

[40] The *Excarpsus* text was unknown to Asbach, *Das Poenitentiale Remense*. The other penitentials are *P. Ps.-Egberti* and *P. Ps.-Bedae*; see R. Haggenmüller, *Die Überlieferung der Beda und Egbert zugeschriebenen Bußbücher* (Frankfurt a.M., Bern, etc., 1991), p. 100.

[41] Kerff, 'Libri paenitentiales', p. 46, n. 68.

[42] For the public of the *Capitula episcoporum*, see P. Brommer, 'Capitula episcoporum. Bemerkungen zu den bischöflichen Kapitularien', *ZKG* 91 (1980), 207–36 (pp. 225–6).

[43] *Liber sacramentorum Augustodunensis*, ed. O. Heiming, CCSL 159B (1984); it concerns Berlin, Deutsche Staatsbibliothek, MS Phillips 1667.

[44] Hägele, *Paenitentiale Vallicellianum*, p. 27.

[45] The date of Halitgar's penitential cannot be established with certainty, see Kottje, p. 5, but if Hartmann's hunch is correct that the canons he discovered are, indeed, Halitgar's, then it may be assumed that Halitgar wrote his penitential towards the end of his episcopacy, i.e. towards 831, see W. Hartmann, 'Neue Texte zur bischöflichen Reformgesetzgebung aus den Jahren 829–31. Vier Diözesansynoden Halitgars von Cambrai', *DA* 35 (1979), 368–94.

relative success of this work in the pastoral field.[46] Its success may indeed be the result of a general need for Halitgar's work – or of a purposeful dissemination by Halitgar himself. In both cases, however, manuscripts including this text obviously reached the level of parish priests.[47] A manuscript written in the tenth or eleventh century in the region of northern Italy and southern France, which has come down to us as part of the codex Paris, Bibliothèque Nationale, MS n.a.l. 281, contains fragments of several penitential texts, including the *Paenitentiale Capitula Iudiciorum*, together with liturgical instructions, so-called *ordines*, for the confessor. Although only parts of the original manuscript remain, it clearly must have contained several penitentials, as well as liturgical material pertaining to the rites of penance.[48] It seems feasible that such manuscripts comprising more than one penitential were intended to serve as pastoral works. In manuscripts apparently meant for a pastoral setting we often also find more than one penitential included. Such manuscripts might also contain penitentials that try to include as much material as possible, such as the *Paenitentiale Vindobonense B*.[49] These combinations of divergent penitential sentences probably were meant to offer the confessor a certain amount of freedom when imposing a specific penance.

Another group of only four manuscripts reflects a monastic background. One of these manuscripts, now divided into two parts, Avignon, Bibliothèque municipale, Cod. 175 and Montpellier, Bibliothèque municipale, MS H.12, was originally conceived as one work when it was put to parchment in the second quarter of the ninth century, in the monastery of Gellone. It contains the Rule of St Benedict, a martyrology, Mass formularies, expositions of the Mass, a chronicle, excerpts from the councils of Neocaesarea and Ancyra and from the *Excarpsus Cummeani*, and the penitentials attributed to Bede and Egbert. Dom Wilmart characterized this manuscript as a sort of monastic Bible, at one and the same time a book for reading, a liturgical book, possibly a book of instruction, a canonical collection and an ascetic handbook.[50]

Excerpts from the penitential of Halitgar were also used in manuscripts

---

[46] See Kottje, *Bußbücher*, p. 85, where he concludes that this work 'in diesem Raum zumindest in den Jahrzehnten nach der Abfassung als besonders geeignetes Hilfsmittel für die Bußpraxis angesehen worden ist und damit den Zweck erfüllt hat, den Erzbischof Ebo ihm zugedacht hatte, als er Halitgar um die Abfassung des Werkes bat'.

[47] Dissemination by Halitgar is implied in Hartmann, 'Neue Texte zur bischöflichen Reformgesetzgebung'. The manuscript evidence, however, suggests that it was Ebo who was responsible for this dissemination; see Kottje, *Bußbücher*, pp. 84–5.

[48] Mahadevan, 'Überlieferung', pp. 32–4.

[49] See Meens, 'Kanonisches Recht', pp. 26–7.

[50] A. Wilmart, 'Un livret bénédictin composé à Gellone au commencement du IXe siècle', *Revue Mabillon* 12 (1922), 119–33 (pp. 132–3): 'une sorte de 'bible' monastique, tout à la fois livre de prime pour la lecture de la Règle et du Martyrologe, livre de messe pour les sollennités, peut-être aussi livre d'édification servant à complies, en tous cas collection canoniques et manuel d'ascèse'. Cf. Haggenmüller, *Überlieferung*, pp. 55 and 74.

which probably served an educational purpose. Parts from books one and two, mainly derived from the writings of Julianus Pomerius and Gregory the Great, appear to have been especially useful in such a context.[51] The Vienna manuscript Österreichische Nationalbibliothek, MS Lat. 956, written in the western part of Germany at the end of the tenth century, contains Halitgar's first two books, Alcuin's *De virtutibus et vitiis*, the *Via regia* of Smaragdus of St Mihiel and Augustin's *De doctrina christiana*, which suggest a royal destination for this manuscript.[52] In two French manuscripts from the tenth and eleventh century, Paris, Bibliothèque Nationale, MSS Lat. 2077 and 2843, Halitgar's penitential is combined with Ambrosius Autpertus' *De conflictu vitiorum et virtutum* to form a new work of moral instruction.[53] Eight manuscripts, all with Halitgar's penitential, can be said to belong to this group of 'educational' manuscripts.

A closer consideration of the manuscript evidence reveals, therefore, three main areas in which penitential texts were employed. They seem to have been used as moral or ascetic treatises in an educational setting, as collections of canonical sentences to be used in an episcopal surrounding such as – but not exclusively – synodical inquisitions, and, last but not least, as practical guides for confessors working in a pastoral context. Halitgar's penitential especially served all these different purposes. The rather general first books of this work made it a suitable vehicle for educational values, while the authority of the work may have been the main reason for its popularity among bishops. But even Halitgar's work was also used in a pastoral setting. Here Kerff's view, that these works were only employed under the authority of the bishop, may be correct, since it may have been Halitgar himself who distributed his work amongst his clergy. In other cases, however, Kerff overestimates the power of early medieval bishops to control the doings of their clergy. If it was that difficult for bishops to provide their priests within their diocese with the necessary books, such as penitentials, it would have been even more difficult to provide them with the right ones! Even as late as the eleventh century the eighth-century *Excarpsus Cummeani* was still used as the main source of the *P. Parisiense compositum*, a text probably composed in the archdioceses of Trier, where in the tenth century Archbishop Ruotger had so strongly condemned the older penitentials.[54] The *Parisiense* penitential was, moreover, combined with extracts of Ruotger's episcopal capitulary, though not his canons on penance.[55]

It is remarkable that while in the ninth century the manuscripts which

---

[51] On the sources of the first two books, see Kottje, *Bußbücher*, pp. 173–81.

[52] See O. Eberhardt, *Via Regia. Der Fürstenspiegel Smaragds von St. Mihiel und seine literarische Gattung*, Münstersche Mittelalterschriften 28 (München, 1977), pp. 125–6.

[53] See Kottje, *Bußbücher*, pp. 50–2.

[54] M. Blasen, 'Die Bußbücher und die Reformbestrebungen des Erzbischofs Ruotger in Trier (915–930) auf dem Gebiet der Bußdiszplin', *Archiv für mittelrheinische Kirchengeschichte* 3 (1951), 56–76.

[55] See Meens, 'Fragmente', p. 168.

prevail are those written with a pastoral intent, that is, those consisting mainly of penitential text or combining penitentials with other pastoral works, in the tenth century the number of juridical manuscripts and those written for an episcopal audience become much more significant. Twenty-eight manuscripts from the ninth century belong to the first group, while juridical and episcopal manuscripts add up to just nine manuscripts. But whereas the latter category remains stable throughout the tenth century (nine manuscripts), the same period sees a marked decline of the number of pastoral manuscripts (three). This picture might be the result of the selection of texts under scrutiny, among which the penitential of Halitgar dominates, especially in the later period, but it could also mean that bishops were indeed gaining control in the tenth century, or even that pastoral care declined radically in that 'iron century'.[56] An examination of the manuscripts of ninth- and tenth-century penitentials, as well as other texts for pastoral use, might provide answers to these questions.

It is notable that all penitentials that have come down to us in only one or two manuscripts are to be found in manuscripts together with other texts of a penitential or pastoral character. This indicates that penitential texts which were connected to canon law texts, such as the *P. Capitula Iudiciorum* or the *Excarpsus Cummeani*, had a better chance of survival than texts merely intended for pastoral use. This seems rather obvious, since the handbooks of confessors were probably not as well preserved as the manuscripts of a juridical nature that were kept in episcopal or monastic libraries or archives. It implies, however, that manuscripts intended to be used by priest confessors were more common than the surviving evidence suggests, and that the penitentials of which only one or two manuscripts exist are to be regarded as representatives of a much larger group.

It is not only the manuscript evidence which reveals that penitentials served a number of purposes. Some penances imposed in penitentials can best be regarded as punishments in which what is stressed is the vindictive nature of the reconciliatory acts rather than the amelioration of the sinner. Again, Halitgar's penitential stands out as an exception. Clerics who had committed serious offenses, such as homicide, fornication or addiction to drink, were to be degraded, which is more of a punishment than a penance. However, although ideas of punishment and judgment play a certain role in penitentials, the paramount metaphors in these texts are penance and healing.[57]

In other words, penitentials were generally intended to be employed in a pastoral context. The manuscripts were composed for parish priests to be consulted in the normal course of their pastoral duties. That they were actually used by confessors is suggested by the appearance of these manuscripts, which

---

[56] A growing importance of episcopal power in the tenth century is suggested by R. McKitterick, 'The Church', in *The New Cambridge Medieval History*, vol. III, *900–1050*, ed. T. Reuter (in press). I thank the author for letting me read her contribution before publication.

[57] R. Kottje, ' "Buße oder Strafe?". Zur "Iustitia" in den "Libri Paenitentiales" ', in *La Giustizia nell'alto medioevo (secoli V–VIII) I*, SSSpoleto 42 (1995), pp. 443–74.

are not only simple, small, unadorned and originally often unbound, but sometimes still bear marks that show heavy use. It can also be shown that priests actually possessed these manuals, for they are mentioned in inventories of priests' possessions, which are extremely precious records for this period. But while these texts are first and foremost pastoral works, they do also have a juridical character, apparent already in the oldest Irish penitentials when they speak of degradation. We noticed that penitentials are often transmitted in manuscripts together with canon law collections. Fragments of penitentials were also incorporated into canon law collections, while sentences from canon law made their appearance in penitentials.

Secret and Public Penance

To understand the conflation of penitentials and canon law, we have to look into the history of this genre of texts. The earliest penitentials were written in Britain and Ireland in the sixth century, in a monastic setting. Confession originated in the monastic practice of the devotional confession, which was intended to guide the monk to perfection, but could also be used as a disciplinary tool, while traditional notions of penance also played a formative role.[58] In the monastically oriented British and Irish churches, where traditional canon law was almost unknown, a confessor would also take disciplinary actions as a matter of course, especially in cases where clerics were concerned. In a missionary context, in which, to gauge from the geography of the extant manuscripts, a lot of penitentials were employed, the role of bishops would also have been limited, and confession may have helped as much to keep up discipline among the clergy as to serve pastoral purposes. Apparently this was quite unproblematic until confession became so strongly advocated throughout the Frankish kingdoms at the close of the eighth century, when penance became a dominant theme in Carolingian discourse. At that moment this practice clashed with the settled interests of the Carolingian episcopacy, which resulted in the discussion of the proper ways of doing penance at the reform councils of 813. The solution to the problem of reconciling the orthodox tradition of canon law as laid down in canon law collections and the insular mode of hearing confession was found in the so-called Carolingian dichotomy, epitomized in the device: public penance for public sins, non-public penance for sins that had remained secret. This new orthodoxy was already expressed in the *Paenitentiale Remense* and in the episcopal capitularies of Theodulf of Orléans, but was incorporated into official Carolingian legislation by the reform councils of 813.[59] One should not forget, however, that this was a

---

58 For a detailed discussion of the context of the earliest insular penitential documents, see L. Körntgen, *Studien zu den Quellen der frühmittelalterlichen Bußbücher*, Quellen und Forschungen zum Recht im Mittelalter 7 (Sigmaringen, 1993), pp. 60–72.

59 See R. Meens, '*Paenitentia publica* en *paenitentia privata*. Aantekeningen bij de

theoretical solution to a probably extremely confusing situation. To dismiss
the only detailed description regarding the practice of early medieval penance
because it does not live up to the expectations of these regulations is, therefore,
questionable.[60]

When Ekkehard IV of St Gall described the penitential acts of the parents of
one of the great teachers of his monastery, Iso, he conformed neither to the
rules of public nor to those of secret penance. After having sexual intercourse
during Easter Saturday, the wedded couple lamented their sins in front of their
entire household, and subsequently confessed their evil deed in ashes and
sackcloth to the parish priest (*presbyter loci*). This priest gave them an
indulgence (*indulgentia*), but ordered them to remain standing outside the
church for a day and a night, and banned them from Easter communion. The
couple then turned to the priest of the next village, who lived in the odour of
sanctity. Still in ashes and sackcloth, they confessed their misdeed in tears to
this priest and his flock (*civibus eius*), and asked him if they could receive
communion the next day. The priest rebuked them for their sinful behaviour,
but gave them his blessing before they returned home. During Mass on Easter
Sunday the couple stood outside the church, until the priest showed them in
when the Kyrie had been sung; he seated them at the back of the church
(*extremos locaverat*). They did not go for communion because this had not found
favour with their priest. After communion, however, the priest from the next
village came in to say another Mass on behalf of his parishioners, and *he* gave
communion to the penitent couple and returned to his flock. When the couple,
grateful for having received communion from his holy hands, sent a horseman
with alms to the neighbouring priest, it turned out that he had never left his
flock that day. It was concluded, and confirmed during a synod, that it must
have been an angel who had appeared to grant the couple communion.[61]

It is clear that we are not dealing with a description of public penance here,
although the ritual as such bears a great resemblance to the ritual of public
penance: sackcloth and ashes, standing outside the church, being led into
church in a ritual way, occupying a special place in church, exclusion from
communion – all are parts of the ritual of public penance.[62] Public penance,
however, belongs to the domain of the bishop, while here the parish priest
conducts the ritual. Of course, Ekkehard tells this story about the exemplary

oorsprong van de zogeheten Karolingische dichotomie', in *Die Fonteyn der ewiger
wijsheit. Opstellen aangeboden aan prof. dr. A.G. Weiler ter gelegenheid van zijn 25-jarig
jubileum als hoogleraar*, ed. P. Bange and P. de Kort (Nijmegen, 1989), pp. 65–74.

60 As Kerff does, 'Libri paenitentiales', p. 36.

61 C. 30, *Ekkehardi IV, Casus Sancti Galli*, ed. H. Haefele, Ausgewählte Quellen zur
deutschen Geschichte des Mittelalters. Freiherr vom Stein Gedächtnisausgabe 10
(Darmstadt, 1980), pp. 70–2.

62 de Jong, 'Boetedoening', pp. 129–32; the author develops her ideas in M. de Jong,
'Pollution, Penance and Sanctity: Ekkehard's Life of Iso', in *The Community, the
Family, and the Saint: Patterns of Power in Early Medieval Europe*, ed. J. Hill and M. Swan
(Turnhout, 1998), pp. 145–58.

behaviour of Iso's parents in order to emphasize the holiness of his hero, Iso. He does this not only by stressing the exemplary behaviour of his parents after their fatal lapse, but also by depicting Iso as someone being conceived in a very special way. It was generally held that children conceived on a holy day would be deformed. Because they were conceived in a way that defied the cosmological order, they would come into the world in an anomalous form. But an anomaly does not necessarily have to be negative. In this case, the exemplary behaviour of his parents turned Iso into a 'good anomaly', that is, into a saintly person.[63] Now, however anomalous the parents' original deed and however marvellous the angel's appearance, the actions of the local priest, characterized by Ekkehard as wise (*discretus*), do not seem to have been at all out of the ordinary run of things.[64] After all, if a story like this was to be plausible, its setting had to be recognisable to its audience. Or are we to believe that the monks of St Gall were unacquainted with the rituals of confession in the lay world?

We could see the ritual portrayed so well by Ekkehard as an illustration of the evolution from the Carolingian dichotomy to a later tripartite stage, where a 'less solemn form of penance', the *paenitentia minus sollemnis*, was formally introduced. After all, Ekkehard was writing in the eleventh century, and though the *paenitentia minus sollemnis* was recognized only late in the twelfth century, it must have had a long prehistory.[65] Ekkehard's description could, on the other hand, represent a very practical state of affairs that might have existed much earlier than the eleventh century.[66] Instead of regarding Ekkehard's tale as being inconsistent with precepts from canon law, we can see it as accurately reflecting the ambiguity of penitentials. Just as public and secret penance have become enmeshed in this story in a peculiar mix of elements found in sentences from canon law and in penitentials, so the two forms of penance appear interconnected in the penitentials themselves and in manuscripts containing such texts. Would not the behaviour of a priest depend in practice on the texts that he had access to, rather that on the theoretical expositions of canon law? And, is it not natural to expect that in small parish communities a certain act that had become notorious would call for a reconciliation with some degree of publicity? If we think of the grave consequences of public penance it would be strange to expect every notorious sin, however small, to be expiated by the episcopal ritual of public penance. Here we should recall the anxious complaints about the absence of episcopal confirmation for the newly baptized: if bishops could not visit all the parishes in order personally to confirm baptisms performed by priests, how could they have intervened in all instances of manifest sins requiring public penance in

---

63 de Jong, 'Boetedoening', pp. 135–7.
64 de Jong, 'Boetedoening', pp. 134–5.
65 See H. Platelle, 'La violence et ses remèdes en Flandre au XIe siècle', *Sacris Erudiri* 20 (1971), 101–71 (pp. 139–69).
66 This is the way M. de Jong sees this story in her 'Pollution, Penance and Sanctity'.

these parishes?[67] Would not the ritual portrayed by Ekkehard live up to the expectations of such a small community, without there being any need to call in episcopal authority?

That even bishops did not always apply the canonical rules concerning penance correctly is illustrated by the adaptation of a chapter from the episcopal capitulary of Gherbald of Liège in a manuscript from Senlis. This adaptation of Gherbald's work by a bishop of Senlis, perhaps Erpuin (840–872), is now known as the *Capitula Silvanectensia I/II*. Both of these texts take over chapters by Gherbald regarding penance in which the final responsibility is taken by the bishop.[68] In the *Capitula Silvanectensia I* the passage ordering sinners to be brought before the bishop is left out, however, so priests seem solely responsible for these people, who in Gherbald's case were still supervised by the bishop.[69] The *Capitula Silvanectensia II*, moreover, give priests the possibility to reconcile mortal sinners who have confessed their sins to them, but only under the supervision of the bishop, if the bishop does not want to do this himself.[70] Most likely this chapter pertains to sins that were secretly confessed to a priest, but the penitents were nevertheless reconciled, if not by the bishop himself, then at least under his supervision. So even in an episcopal capitulary the Carolingian dichotomy was not followed to the letter.

The Communal Nature of Secret Penance

If we think of secret penance in terms of a kind of communal ritual and not of a private act (as is suggested by the use of the term 'private penance'), it becomes much easier to understand that priests could act as a 'police des moeurs' as well as hear confessions.[71] That hearing confession was a sort of communal ritual, is implied by the close link between confession and communion. If confession was heard regularly at a certain period of the liturgical year and if penance was normally undertaken during one of the fasting periods associated with the three principal liturgical feasts, penance must have had some communal aspects. The visibility of some forms of penance – for instance, fasting, alms giving and exclusion from communion – fits very well into such a picture. This would mean that in such a small community strong

---

[67] S. Foot, ' "By Water in the Spirit": the Administration of Baptism in Early Anglo-Saxon England', in *Pastoral Care Before the Parish*, ed. J. Blair and R. Sharpe (Leicester, London etc., 1992), pp. 171–92 (p. 179); cf. Thacker, 'Monks', p. 138.

[68] Gherbald II, c. 11 and Gherbald III, c. 10, ed. Brommer, *MGH Cap. Ep.* I, 30 and 40.

[69] C. 12, ed. *MGH Cap. Ep.* III, 83.

[70] C. 19, ed. *MGH Cap. Ep.* III, 90–1. I follow the editor's interpretation as set forth in note 70.

[71] Murray, '1215', p. 59, questions the dual, policing and pastoral, function of the parish priest.

pressure could be exerted by both the priest and the community at large to confess one's sins, much as in the later middle ages.

Bede's description of St Cuthbert travelling around through small villages, preaching the word of God and hearing confession afterwards, also reveals the communal nature of confession. Because of Cuthbert's eloquence nobody could hide the secrets of his heart from him, and 'all confessed their sins openly (*omnes palam quae gesserant confitendo proferrent*) and they cleansed their sins by the worthy fruits of their penance, as he had ordered'. Bede may here, of course, describe an idealized past, when 'it was the custom amongst the English people at that time, when a clerk or a priest came to a village, for all to gather at his command (*ad eius imperium*) to hear the Word, gladly listening to what was said and still more gladly carrying out in their lives whatever they heard and could understand'.[72] But on the other hand, though Cuthbert is presented as especially holy in visiting 'those villages that were far away on steep and rugged mountains, which others dreaded to visit and whose poverty and ignorance (*rusticitas*) kept other teachers away', the picture of pastoral care as presented here, carried out from a monastic setting with preaching and confession as main instruments, must somehow have been familiar to Bede's audience. Noteworthy in this context is the case of Aidan, when it was decided that he should go to Northumbria to preach the faith, after an unnamed Irish bishop had failed in this task because of his austerity: what Bede stresses in Aidan is the quality of discretion, 'the mother of all virtues'. Discretion was, after all, of the utmost importance for a priest when hearing confession.[73]

It has been assumed that the monastic flavour of penance that we encounter in the works of Bede and Theodore, provoked 'indifference, or even resistance' among the people, especially among the rich.[74] This resulted in a far flung practice of commutation, to be sharply criticized at the council of Clovesho (747).[75] Together with the apparent lack of manuscripts containing penitentials written in early Anglo-Saxon England, the absence of a firm tradition of composition of such works has been interpreted as evidence for a very limited application, indeed, of penitential prescriptions. This would be due to their austerity, or to use the author's words, to the 'horrors of penance'.[76] It should not be forgotten, however, that commutation was from the start a means by which the confessor could accomodate the rules he found in his penitential to the specific circumstances of the sinner. And although Theodore's penitential

---

72 See *Bede's Ecclesiastical History of the English People* IV, 27, ed. B. Colgrave and R. A. B. Mynors, 2nd edn (Oxford, 1992), p. 432; for Bede's idealized past, see A. Thacker, 'Bede's Ideal of Reform', in *Ideal and Reality in Frankish and Anglo-Saxon Society. Studies presented to J. M. Wallace-Hadrill*, ed. P. Wormald and R. Collins (Oxford, 1983), pp. 130–53.

73 *Bede's Ecclesiastical History* III, 5, pp. 228–9.

74 Thacker, 'Monks', p. 162.

75 C. 26–7. For this council see C. Cubitt, *Anglo-Saxon Church Councils c.650–c.850* (London and New York, 1995), pp. 99–152.

76 Thacker, 'Monks', pp. 162 and 169.

is the only one that can be safely assumed to have originated in Anglo-Saxon England, there must have been penitentials from Ireland in use at the time of its composition, as the *Discipulus Umbrensium* himself admits in his prologue.[77] Theodore's penitential, moreover, exists in five recensions, which may well have originated in England, and this in itself is evidence of a lively interest in this text. The text itself, moreover, smacks of penitential experience and thus gives evidence of an existing penitential practice. How far this practice was disseminated and how far it lived up to Bede's expectations, is a question that is difficult to answer. Yet, the fact that on the continent we find a lot of manuscript evidence for penitentials originating from the field of the Anglo-Saxon mission, suggests that penitentials must have been quite common in eighth-century Anglo-Saxon England. That these texts often travelled under the flag of Anglo-Saxon ecclesiastical celebrities, such as Theodore, Bede and Egbert, is another indication of a rather widespread use in Anglo-Saxon England.[78]

It has been observed that the term private confession is an anachronism.[79] Early medieval sources speak of *paenitentia occulta, secreta*, or *paenitere absconse*. It is hard to assess what this type of penance entailed in practice. This 'secret' form of penance can perhaps best be characterized by what it is not: it is not public penance, in the sense of a highly ritualized form of penance imposed by the bishop. Apart from this it probably could take on many forms. The use of the word 'private' evokes modern sensitivities, with regard to privateness, that are hard to imagine in an early medieval context, and it is, therefore, to be avoided. Early medieval penance was not necessarily private. It included various elements taken from the context of public penance that must have made it visible to all and thereby, to a certain degree, public.[80] The act of confession proper was normally part of the ritual for the beginning of Lent or one of the other periods of preparation for a major feast at which one was expected to receive communion, and it was thus also a communal act. Apart from this, confession also played an important part in the ritual for the sick and the dying.[81]

---

[77] Haggenmüller, *Überlieferung*, p. 298, concludes from the manuscript tradition that both the penitentials attributed to Bede and Egbert were composed on the Continent, though there are reasons to assume that the penitential attributed to Egbert might be of Anglo-Saxon origin; *P. Theodori, Discipulus Umbrensium* in: P.-W. Finsterwalder, *Die Canones Theodori Cantuariensis und ihre Überlieferungsformen* (Weimar, 1929), p. 287.

[78] Cf. A. Frantzen, 'The Tradition of Penitentials in Anglo-Saxon England', *Anglo-Saxon England* 11 (1982), 23–56 (p. 35).

[79] See for this and what follows de Jong, 'Public'.

[80] See also Körntgen, *Studien*, pp. 71–2.

[81] See F. Paxton, *Christianizing Death. The Creation of a Ritual Process in Early Medieval Europe* (Ithaca and London, 1990).

Narrative and Normative Sources

Why then is early medieval confession so seldom mentioned in narrative texts?[82] Murray argues that this is so because confession was just as rare as references to it in medieval literature. This fact might equally well suggest, however, that confession was quite an ordinary thing at the time. Ekkehard mentions the penance of Iso's parents' because they were exceptionally devout. If they had acted normally and confessed in secret, this rare example of early medieval penance probably would not have been considered worth remembering. It is the dramatic which is recorded, and this may also be the reason for the stress on deathbed penance in narrative sources. For it is usually only when a sinner is dying that his acceptance or refusal of confession becomes dramatically interesting. I find it hard to use narrative sources as indicators of the frequency of certain acts. How many references do we find to priests preaching or saying Mass? Or how often do narrative sources inform us about everyday practices like clothing and food? Still, Murray's findings that information about confession is mostly found in narrative sources originating from important centres of pastoral care, like Fulda under Hrabanus or the surroundings of Grenoble during the episcopacy of Hugh of Grenoble (1080–1132), are food for thought. In these cases penance probably was indeed part of a movement of reform.[83] It is not clear, however, whether such a reform entailed an introduction of penitential discipline from scratch, or just a reform of an existing penitential practice.

It is also striking that narrative sources hardly ever inform us about authors of penitentials. In his portrait of Theodore of Canterbury and the account of the archbishop's achievements, Bede does not refer to the penitential which went under Theodore's name. Neither does Jonas of Bobbio mention that Columbanus had written a penitential, though this text was definitely used in Columban's foundations. Hearing confession and composing a penitential, therefore, simply do not seem to have been regarded as deeds worth recording in narrative texts. There are, however, other texts which presuppose an existing penitential practice. Visionary literature, depicting the harrowings of hell and the pleasures of paradise, was obviously used to stir people to repent and confess their sins.[84] The visionary parts of Bede's *Ecclesiastical History* are transmitted separately from Bede's work in manuscripts containing sermons.[85] With this we touch upon another genre in which penance and confession abound. Early medieval sermons never grow tired of reminding their audience of the importance of confessing and amending one's sins. Early

---

[82] See Murray, '1215', pp. 65–79.

[83] Murray, '1215', pp. 72–4.

[84] Y. Hen, 'The structure and aims of the *Visio Baronti*', *JTS* n.s. 47 (1996), 477–97.

[85] As e.g. in St Gall, Stiftsbibliothek, MS 150 (I), pp. 1–64, where Bede's *Ecclesiastical History* V, 12–14, is combined with sermons of St Augustine and Valerianus Cemeliensis.

medieval sermon literature still is a neglected field of study, but those sermons available in print are full of preachers exhorting their audience to come to confession. See, for example, the *Scarapsus Pirminii*, the collection of sermons known as *In nomine Dei summi*, and the sermons attributed to Eligius of Noyon and Boniface.[86] Of course, these are all normative sources telling us how people ought to behave, instead of how they behaved. One may, however, wonder whether any medieval sources exist which are not, in one way or another, of a normative kind. The quantity and congruence of these normative sources, however, suggest that penance and confession were important features of early medieval religious life.

In the end, the phenomenon of early medieval confession will because of its very nature remain elusive. Our sources do not permit us to recreate the procedure of penance as it functioned in practice, let alone to establish its frequency with any precision, since such texts are normally of a normative type. We must also reckon with considerable chronological and geographical variety. Nevertheless Murray's dictum, 'Anyone acquainted with theology, however briefly, knew of this corrolary of the "cure of souls"', also holds true for the Carolingian period.[87] It even seems that hearing confession together with dispensing baptism was regarded as one of the principal functions of a priest.[88] Penitential texts do provide clues as to the nature of early medieval penance, while the manuscripts in which these texts have come down to us suggest a public for which these *codices* were intended. They make it possible to conclude that early medieval penance was primarily a communal activity and that the forms it took in practice consisted of a mixture of public and private acts. As such penance was administered by simple parish priests as well as by bishops. Bishops used penitential texts not only when hearing confessions, but also when judging cases in synodical procedures. Probably

---

[86] I stressed the importance of the theme of confession in the *Scarapsus Pirminii* and its textual links with penitential texts in Meens, 'Volkscultuur', pp. 10–14. See also R. E. McNally, ' "In Nomine Dei Summi": Seven Hiberno-Latin Sermons', *Traditio* 35 (1979), 121–43, especially sermon II (p. 136), which begins: 'Ad ecclesiam frequenter conuenite! Confessiones uestras sacerdotibus confitete, et illos rogate ut pro peccatis uestris rogent Deum ut indulgeat uobis.' *Praedicatio Eligii de supremo iudicio*, c. 13, ed. B. Krusch, *Passiones vitaeque sanctorum aevi Merovingici*, *Monumenta Germaniae Historica*, *Scriptores rerum merovingicarum* IV (Hannover, Leipzig, 1902), p. 758: 'Recurrat ad confessionem et agat paenitentiam nec erubescat publicae paeniteri super inmunditiis quae gessit, quia re vera multo melius est hic pauco tempore paeniteri quam per tot milia annorum inferni supplicia sustinere.' Or Ps.-Boniface, sermo II (*PL* 89, 847): 'Igitur illi qui peccare non metuunt, nec sua peccata curant confiteri, vel per poenitentiam emendare, servi sunt diaboli.' Or Sermon III (col. 849): 'Et si quis in quolibet peccato lapsus ceciderit, citius per confessionem resurgat et purget se in poenitentiam'.

[87] Murray, '1215', p. 64.

[88] *Capitula Franciae occidentalis*, c. 8: 'Laici homines venerari debent sacerdotes dei, per quorum officium baptisma consecuntur, paenitentiam accipiunt et benedictionem et, quando necessitas incubuerit, eorum visitationibus recreantur', ed. *MGH Cap. Ep.* III, 44.

because of this, canons from penitentials found their way into early medieval collections of canon law. In the final analysis, therefore, the influence which penitential practice had in the building of canon law was greater than the power which could be exercised by theorists of the Carolingian church reform when trying to change the way priests heard confession.

Appendix

Classification of Manuscripts containing Tripartite Penitentials[89]

I. Manuscripts of a Penitential Nature

Bamberg, Staatliche Bibliothek, Can. 2 (A.I.35) (fols. 33–86) (s.IX med., N.E. France):
  P. Halitgarii.
Brussels, Koninklijke Bibliotheek, 10034–37 (fols. 117–42) (s.IX med., N.E. France):
  P. Halitgarii.
Einsiedeln, Stiftsbibliothek, 281 (886) (pp. 271–322) (s.IX 2/4, France):
  P. Halitgarii.
Einsiedeln, Stiftsbibliothek, cod. 326, (fols. 35–66): s.IX ex. or IX–X, Germany):
  Excarpsus Cummeani.
Ghent, Bibliotheek der Rijksuniversiteit, 506 (551) (pp. 3–132) (s.IX 3/4, 'westrheinisch'):
  P. Halitgarii.
Novara, Biblioteca Capitolare, 18 (LXXI) (s.IX med.–3/4, N. Italy):
  P. Halitgarii.
Orléans, Bibliothèque Municipale, 216 (188) (s.IX², N.E. France):
  P. Halitgarii
Oxford, Bodleian Library, Laud.Misc. 263 (fols. 66–81) (s.IX in., Mainz):
  Excarpsus Cummeani.
Oxford, Bodleian Library, Bodley 311 (s.X, N. or N.W. France):
  P. Remense.
Paris, Bibliothèque Nationale, Lat. 2341 (fols. 204–34) (s.IX 2/4, Orléans):
  P. Halitgarii.
Paris, Bibliothèque Nationale, Lat. 2373 (fols. 7–26) (s.IX 3/4, N.E. France, court of Charles the Bold?):
  P. Halitgarii.

---

[89] This appendix only intends to inform on the manuscripts that were studied and their classification. For a full presentation of the evidence see Meens, *Tripartite*, pp. 220–66.

Paris, Bibliothèque Nationale, Lat. 2999 (fols. 1–32) (s.IX med., St Amand):
P. Halitgarii.
Paris, Bibliothèque Nationale, Nouv. acq. lat. 281 (fols. 92–4, 99–101, 110, 119) (s.X/XI, N. Italy/S. France):
P. Capitula Iudiciorum.
St Gall, Stiftsbibliothek, 550 (pp. 162–234) (s.IX med., Switzerland):
Excarpsus Cummeani.
Vatican, Biblioteca Apostolica Vaticana, Reg. lat. 207 (s.IX 2/4, N.E. France, Rheims?):
P. Halitgarii.
Vatican, Biblioteca Apostolica Vaticana, Vat. lat. 5751 (s.IX ex., N. Italy, possibly Bobbio):
P. Merseburgense A, P. Capitula Iudiciorum, P. Halitgarii.
Vercelli, Biblioteca Capitolare, CCIII (32) (s.IX 4/4, Italy/N.E. France?):
P. Capitula Iudiciorum, P. Halitgarii.
Vienna, Österreichische Nationalbibliothek, Lat. 2233 (s.VIII ex., Salzburg):
P. Vindobonense B.
Zürich, Zentralbibliothek, Rh.XXX, (fols. 14–24) (s.VIII ex., Switzerland):
Excarpsus Cummeani.

II. Pastoral Manuscripts

Barcelona, Biblioteca de la Universidad, 228 (s.X², N. Italy):
P. Vallicellianum I, P. Halitgarii.
Brussels, Koninklijke Bibliotheek, Burgund. 10127–10144 (s.VIII ex., N.E. France, Belgium):
P. Remense or the 'mixed version' of Excarpsus Cummeani and Remense.
Cologne, Dombibliothek, 117 (Dart. 2116) (fols. 61–92) (s.IX med.–², E. France?):
P. Halitgarii.
Florence, Biblioteca Medicea Laurenziana, Ashburnham 82(32) + Orléans, Bibliothèque municipale, 116 (s.IX², W. France, possibly Fleury):
P. Remense (praefatio).
Merseburg, Dombibliothek, 103 (s.IX¹, N. Italy):
P. Merseburgense A.
Milan, Biblioteca Ambrosiana, L 28 sup. (s.IX 3/3, prov.: N.E. Italy):[90]
P. Halitgarii.

---

[90] I owe my knowledge of this manuscript to Raymund Kottje, who got to know it only after publishing *Bußbücher*. The manuscript is dated and localized in S. Keefe, 'Carolingian Baptismal Expositions: A Handlist of Tracts and Manuscripts', in *Carolingian Essays. Andrew W. Mellon Lectures in Early Christian Studies*, ed. U.-R. Blumenthal (Washington, 1983), pp. 169–237 (p. 221).

Munich, Bayerische Staatsbibliothek, Clm 14532 (s.IX ex., N.E. France, possibly Lotharingia):
P. Halitgarii.
Munich, Bayerische Staatsbibliothek, Clm 17068 (1152–1158, Schäftlarn or written for this monastery):
P. Halitgarii.
Munich, Bayerische Staatsbibliothek, Clm 17195 (s.XII med., Schäftlarn or written for this monastery):
P. Halitgarii.
Munich, Bayerische Staatsbibliothek, Lat. 22288 (fols. 1–81) (s.XII^1, possibly Bamberg):
Excarpsus Cummeani.
New York, Library of the Hispanic Society of America, HC 380/819 (s.XI, Catalonia):
Excarpsus Cummeani.
Oxford, Bodleian Library, Bodl. 516 (2570) (fols. 40–104) (s.IX 3/4, N. Italy):[91]
P. Halitgarii
Oxford, Bodleian Library, Bodl. 572 (fols. 51–106) (s.IX 1/3, N. France):
Excarpsus Cummeani.
Paris, Bibliothèque Nationale, Lat. 614a (s.X in., S. France):
P. Halitgarii.
Paris, Bibliothèque Nationale, Lat. 1207 (fols. 2–9) (s.XI^2, N. France):
P. Parisiense compositum.
Paris, Bibliothèque Nationale, Lat. 1603 (s.VIII/IX, N.E. France, 'Nähe des Hofes Karls des Großen'):
P. Remense.
Paris, Bibliothèque Nationale, Lat. 2998 (s.X/XI, Moissac):
P. Halitgarii.
Paris, Bibliothèque Nationale, Lat. 12315 (s.XII^2, N.E. France, Corbie?):
P. Halitgarii.
Paris, Bibliothèque Nationale, Lat. 18220 (s.X^2, prov. St Martin-des-Champs, Paris):
P. Halitgarii.
Séléstat, Bibliothèque Municipale, 132 (s.IX 2/3, Mainz?):
Excarpsus Cummeani.
St Gall, Stiftsbibliothek, cod. 150 (pp. 273–322) (s.VIII/IX of IX in., St Gall):
P. Capitula Iudiciorum.
St Gall, Stiftsbibliothek, 150 (pp. 323–84) (*c.* 820–840, St Gall):
P. Sangallense tripartitum.
St Petersburg, Publičnaja Biblioteka im. M.E. Saltykova-Ščedrina, cod. Q. v. I. Nr. 34 (Corbie 230; Sangerm. 686) (fols. 45–88) (s.IX ex., prov. Corbie):
P. Halitgarii.

---

[91] From Kottje, *Bußbücher*, p. 48, it is unclear whether this manuscript is a codicological unity or a composite one.

Troyes, Bibliothèque Municipale, 1979 (s.X/XI, E. France/W. Germany?):
P. Halitgarii.
Vatican, Arch. di S. Pietro, H 58 (s.XI/XII, Central Italy, probably Rome):
P. Halitgarii.
Vatican, Biblioteca Apostolica Vaticana, Reg. lat. 191 (fols. 54–75) (s.IX[2],
around Rheims):
P. Halitgarii.
Vesoul, Bibliothèque de la Ville, 73 (s.X–XI):
Excarpsus Cummeani.
Vienna, Österreichische Nationalbibliothek, Lat. 2171 (s.IX 3/4, S.W.
Germany):
Excarpsus Cummeani.
Vienna, Österreichische Nationalbibliothek, 2223 (*olim* iur. can. 116) (s.IX
in., Maingebied):
P. Capitula Iudiciorum.
Vienna, Österreichische Nationalbibliothek, Lat. 2225 (s.IX–X, S. Germany):
P. Merseburgense A; Excarpsus Cummeani.
Würzburg, Priesterseminar, Membr. 1 (burned in 1944) (s.IX?):
P. Halitgarii.
Zürich, Zentralbibliothek, Car. C 123 (fols. 159v–69v) (s.X, Zürich?):
P. Halitgarii.
Zürich, Zentralbibliothek, Car. C 176 (D 64) (fols. 1–136) (s.IX (med.–3/4, E.
France, Alsace?):
P. Halitgarii.

III. Liturgical Manuscripts

Berlin, Deutsche Staatsbibliothek, Phillipps 1667 (s.VIII–IX, France):
Excarpsus Cummeani.
Paris, Bibliothèque Nationale, cod. lat. 2296 (fols. 1–8 en 16–27) (s.IX 2/4, St
Amand):
Excarpsus Cummeani.
Rome, Biblioteca Vallicelliana, E 15 (fols. 1–197) (s.XI[1], Rome?):
P. Vallicellianum I.
Vercelli, Biblioteca Capitolare, CLXXIX (152) (s.XII/XIII, Vercelli):
P. Vallicellianum I.

IV. Juridical Manuscripts

Cologne, Dombibliothek, 91 (s.VIII–IX, Burgundy):
Excarpsus Cummeani.
Copenhagen, Kongelige Bibliothek, Ny.Kgl.S.58 8º (s.VIII in., Septimania):
Excarpsus Cummeani.

Florence, Biblioteca Medicea Laurenziana, Ashburnham 1814 (s.XI^2, Poitiers?):
P. Vallicellianum I, P. Halitgarii.
Kynžvart, Zámecká Knihovna, 20 K 20 (fols. 1–78) (s.XII^1, St Blasien):
P. Capitula Iudiciorum, P. Halitgarii.
Milan, Biblioteca Ambrosiana, Trotti 440 (s.XII^1, N. Italy, Milan?):
P. Halitgarii.
Munich, Bayerische Staatsbibliothek, Lat. 6243 (fols. 1–199 en 217–232) (s.VIII ex., around Lake Constance):
Excarpsus Cummeani.
Oxford, Bodleian Library, Can. Patr. lat. 49 (s.XII med., N. Italy):
P. Halitgarii.
Paris, Bibliothèque Nationale, Lat. 8508 (fols. 57–163) (s.IX ex., S. France):
P. Halitgarii.
Paris, Bibliothèque Nationale, Lat. 10588 (s.IX^1 or med., Burgundy or S. France):
Excarpsus Cummeani.
Paris, Bibliothèque Nationale, Lat. 12444 (s.VIII–IX, possibly Fleury):
P. Remense.
Paris, Bibliothèque Nationale, Lat. 14993 (s.XII/XIII):
P. Vallicellianum I.
Rome, Biblioteca Vallicelliana, F 54 (fols. 131–69) (s.XII^1, Central Italy):
P. Vallicellianum.
Rome, Biblioteca Vallicelliana, T. XVIII (s.X^2, Central Italy):
P. Halitgarii.
St Gall, Stiftsbibliothek, 675 (s.IX^1, Bavaria):
Excarpsus Cummeani.
St Gall, Stiftsbibliothek, 676 (s.XI ex., St Blasien/Schaffhausen):
P. Halitgarii.
St Gall, Stiftsbibliothek, 679 (s.IX/X, St Gall?):
P. Halitgarii.
Stuttgart, Württembergische Landesbibliothek, HB VI 107 (s.XI ex., S.W. Germany, near Lake Constance):
P. Halitgarii.
Stuttgart, Württembergische Landesbibliothek, HB VI 112 (fols. 1–124r) (s.X, near Lake Constance):
Mixed version Excarpsus Cummeani and P. Remense.
Vatican, Biblioteca Apostolica Vaticana, Reg. lat. 263 (fols. 205–226) (s.XII med. or XII^2, France or N. Italy):
P. Halitgarii.
Vatican, Biblioteca Apostolica Vaticana, Reg. lat. 407 (fols. 54–101) (s.IX med.–3/4, S. Germany, near St Gall):
P. Halitgarii.
Vercelli, Biblioteca Capitolare, CXLIII (159) (s.X^2, N. Italy):
P. Vallicellianum I, P. Halitgarii.

Verona, Biblioteca Capitolare, LXIII (61) (s.X med. or X^2, N. Italy, Verona?):
P. Halitgarii.

V. Monastic Manuscripts

Avignon, Bibliothèque municipale, 175 + Montpellier, Bibliothèque Municipale, H. 12 (s.IX 2/4, Gellone):
Excarpsus Cummeani.
Berlin, Deutsche Staatsbibliothek, Hamilton 290 (s.X^2, N. Italy):
P. Halitgarii.
Karlsruhe, Badische Landesbibliothek, Aug. IC (fols. 1–36) (s.IX^2, W. Germany):
Excarpsus Cummeani.
Vienna, Österreichische Nationalbibliothek, Lat. 2195 (fols. 2v–57r) (s.VIII ex., Salzburg):
Excarpsus Cummeani (praefatio).

VI. Episcopal Manuscripts

Cambridge, Corpus Christi College, 265 (pp. 1–268) (s.XI^1, England):
P. Halitgarii.
Châlons-sur-Marne, Bibliothèque Municipale, 32 (s.XI^2, W. Germany, Lotharingia):
P. Halitgarii.
Heiligenkreuz, Stiftsbibliothek, 217 (fols. 30–330) (s.X ex., W. Germany):
P. Halitgarii.
London, British Library, Add. 16413 (s.XI in., S. Italy):
P. Capitula Iudiciorum.
Munich, Bayerische Staatsbibliothek, Clm 3851 (s.IX ex., E. France, Lotharingia?):
P. Halitgarii.
Munich, Bayerische Staatsbibliothek, Clm 3853 (fols. 1–128) (s.X^2):
P. Halitgarii.
Munich, Bayerische Staatsbibliothek, Clm 3909 (1138–1143, Augsburg):
P. Halitgarii.
Munich, Bayerische Staatsbibliothek, Clm 12673 (fols. 17–182) (s.X, Salzburg?):
P. Halitgarii.
Münster, Staatsarchiv, c. VII 5201 (s.X^1, Corvey):
P. Halitgarii.
Paris, Bibliothèque Nationale, Lat. 3878 (s.X ex., N.E. France, Liège?):
P. Halitgarii.

St Gall, Stiftsbibliothek, 277 (s.IX 2/4, probably Weißenburg):
P. Halitgarii.
St Gall, Stiftsbibliothek, 570 (pp. 23–197) (s.IX med., E. France, Lotharingia):
P. Halitgarii.
Stuttgart, Württembergische Landesbibliothek, HB VI 113 (s.VIII ex., Rhaetia):
Excarpsus Cummeani.
Vatican, Biblioteca Apostolica Vaticana, Ottob. lat. 3295 (fols. 14–84) (s.IX 3/4, Rhine-Main-area, Mainz?):
P. Halitgarii.
Wolfenbüttel, Herzog-August-Bibliothek, 656 Helmsted. (s.IX med., partly written in Mainz):
P. Halitgarii.

VII. Manuscripts of a Didactic Nature

Monte Cassino, Archivio dell'Abbazia, 557 bis 0 (s.XI[1], Monte Cassino?):
P. Halitgarii.
Paris, Bibliothèque Nationale, Lat. 2077 (s.X[2], Moissac):
P. Halitgarii.
Paris, Bibliothèque Nationale, Lat. 2843 (fols. 57–160) (s.XI, Limoges?):
P. Halitgarii.
St Gall, Stiftsbibliothek, 184 (pp. 188–262) (856, connected to Grimald, Weißenburg, St Gall?):
P. Halitgarii.
Troyes, Bibliothèque Municipale, 1349 (fols. 57–120)(s.XII med., Liège?):
P. Halitgarii.
Vatican, Biblioteca Apostolica Vaticana, Reg. lat. 215 (s.IX[2], Tours):
P. Halitgarii.
Wenen, Österreichische Nationalbibliothek, Lat. 956 (Theol. 320) (s.X ex., W. Germany):
P. Halitgarii.
Zürich, Zentralbibliothek, Rh. 102 (fols. 64–136) (s.X in., Rheinau):
P. Halitgarii.

VIII. Manuscripts of an Uncertain Character

Milan, Biblioteca Ambrosiana, I 145 inf. (s.XII, Milan?):
P. Vallicellianum I.
Arezzo, Biblioteca Consorziale, 312 (s.XII[1]):
P. Halitgarii.

Counselling in Medieval Confession

Alexander Murray

For the general run of historians, until about twenty years ago, confession was among the abused and neglected children of historiography; abused for one reason, neglected for another. It was abused because its parents were divorced, as private conscience and the institutional church went through their long and painful separation after the Reformation, being destined to wrangle over confession ever since. One partner, admitting that sacramental confession was by some oversight not mentioned in the Bible, insisted its lineage was still respectably early, while the other, that confession had been invented by priests in 1215.[1] Since both positions could be sustained simultaneously – because there was little evidence to prove either – the subject was also neglected. Even the theory of confession is fairly short of evidence before the late twelfth century. The practice is shorter, above all when it comes to what was said *in* confession, where there is next to no evidence at all, since confession was meant to be secret.[2] One church historian, standing up for one partner in the divorce, thought the secrets so well kept as to prove that confession had a divine origin.[3]

In the last twenty years the complexion of this miserable child has improved with care and food. Work by Roberto Rusconi, Joseph Avril, John Bossy, Thomas Tentler, Joseph Goering, Lester Little, Nicole Bériou and the Groupe de la Bussière, and still others, and the editing of some of the main confessors' handbooks, have rescued confession from Reformation wrangles and penetrated a few of its secrets.[4] Whether the reviving infant will heal the divisions that blighted it remains to be seen. The improvement is in any case good news. So the Regent History Masters of York, as usual in the front line

---

1 Some of the debate is documented in Murray, '1215', pp. 52–4.
2 The seal and its leaks are discussed in Murray, 'Confession', pp. 281–6.
3 The historian was Suarez: see Honoré, p. 124.
4 From each of the above-named recent writers on medieval confession a single title will serve as guide to others: Rusconi, 'Prédication'; Avril, 'Pratique'; Bossy, 'Social'; Tentler, *Sin*; J. Goering, 'The Internal Forum and the Literature of Penance and Confession', in *The New History of Canon Law*, ed. K. Pennington and W. Hartmann (Washington, D.C., 1997), pp. 1–75; L. K. Little, 'Les techniques de la confession et la confession comme technique', in *Faire croire*, pp. 87–99; Bériou, 'Latran'. Two recent editions are those of Chobham, *Summa*, and Flamborough, *Liber*. For others see below, at notes 9, 13, 22 and 38, and for general list of late medieval handbooks, Tentler, *Sin*, pp. 373–9.

with good ideas, are to be thanked for convening us all to give the subject milk and exercise. From us all, thank you.

My own part here concerns medieval *minds*. It used to be thought that there was *The* Medieval Mind.[5] We in this room know there was no such thing but rather that there were many medieval minds. To forget that fact is to lose the key to an understanding of the entire *machina* of medieval society, since it is the interaction of different minds that engenders change. Hegel's dialectic was at work in the Middle Ages as at other times, and there is no dialectic when everyone thinks the same.

The zone in which I shall explore this principle is a small one within a large, the large one being, naturally, the church. The word 'church' has two meanings, and switches between them according to the angle of our knees. Knees bent, in prayer, 'the church' means the baptized. Knees straight, walking about, 'the church' means the clergy. Even that word clergy has more than one meaning, depending partly this time, on whether one is in it or out of it, and here I shall understand 'clergy' sometimes in the narrowest sense that means priests, but occasionally, also, in a broad one that includes minor orders and especially monks and nuns. Now we all know that in the Middle Ages the clergy in the broad sense were 'those who prayed'. But let us not forget they were something else too. They were also those who studied. Until the end of the Middle Ages *Sacerdotium* was roughly the same as *Studium*.[6] What this meant was that, for all its blurred cultural edges, the clergy had a distinct 'mind', a mind distinguished mainly by committal to Christian belief and practice, and by better education in their regard. The church in one sense (legs straight), that is to say, had one mind; the rest of the church in the other sense (legs bent), the laity, another. The two minds interacted; and it is precisely in their interaction, along the long, varied interface between priesthood and laity, that we must expect to find the dialectic that imparted movement to medieval religion.

Find it, and not find it. Where do we find it? Much of the priest-lay interface was economic and social: a matter of tithes, rents, and meetings in the street. But it is the areas of ecclesiastical encounter that concern us, and for today's purpose these divide into three. The first included the celebration of Mass; burials and marriages, and ceremonies like processions with relics. Here the priest's function was more or less ritualized since both priest and laity used actions and formulae whose meaning was understood before the performance began. In the second and third areas the encounter was intellectual. Someone had to wait to hear what someone else was going to say. In one area were sermons, whether within Mass or outside it, where the preacher sought to put

---

5   A list of books with this or a similar title is given in my 'Nature and Man in the Middle Ages', in *The Concept of Nature. The Herbert Spencer Lectures*, ed. J. Torrance (Oxford, 1992), pp. 25–62 (pp. 29, 57).

6   The theme developed in H. Grundmann, 'Sacerdotium – Regum – Studium: Zur Wertung der Wissenschaft im 13. Jh.', *Archiv für Kulturgeschichte* 34 (1951), 5–21.

a message across by argument and authority. The sermon was a meeting of minds, for that very reason an excessive challenge for some clergy – of which more in a moment. The third section was confession. Confession was distinguished in this context by four peculiarities. It was individual. The priest had to improvise his words in confession for one person as distinct from a general audience; here was a tailor-made suit, not one mass-produced and bought off the peg. Second, it was instant. The tailor had to measure and make the suit in as long as it took to conduct the confession. Third, confession was secret, with consequences for our understanding of the subject I have mentioned and shall come back to. Last, but most important, it was unscripted.

This last point deserves explanation. All of us here know enough of the history of preaching to know that, as the practice became general in the twelfth and thirteenth centuries, the clergy usually had to be stirred to undertake the task at all. The friars organized systematic training for preachers. Before then, many secular clergy had found spontaneous preaching too difficult and fulfilled their obligations, when at all, by reading out standard sermons, merely translating them into the vernacular as they did so. Humbert de Romans tells a credible story of Innocent III's doing this as an example to lower clergy. The pope, that is, read from a Latin homeliary by Gregory the Great and translated the Latin into the vernacular as he did so. When asked afterwards why he did this, when he could have written his own sermons, he replied that it was to shame ignorant clergy who, unable to write decent sermons themselves, were still too proud to read the sermon-for-the-day from a homeliary composed by someone else.[7] Among the great mass of clergy, especially away from big towns, that was a normal way of giving sermons, a fall-back for clerical minds unequal to the challenge. In that measure, for any priest who chose, preaching was scripted.

But confession was different. Books could play only a limited part. Tariffs for particular sins were prescribed in the penitential books of the Carolingian period, laying down penances of days, months or even years, for sins according to their gravity. The tariffs seem severe, and whether priests actually followed them, or commuted them in some way, has puzzled scholars from the late twelfth century until now. What is certain is that, as the idea of inner contrition – being distinct from external penance – gained ground in confession, the priest's role became increasingly a matter of judgement.[8] The priest had to judge whether an act was sinful at all, how bad it was, the circumstances, and how far the penitent's contrition had excused him from an external act of penance. Let me quote a typical thirteenth-century handbook on the subject. It says 'penances are to be gauged, heavier or lighter, by the

7   Humbert of Romans, *Liber de eruditione praedicatorum* I.vii, in Humbert's *Opera de vita regulari*, ed. J. J. Berthier, 2 vols. (Turin, 1956), II, 397; quoted by Rusconi, 'Prédication', p. 74.
8   On contrition see B. Poschmann, *Penance and the Anointing of the Sick*, trans. T. Courtney (Freiburg and London, 1964), p. 163; and Murray, '1215', p. 62.

discretion of a confessor as he considers the quantity and quality of the offences and the person's condition'.[9] A score of similar acknowledgements could be quoted. It was axiomatic, in fact, that penances must be tailor-made on the basis of certain – or sometimes uncertain – principles, in interpreting which the confessor had to think for himself. The same handbooks says: 'if a penitent is involved in farmwork, the army, or travel, and cannot fast, he should give money to feed or clothe or redeem the poor or for the building of a church or bridge, or some other work of charity; and if he is too poor for that but still cannot fast, let him say forty paternosters on each day when he should be fasting'.[10] Again there are scores of prescriptions of this kind. No doubt the priests found them useful guides. But guides only: they are not, as the homeliaries were, scripts.

In the matter of church organization a further consequence follows. *Qua* confessor, the priest must be wise. Whatever qualities might be demanded by a priest's other duties, wisdom was the demand put on him by his part in confession. I call it wisdom. But the wisdom actually comprised three qualities which together composed it: a holy life; instruction; and prudence. They are the three which, in one form or another, often come together in thirteenth-century prescriptions for confessors. Thus Innocent III's famous canon on confession, *Omnis utriusque sexus*, says the confessor priest

> should be discerning and prudent ['discretus et cautus'] so that like a practised doctor ['more periti medici'] he can pour wine and oil on the wounds of the injured, diligently enquiring into the circumstances both of the sinner and of the sin, from which to choose intelligently ['per quas prudenter intelligat'] what sort of advice he ought to give him and what sort of remedy to apply ['quale illi consilium debeat exhibere et cuiusmodi remedium adhibere'], among the many available for healing the sick.[11]

Episcopal statutes echo this demand. Those of Walter Cantilupe, for instance, in 1240, say the priest 'must be able to teach his parishioners how they should confess, and know how *eorum conscientias perscrutari*, and choose appropriate remedies'.[12] Nor is the confessor's handbook less insistent. The confessor, besides being pious, writes Alan of Lille, 'must not lack the gift of science, and

---

9   *De modo confitendi*, in Oxford, Bodleian Library, MS Bodley 828, fol. 215v: 'iste quidem penitentie taxande sunt levius vel gravius per discrecionem confessoris considerantis quantitatem et qualitatem delictorum et personarum condiciones'. On this work see S. Harrison Thomson, *The Writings of Robert Grosseteste* (Cambridge, 1940), p. 126, §83. I have kept Thomson's name for the tract. But it has been renamed and redefined in the new edition, by Goering and Mantello, Grosseteste, *De modo*. (I quote from a coda in MS Bodley 828, external to the main text.)

10 *De modo confitendi*, MS Bodley 828, fol. 212v, as in note 46 below.

11 Canon 21, in *COD*, p. 221.13–17; translated in *English Historical Documents, 1189–1327*, ed. H. Rothwell (London, 1975), pp. 654–5.

12 Quoted by Rusconi, 'Prédication', p. 73.

should know how to recognize whatever matter comes under his judgement, for the power to judge demands discernment of those matters to be judged'.[13] The priest must be 'dulcis in corrigendo, *prudens in instruendo*, pius in puniendo', in the words of yet another handbook.[14] If the priest felt at all short of learning during a confession it became standard doctrine that he could postpone confession for the consultation of books.[15] Sensitive confessors were so aware of their shortcomings in this respect that some wished confessors could have second sight to know the penitent's psychology by 'prophecy'. That just shows how aware they were of the high demands confession put on a priest's wisdom. As it was, they knew, the church must be content with well-educated, judicious holiness.[16]

It was largely the demands of confession that made the cure of souls the most testing of all disciplines. *Cura animarum est ars artium*, as the Council of 1215 acknowledged, the same Council that made annual confession general, using a dictum of St Gregory Nazianzen to explain the importance it attached to the choice, education and discipline of priests.[17] All involved in confession knew how testing it was for the priesthood, and how disastrous things could be when priests fell short. Thus Caesar of Heisterbach's *Dialogus miraculorum* has several stories in which priestly ignorance or fraud leads to confusion and anger among the laity.[18] Caesar's *exempla* on this topic have a Chaucerian tone, and perhaps we should not put too much weight on them. But logic alone puts weight on the basic confrontation. A penitent who exposed his soul to a priest was at his most sensitive, and even the slightest failure in judgement could wound. Peter Quivel, bishop of Exeter, remembered across years his experiences when confessing to secular priests. His statutes of 1287 included a *Summula* on penance and he recalled with a shudder the flaws of confessor-priests, 'quorum ignorantiam, proh dolor! sepissime sum expertus'.[19]

Confession, then, was individual, secret, and unscripted; and it was each of these things because it was the other two. Added together, the consequences of this trio suggest a conclusion which may blow like a draft of cold air over our proceedings. For they suggest it was precisely in that area of church life from

---

13 *Liber poenitentialis* III.xlvii, ed. J. Longère, AMN 18, 2 vols. (1965), I, 156; quoted by Goering, 'The Internal Forum', p. 30, note 64.

14 Andreas de Escobar, *Interrogationes*, quoted by Tentler, *Sin*, p. 95.

15 Tentler, *Sin*, pp. 100, 102.

16 Notably Caesar, *Dialogus* III.xxxii; I, 155. Cf. Grosseteste, *De confessione* I, in Oxford, Bodleian Library, MS Bodley 52, fol. 151r: 'Unde cum alius mediator non sit nisi homo *et homo non sit cognitor occultorum*, oportet ut illi confiteamur ut sciat super que debet vice dei satisfaccionem iniungere'. The words I have italicized are absent from the same text in MS Bodley 830, fol. 168v. For the work see Thomson, *Writings of Robert Grosseteste*, p. 172, §15; p. 125, §79.

17 Canon 17, in *COD*, p. 244.4; *English Historical Documents*, ed. Rothwell, p. 657.

18 Caesar, *Dialogus* III, I, 110–70 : e.g. III.xxiv, I, 139–41; III.xl, I, 160–1; III.xlii, I, 162; III.xlv, I, 164.

19 Quoted by Rusconi, 'Prédication', p. 76.

which the historian is most systematically excluded that the dialectic of priest-lay relations was most potent. How discouraging. Even to recognize this much is useful, however, as it is always useful to know where we are ignorant, and the mere recognition of this hidden mechanism must be a useful tool in our interpretation of the fortunes of the late medieval church. Steven Ozment has already so used it, by proposing that Luther's detestations of 'works' was a reaction specifically to consequences of confession, at a time when confession in Germany was handled thoroughly, and perhaps prudently, but not prudently enough for the high demands it put on priests.[20] Students of Luther must discuss that theory. For my part I shall formulate a more general hypothesis, touching the ways the hidden mechanism in question *may* have worked.

Let me frame the hypothesis in the light of a famous heresy. The most widespread of official medieval heresies – like Waldensianism or Hussitism – had at their heart the doctrine of Donatism, which equates the efficacy of sacraments with the moral stature of the priest. Since that doctrine must have the effect of dissolving an institutional church, the latter naturally defended the contrary view, and taught that the efficacy of priest's sacraments depended not on his personal qualities but on his office, of which he could be deprived if he was bad but which, while he had it, guaranteed all he did in its exercise.

The church authorities often had to insist on that doctrine. But their insistence on it by-passed an important problem: the ever-changing relation between the intellectual levels of priesthood and laity. These changes would occupy several colloquia, let alone one half-hour contribution to one colloquium. I call the relationship ever-changing because the levels changed. The education of both the priesthood in general, and the laity in general, are complex subjects. One could change more than the other, and in different directions, and all this could not but change their relationship. There were numerous local variations and indeed personal variations: one priest who was wise, holy and learned could make his parish an island of one sort of relationship, while its neighbour was in the opposite condition. None of this had much effect on most sacerdotal duties. The Eucharist, marriage, last rites, worked just the same. Even the sermon, if it was one by Gregory the Great, orally translated into a dialect, was much the same whether the priest was *fatuus* or learned. Even, let it be added, absolution: the end, and sacramental substance, of confession, worked even if the priest were ignorant.

But this did not apply to the meeting of minds in confession. Here the relative intellectual development of the two *did* matter; intellectual, that is, in the sense of the triple compound of education, wisdom, and holiness. I repeat

---

20 S. E. Ozment, *The Reformation in the Cities* (New Haven, Conn., and London, 1975), pp. 17, 26–32, 50–6, 67–8, 72–6, 100, 153–60; cf. Tentler, *Sin*, especially pp. 352–72, and the same author's 'The *Summa* for Confessors as an Instrument of Social Control', in *The Pursuit of Holiness*, ed. C. Trinkaus and H. A. Oberman (Leiden, 1974), pp. 103–37 (with comments by L. E. Boyle and W. J. Bousma on pp. 105 and 123–4).

that the compound could vary from priest to priest and layman to layman, and generically between collectivities of both. A pious layman in Medicean Florence might have *more* of these qualities than an ill-educated country priest. Who was *medicus animarum* then? The sacrament, with its immeasurable healing power, remained the same. But the mind-to-mind encounter could put strains on the priest-lay relationship. The historian will not normally see the strains themselves, only the results.

So let me identify one result. Historians of medieval confession are surely familiar with the official insistence, made in *Omnis utriusque sexus* and elsewhere, that the penitent confess to his own parish priest.[21] The insistence betrays that people might not wish to do so, and there were two possible grounds for their reluctance. One, tied up with the whole matter of 'social control', was that the parish priest was part of the village community. St Bonaventure, defending the right of friars to hear confessions, said there were too many complaints that priests revealed their penitents' secrets in the local community; and his is far from the only such testimony.[22] Breach of confidence was bad enough, with or without the kind of social control exercised by Pierre Clergue at Montaillou, or by lecherous priests whose young women-penitents were so much at risk that some experts recommended young women to take a parent into confession with them.[23]

But there was a second reason why some people might shy from confessing to their own parish priest. He might not have the wisdom, holiness and education required to make any sense of their problems. The *medicus animarum* might not know what oil to pour to soothe people's souls. No wonder some of them wished for second sight. One assuredly expert confessor, the Franciscan David of Augsburg, illustrates a general rule that the wiser a man is the more he knows his limitations. No doctor, David said, can fully recognize all the malfunctions that afflict the body, and since the soul is subtler than the body how much less can anyone fully understand [*plene discernere*] all the spiritual sicknesses arising from human passions and temptations?[24] For the priesthood at large, the *medicus* analogy was a pious image coined with good intentions.

---

21 The background and substance are explored by Avril, 'Pouvoirs du prêtre'.
22 Bonaventura, *Quare fratres minores praedicent et confessiones audiant*, in his *Opera omnia*, 8 (Quaracchi, 1898), pp. 375–85; esp. para. 15 [p. 379L] and para. 19 [p. 381L]. For more evidence of violations see H. C. Lea, *A History of Auricular Confession and Indulgences in the Latin Church*, 3 vols. (London, 1896), I, 450–56; and Courçon's *Summa*, p. 304: 'qui presens est sacerdos aut omnino fatuus est aut confessionum revelator'.
23 E. Le Roy Ladurie, *Montaillou* (Paris, 1975), pp. 98–102, 235; cf. 525, note 1. Courçon, *Summa*, p. 305; 'consilium sanum est ut adducat patrem aut matrem vel aliquem carum suum ante sacerdotem et coram illis simul confiteatur ne ante testem illum audeat sacerdos a luxum provocare quod faceret si in secreto'.
24 David of Augsburg, *De exterioris et interioris hominis compositione* (Quaracchi, 1899), p. 180: 'Sunt et aliae plurimae tentationum species quarum naturas, origines, et curas prosequi longum esset. Si enim nullus medicorum omnes morborum corporalium

The good intentions may or may not have paved the road to Luther's Reformation. What is certain is that failures in this area compromised the structure and effect of the priesthood and could not do otherwise. In this field alone, it was *legal* to be a 'Donatist'; and people were.

They can be proven to have been, in that a popular drift is detectable, away from confessors qualified by law, to those qualified by wisdom and holiness. A saintly bishop will attract a lot of confessions just because he is saintly.[25] The same will be true of a monk or nun renowned for holiness.[26] Saintliness apart, as a general rule the drift was towards religious orders. How far monks and canons had pastoral functions is a question on which more light is gradually being thrown, though in respect of friars it is substantially closed, because the siting of mendicant convents in towns is alone enough to reveal a purpose supplementary to the parish.[27] But the whole question is commonly seen from the viewpoint of church authority, which found it convenient to have 'group practice' clergy to fill deficiencies in the parish system. The laity also had a viewpoint. The viewpoint is especially distinct in respect of confession in that the laity might prefer to confess to religious if they could.

Again, signs survive that some did prefer it. The whole issue can be observed in the confessional manuals. According to Gratian's *Decretum*, St Augustine had said:

> just as we should seek out the more experienced doctor for a bodily cure, so, for the same reason, for the cure of souls, we should seek the wiser priest. (Sicut peritior medicus querendus est cure corporali, ita discretior sacerdos cure animarum.)[28]

That is, a penitent *should* shop around. The manuals quoted this principle while acknowledging the difficulty it presented. Unmodified, it would dissolve the parish and indeed the church, and since the dilemma offered no escape, each writer had to feel for his own answer. Among writers to see the

veritates, et dolores, plene potest cognoscere, quanto minus spirituales morbos tentationum, et passionum, quae subtiliores sunt, valet aliquis plene discernere.'

25 E.g. St Hugh of Grenoble, as in my 'The Temptation of St Hugh of Grenoble', in *Intellectual Life in the Middle Ages. Essays presented to Margaret Gibson*, ed. L. Smith and B. Ward (London and Rio Grande, 1992), pp. 81–101 (p. 93).

26 E.g. *Die Offenbarungen der Adelheid Langmann*, ed. P. Strauch (Strasbourg, 1878), pp. 45–6.

27 J. Avril, 'Recherches sur la politique paroissiale des établissements monastiques et canoniaux (xie–xiie siècle)', *Revue d'histoire de l'Église de France* 59 (1976–80), 453–517; G. Constable, 'Monasteries, Rural Churches and the *cura animarum* in the Early Middle Ages', in *Cristianizzazione ed organizzazione ecclesiastica delle campagne nell'alto medioevo: espansione e resistenze*, SSSpoleto 28 (1982), pp. 349–89. On mendicants see J. Le Goff, 'Apostolat mendiant et fait urbain dans la France médiévale: l'implantation des ordres mendiants. Programme – questionnaire pour une enquête', *AESC* 23 (1968), 335–52.

28 *Decretum*, c. 7, C. III, Q. VII; ed. Friedberg, I, 528. Cf. Ps.-Augustine, *Liber de salutaribus documentis*, LII; *PL* 40, 1066D.

dilemma clearly was Robert of Courçon. To him the Augustinian principle was decisive. Robert said that if a penitent had reason to mistrust the parish priest it was right to go to another priest.

> And if he or she is excommunicated for going to a more discreet priest for the remedy of penance, let this be borne patiently. (Et si excommunicatur quia ad discretiorem transit in remedium penitentie, patienter sustinat.)

Robert was well aware his recommendation *sounded* like Donatism, but he answered his imagined critics. Confession was different from baptism and the Eucharist, he insisted,

> for in respect of these, even moderate learning is not required, only a form of words, and the order and substance of the elements. Whereas the administration of penance calls for wise and discreet counsel [*sanius et discretius consilium*], according to the authority of the fathers and the understanding of the Bible.[29]

The peculiarity of confession could not be put more clearly.

Robert's early contemporary Peter the Chanter was meanwhile more fastidious, insisting the bishop's permission always be obtained for a change of confessor. But his very insistence on this rule shows people broke it, and Peter actually mentions some of the culprits, especially clerks, who habitually avoided confessing to their own deacon on grounds that they are not bound by the parish law. But the lawlessness was widespread.

> Many are therefore deceived [Peter says] in running to religious [*claustrales*] to confess, rather than to those set over them. (Multi ergo decipiuntur currentes ad claustrales et non suos prelatos ut confiteantur.)

If such people had to go off to *claustrales*, let them be quite clear they did so only for *consilium*, or to incur salutary embarrassment by confessing twice, but

---

[29] Courçon, *Summa*, p. 305: 'Praeterea, sicut in cura corporis debet expectari aliquamdiu discretior medicus, antequam ab indiscreto sumatur potio, ita discretus sacerdos debet expectari etiam longo tempore antequam secundum stultum agatur consilium sacerdotis fatui. [The girl who fears a priest's advances is given the advice quoted in note 23 above]. . . . in secreto. Et si excommunicatur quia ad discretiorem transit in remedium penitentie, patienter sustineat illam iniustam excommunicationem. Et secus est de baptismate et de confectione quam de confessione et penitentia quia in celebratione tam baptismatis quam eucharistie non requiritur maior aut minor scientia sed tantum forma verborum et ordo et substantia elementi. Sed in penitentia iniungenda coexigitur sanius et discretius consilium secundum auctoritates patrum et intelligentiam scripturarum.' On theologians' recommendations to bear excommunication patiently, see my 'Excommunication and Conscience in the Middle Ages', The John Coffin Memorial Lecture, 1991 (University of London, 1991), pp. 38–43.

they should not imagine any priest but their own had the power of binding and loosing.[30]

To give worthwhile counsel to a worried penitent, then, a confessor had to have these three qualities that he was learned, wise and holy; and this trio did not necessarily go with the legal right to conduct a particular person's confession. Even the authors of the manuals were aware that the principle thus placed at the heart of the church was at odds with its structure. To borrow a distinction from Evans-Pritchard, medieval religion was mainly one of priests rather than prophets.[31] Even preaching was no exception to that rule, since when charismatic prophet-preachers did appear they might be suppressed. Confession was the odd man out. It was restive under the rule, as penitents, not without encouragement from confessors who saw the point, drifted up the spiritual scale towards confessors they preferred.

We have identified one principle of movement within the church, then, generated by the secret dialectic of confession. I wish now to identify a second, in the other direction. The same strains that drove some penitents away from their legal confessors, that is to say, helped modify the confessors' own approach to moral problems. We can all change, all repent; even parish priests. And in two ways, change is detectable on this side, too.

The first is a case of individual change, as a parish priest, after struggling with demons in his own life, grows older and wiser, and a better confessor. The tell-tale example here comes in one of Caesar of Heisterbach's stories about Cologne and the Rhineland.[32] There was a parish priest, Everard, *plebanus* of St James the Apostle in Cologne. Everard had all the priestly qualities: he was 'literatus, humilis, castus, affabilis, pauperum pater, religiosorum susceptor, totius Christianiae religionis amator, Deo carus, toti civitati acceptus'. He had only one blemish.

> During Lent, the well-to-do and delicate young men of Cologne, sons of the burghers, came to confess their sins and confessed especially to those stirrings of the flesh commonly brought on by fine diet. But Everard had not had much experience of these feelings, so he could be excessively severe on them and say it was disgraceful for Christian men to be

---

[30] Chanter, *Summa* II, 323, lines 22–4: 'Sicut peritior medicus querendus est cure corporali, ita discretior sacerdos cure animarum' [see note 28 above]. II, 323, lines 25–8: 'dissonat etiam consuetudo quarumdam ecclesiarum in quibus clerici vitant suum decanum, unde et eis indulgetur licentia aliis confitendi. Dicit etiam clericus quilibet se iure parrochiali non teneri.' A pilgrim or scholar should confess to the bishop of the place he is in or to his representative 'sive presbytero parrochiali vel religioso', II, 323, lines 40–1. II, 324, lines 50–2: 'In querendo discretum sacerdotem licentia prelati sui mediante, licetne eligere clericum tantum, an etiam monachum?' (clearly an issue of current interest); lines 69–71: 'Multi ergo decipiuntur currentes ad claustrales et non suos prelatos ut confiteantur.'
[31] E. E. Evans-Pritchard, *Nuer Religion* (Oxford, 1956), pp. 287–310.
[32] Caesar, *Dialogus* IV.xcviii; I, 266–7.

troubled by such improper desires. He thus scandalized the weak and drove some of them some way to despair.

But Everard was to learn by experience. God allowed the Apostle Peter to fall for the sake of his flock. In the same way

> he taught his beloved servant Everard a lesson by the scourge of temptation, so that by suffering similar feelings he should learn to sympathize with those under his care . . . and come to understand, through his own experience, how he should heal others [*ex hoc in se ipso didicit, quomodo aliis deberet mederi*].

Caesar had discovered this secret through one of his own fellow-monks, Hermann. Years before, when Hermann was about to enter the order, he had suffered from sexual temptation and decided to go and confess to the well-known, saintly priest Everard, to get the help of his prayers. He found Everard preparing for Mass.

> There was no time to make confession as he had proposed. But instead he whispered secretly into the priest's ear, 'Father, I am seriously disturbed by the goad of the flesh [*stimulum carnis*]. Pray to God that he liberate me.' Everard looked at him for a moment and then suddenly burst out: 'be assured, I suffer the same, so why will *I* be able to pray for you? [*Certe ego simile patior; quid ergo pro vobis orare potero?*]'

Hermann added that he went away edified to know that so holy and senior a man should suffer likewise.

The moral of that story, drawn by the Cistercian Caesar, himself a novice-master and experienced confessor, was that personal difficulty made Everard a better confessor. Age brought wisdom. There is no reason why the case of Everard should have been unique. Within religious orders, where documentation is better than in parishes, we know of old monks who reflect that the temptations they suffered, years before, has proved helpful to them later, as novice-masters or otherwise in counselling the young.[33]

If individual confessors learned how to handle temptations through their own painful experiences, the profession as a whole could learn similar lessons by the experiences of their penitents. In a paper published in 1981 I considered how confessors learned from the experiences of their penitents. Several of Thomas of Chantimpré's stories, I suggested, and some of Stephen of Bourbon's, must have started in this way.[34] The same paper argued that it was practical difficulties in the moral life heard about largely through friar confessors that goaded Grosseteste to make a state-of-the-art translation of

---

33 For examples see my 'The Temptation of St Hugh of Grenoble' [as in note 25], pp. 96–9.
34 Murray, 'Confession', pp. 287, 289–94.

Aristotle's *Nicomachean Ethics*. (Grosseteste referred to the 'new questions' that the confessor-friars brought him 'daily', and sent what appears to be the first copy of the translated *Ethics* to a strict Franciscan whose library was restricted to books with a pastoral purpose.)[35] Compared with the Penitential Books, or even with the Roman Stoics whose adages filled the moral handbooks, Aristotle's ethics are those of moderation and commonsense. It is as if confessors were learning, *via* penitents' experiences, of the practicalities of lay moral life. Let us now look more closely at the process by which this understanding may have been imparted.

To do so we must penetrate the secrecy of confession. This can be done to some extent by the careful use of handbooks and *exempla*. We learn first of all that priests often found penitents ignorant and careless about their moral life, and hence needful of instruction. The priest had to draw out the events in the life of a penitent who may, to quote Giordano of Rivalto, have taken no thought of it beforehand.[36] There were questionnaires a priest could use, questionnaires which both got the necessary information and put it in systematic order – as distinct from the vague chronological order in which some penitents told their story, according to a complaint by Robert of Flamborough.[37] Then the priest had to tell the penitent which sins were mortal and which venial, since many penitents – according to Grosseteste – considered as venial sins which were in fact mortal, like fornication, drunkenness and suchlike (huiusmodi).[38] Some penitents had to be persuaded that Hell and damnation actually existed, according to several authorities.[39] So there was much basic teaching to do.

Having thus taken his horse to water the priest had then to make it drink,

---

[35] Murray, 'Confession as a Historical Source', pp. 306–7, 310–17.

[36] *Prediche inedite del beatu Giordano da Rivalto*, ed. E. Narducci (Bologna, 1867), p. 149: 'Sono molti e molte che vengono a confessione, e non hanno pensato nulla inanzi: questi non si salvano bene.'

[37] Flamborough, *Liber* I.ix, p. 62, lines 68–78; quoted in Rusconi, 'Prédication', pp. 79–80.

[38] Grosseteste, *Deus Est* II [cf. Thomson, *Writings of Robert Grosseteste*, p. 125, §80; p. 176, §32], p. 287: 'Hic querendum est de mortalibus que a laicis pro venialibus habentur ut fornicatio, ebrietas, et huiusmodi. Postea si incautus fuerit querendum, ut si vitium pro virtute reputat, sicut dicunt quidam habundanciam temporalium esse virtutem'; cf. p. 280: 'quia tam clerici quam laici opinantur gulam non esse peccatum mortale ex quo nichil male consequitur'. For continental sources, cf. *Les lettres de Jacques de Vitry*, ed. R. B. C. Huygens (Leiden, 1960), p. 86, lines 166 and 170–4: '[facta confessione] . . . non enim fornicationem credebat esse mortale peccatum'; and two papers of my own, 'Piety and Impiety in Thirteenth-Century Italy', in *Popular Belief and Practice*, ed. G. J. Cuming and D. Baker, SCH 8 (1972), 83–106, especially pp. 95–6; and 'Archbishop and Mendicants in Thirteenth-Century Pisa', in *Stellung und Wirksamkeit der Bettelorden in der städtischen Gesellschaft*, ed. K. Elm, Berliner Historische Studien 3 [Ordensstudien, 2] (Berlin, 1981), pp. 19–75, especially pp. 49–50, 56–7.

[39] Grosseteste, *Deus est*, II, 261: 'Talis [presumptuosus] credit Deum velle neminem damnare dicendo, "Non me fecisset si damnandum me cognovisset".' Cf. the 'Theological Miscellany' in London, British Library, MS Add. 11,579, fol. 27v: 'Ita

and this was harder. We read in Antony of Padua and Remigio de' Girolami, for instance, of the resistance penitents put up to avoid recognizing their sin or accepting penance for it.[40] Frère Laurent, author of the influential *Somme le Roi*, compared one kind of penitent to a wild boar at bay, fighting to defend his moral position.[41] Federigo Visconti, archbishop of Pisa, compared the confessor's battles with those of a knight.

> For the sinner says, 'I will do all you wish; but I will on no account give up such-and-such a mistress – or usury, or my hatred or envy for such-and-such people.' Hence it is that, just as the knight struggles with some tough rebel, so the friar wrestles and battles – his divers reasons and arguments serving as so many arrows – against the sinner, so that he may first conquer and then spiritually fortify him.[42]

A day spent hearing confessions could thus be exhausting, as several confessors testify. The fifteenth-century Carthusian James of Clusa – to name only one – was to claim that he knew no more 'dangerous or difficult work' than the hearing of confessions, and said this was not widely understood by those without experience.[43]

Thesis, antithesis, synthesis. Penitent and priest both had their difficulties. But where there was labour there was result, and this applied on both sides. 'Thou canst not speak of that which thou dost not feel', cried Romeo to his friar. Struggle had to end in compromise, and we again find evidence that it did. The same Robert of Flamborough advises on how to bargain with the penitent, to see what he can bear: he does not wish to hinder 'a scholar in his studies, a

---

aliqui non timent penam purgatorii, nec inferni, set penitenciam'; and Remigio de' Girolami, *Sermones quadragesimales*, in Florence, Naz. MS Conv. Soppr. G. 7. 939, fol. 3v: 'concupiscentia reviviscente et invalescente ligat consuetudo et ratio consopitur et sic trahitur homo in profundum malorum tyrannidi viciorum ira ut carnalium voragine desideriorum absortus rationis sue divini nominis oblitus'.

40 St Antony of Padua, *Sermones dominicales*, ed. A. M. Locatelli, 3 vols. (Padua, 1895–1913), I, 48a: 'si de peccato perpetrato redarguere volueris, statim se intra se recolligit et culpam, quam commisit, excusando abscondit . . . Quum enim redarguitur, aut excusat se ignorantia aut diaboli suggestione aut sueae carnis fragilitate aut proximi occasione'. Remigio de' Girolami, *Sermo pro feria quarta post Dominicam quartam*, in *Sermones quadragesimales*, Florence, Naz. MS conv. Soppr. G. 7. 939, fol. 73r: 'Sepellitur enim anima in defensione peccati. Nam ex tali necessitate homo cadit in defensionem ipsius peccati volens statum sui sceleris excusare. Sepe enim inveniuntur homines scelerati dicentes, quod peccatum [non] est usura, assignantes rationes suas. Alii dicunt quod peccatum [non] est inter solutum et solutam [coitio]. Alii dicunt quod peccatum [non] est ire in alex[iteriam], non reputo me excommunicatum, credo quia peius facit papa me excommunicando. In ista tali defensione peccati sepellitur anima.'

41 *Somme le roi*, edition of Anthoine Berard, Paris, n.d., fol. 32v: 'quant on les chastie et reprent ilz se defendent come le sanglier, si que ilz ne recognoistront la leur folie, et tant plus s'excusent tant plus engrege le peche. Ainsy est il quant dieu les chastie maulgre eulx et dient souvent, Que ne fait dieu, que luy aiye mesfait.'

42 Murray, 'Archbishop and Mendicants', p. 72.

43 Quoted by Tentler, *Sin*, p. 126.

smith in his workshop, or a peasant or other worker, so that he cannot support his family by working, for the sake of an incautiously-given penance'.[44] Grosseteste tells a priest how he can discuss with a married woman how she can best atone for her adultery without arousing her husband's suspicions, as she might, for instance, by outright fasting on certain days. Let her eat, Grosseteste allows, but eat only a little, especially with meat dishes. Even this prescription is subject to the woman's agreement.[45] And Grosseteste, too, says farmwork, travel, or military service can excuse a penitent from fasting.[46] In such cases he should give alms for the poor, or a church or a bridge, and, if too poor for that, say forty paternosters on each day he should have been fasting.

The title of this paper refers to counselling in confession. I may have implied throughout that all the impromptu part of the priest's contribution was to be understood as 'counsel'. That may be too broad a reading. Questioning, teaching moral theology, struggling with penitents to make them believe it, thinking up a fair penance and then bargaining about *that*, may not all count as counsel. But some of it did and our sources not infrequently use the term *consilium* in this connection. I am not speaking now of the *consilium* for which parishioners in difficulties commonly asked priests, and which could be given in close proximity to sacramental confession.[47] I am speaking of counsel given *in* confession. We have already seen the term *consilium* used in the canon of 1215 and in other legislation, and we find it also used in *exempla* about the sacrament. Thus Thomas of Chantimpré admits to having, in confession, persuaded some of his penitents 'secrete *in consilio* ad orandum pro eo',[48] and

---

44 Flamborough, *Liber* V, prologue §235, p. 204, lines 27–31: 'Nolo ut sub pondere penitencie incautum gemat quis ut a studio cessare scolaris a scola, vel ab officio suo faber, vel agricola, vel alius laboriosus ut domui sue providere non possit vel ut dominum suum sequi non possit cursor, vel claustralis conventum'; quoted by Rusconi, 'Prédication', p. 79. The subject was close to Robert of Flamborough's heart: *Liber* IV.ix, §231, p. 201; V.xii, §351, pp. 273–4; V.xvi, §355, pp. 276–1.

45 Grosseteste, *De modo*, p. 96 [= II, §15]: 'Si mulier fecerit adulterium et non audeat ieiunare ne suspecta sit viro suo, consilium nostrum est, ut suscipiat ieiunium quod pro adulterio est iniungendum, ita ut in die ieiunii commedat ne suspecta viro sit, unquam tamen saciet se nisi semel in die, nec comedat carnes ad satietatem in diebus penitencie sue. Si autem induci non poterit ad hoc . . .'.

46 Grosseteste, *De modo*, p. 94 [= II, §10]: 'Qui autem pro labore autumni, itineris, vel exercitus ieiunare non potest, det singulos denarios ad pauperes pascendos vel vestiendos, vel redimendos, vel ad structuram ecclesie vel pontis, aut aliud opus caritatis, pauper autem qui hoc facere non potest; pro quolibet die quo iuiunare deberet, dicet xl paternoster.' Cf. p. 99 [= II, §28]: 'Ex his poterit discretus sacerdos perpendere quomodo possit alias paenitentias, de quarum temperamento in hoc tractatu non agitur, temperare. Hoc autem modis omnibus studeat sacerdos confitenti persuadere ut cesset ab actu et voluntate criminalis peccati et iuste vivat.'

47 Murray, 'Confession', pp. 290–1. Another case in the miracles of St Gerard Cagnoli (†1342): a pregnant lady comes to a priest 'seeking counsel' and he has her confess. See M. Goodich, *Violence and Miracle in the Fourteenth Century* (Chicago and London, 1995), p. 88. Goering, 'The Internal Forum', p. 23, quotes an Italian folktale which hinges on practical advice given by a confessor as if this were normal.

48 *Bonum universale de apibus* II.lii, §32, ed. G. Colvenerius (Douai, 1627), p. 513.

the word *consilium* is frequent in Caesar's confession stories. A usurer is tempted to confess by the promise of a light penance and replies 'if you keep your promise I will be happy to use your *consilium'*.[49] A dishonest businessman is advised by his priest, *'utere consiliis meis* and you will become rich'.[50] Another is told not to lie and swear but to *utimini consilio meo*.[51] A secular priest refuses to hear the confession of a monk on the grounds that the latter was outside his jurisdiction but conceded 'I will gladly hear you and *bene consilium do'*, as if these non-sacramental elements in confession were normally dispensed within it.[52] Almost as often, Caesar uses in the same context words with a similar meaning like *edocere*[53] or *[ad]monere*,[54] or – in the case of a penitent who has confessed to fornication with the priest's own concubine – *durius arguere*.[55]

To sum up: the confessor's handbook, unlike liturgical books, gave the priest only a minimal script, from which he had to improvise in conversation with his penitent. Together they had to forge a morality practicable as well as consonant with Christian profession. Their battles in doing so have almost entirely vanished from any historical record. We are left only with the battlefield. But that is enough to prove that the struggles took place, extensively, in the later Middle Ages, at this one point on the priest-laity boundary where the part of the church was represented by the initiative of a fallible individual. Half an hour is too little to identify all the possible consequences of this private dialectic, all the less because part of it would go on reaffirming, despite the failures, the positive values of confession in all its parts. Supernatural sacraments apart, the *medicus animarum* may often have been that. The system could not have lasted at all otherwise. But the effect of the mind-to-mind encounter between priest and lay must in the nature of things have varied, and in doing so set up tensions, with necessary results. Reformation experts may speculate how far the tensions led to Luther's contempt for works; students of scholastic ethics, how far they account for its Aristotelian modifications in the late thirteenth century. But beyond particular effects, found or to be found, the mere consideration of this aspect of confession provides us with an instrument for the reading of late medieval church life. Much in it was the outcome of a dialectic, between, at any moment, two types of medieval mind, that of the instructed priest and that of the uninstructed layman, producing a synthesis to which both had contributed.

---

49 Caesar, *Dialogus* III.lii; I, 169.
50 Caesar, *Dialogus* III.xxxvi; I, 157.
51 Caesar, *Dialogus* III.xxxvii; I, 158.
52 Caesar, *Dialogus* III.liii; I, 170.
53 Caesar, *Dialogus* III.vi; I, 16: 'a quo satis edocta ne maligno consentiret'; also III.vi; I, 119: 'quid dicere deberet diligenter edocta'.
54 Caesar, *Dialogus* III.xiv; I, 129: 'ut de cetero cautior foret monuisset'; also III.xxxv; I, 156: 'admonitus ab eo, ut peccata confessa deseret'.
55 Caesar, *Dialogus* III.xxix, I, 146.

Gendered Souls in Sexed Bodies:
The Male Construction of Female Sexuality
in Some Medieval Confessors' Manuals

Jacqueline Murray

One of the fundamental tenets of Christianity is the spiritual equality of all believers. This doctrine received its definitive articulation in Paul's letter to the Galatians. He wrote: 'There is neither Jew nor Greek, there is neither bond nor free, there is neither male nor female; for you are all one in Christ Jesus' (Galatians 3.28). In the world social distinctions might persist but within the order of salvation the souls of all believers have the same merit. While this doctrine of the spiritual equality of sexless souls could be understood to be immutable and transhistorical, it nevertheless has a history.

The notion of a sexless soul was conceived in a certain religious and intellectual climate. In the world of the first century CE, it harmonized with the dominant neoplatonic philosophy of the time, a philosophy that separated body and soul and somewhat minimized the essential differences between human beings on the basis of sex.[1] Yet, even for Neoplatonists, who believed that women and men had the same eternal souls, women's physical bodies rendered them weaker because they were tied more closely to the inferior physical realm.[2]

In the centuries following Paul's assertion of a sexless soul, theologians developed a remarkable array of misogynistic evaluations of women and female nature.[3] Social inequality combined with theoretical arguments to modify and undermine women's spiritual equality. While Paul's assertion could not be ignored, it was modified under layers of interpretation that sought to reconcile its utopian theory with a sharply divergent social reality. Augustine noted that woman was made in the image of God insofar as she had a rational soul. Sex differences only pertained to the physical body which

---

1 C. G. Allen, 'Plato on Women', *Feminist Studies* 2 (1975), 131–8 (p. 135) and P. Allen, *The Concept of Woman. The Aristotelian Revolution 750 BC–AD 1250* (Montreal, 1985), pp. 57–75 and 79–81.
2 E. V. Spelman, 'Woman as Body: Ancient and Contemporary Views', *Feminist Studies* 8 (1982), 109–31 (pp. 117–18).
3 See the survey in M. T. d'Alverny, 'Comment les théologiens et les philosophes voient la femme', *Cahiers de civilisation médiévale* 20 (1977), 105–29.

certainly rendered women inferior.[4] Jerome was less able to accommodate the
seeming contradictions between spiritual equality and physical inferiority. He
insisted that a faithful and holy woman will, in fact, shed her sex and become a
man.[5]

The weighting of the sexless soul towards an increasingly male definition
continued, despite the fact that generally medieval people formally believed
that women were included in the universal and normative 'man' (homo).[6]
However, as Kari Elisabeth Børresen has noted, 'in spite of the possession by
both man and woman of a rational asexual soul, there remains a kind of
congruity between the male body and the asexual soul'.[7] By the twelfth
century, scholastic theology considered that a sexless soul could in fact
develop better in a male, as opposed to a female, body.[8] Thus, the symbolic
transsexualism discussed by the Fathers, which had urged women away from
the physical world and towards the spiritual, gradually became transformed
into a more stringently antimaterialistic and misogynistic marginalization not
only of female bodies but also of female souls. Consequently, although there
were strong theological and philosophical roots for a Christian notion of a
truly sexless soul, the influence of social inequality and body/soul dualism
combined to create in medieval thought what may be termed a gendered soul;
a soul that while perhaps not explicitly sexed female nevertheless carried with
it the implications of being gendered female because it was housed in a female
body.[9] This had numerous ramifications for the cura animarum, especially as it
was effected through the sacrament of confession.

Confession and penance was in itself a singularly androcentric sacrament.
Evolving as a means by which to reconcile the believer, separated by sin, with a

---

4   Augustine, De Genesi ad litteram III.xxii; CSEL 28.1, 89.
5   'mulier esse cessabit, et dicetur vir': Jerome, Commentarius in Epistolam ad Ephesios
    III.5; PL 26, 567.
6   Very early on there was some doubt whether 'homo' in fact included women. This
    was debated at the Council of Mâcon (585); see Gregory of Tours, Historia francorum
    VIII.xx, in The History of the Franks, trans. L. Thorpe (Harmondsworth, 1974), p. 452.
    Some doubt must have lingered, however, despite the Council's affirmation. For
    example, in the early thirteenth century, Caesar of Heisterbach affirmed that both
    sexes were included in the term 'homo' and both were subject to the same desires:
    Caesar, Dialogus, IV.ci; I, 272. Clearly, the need to affirm that 'homo' referred to both
    men and women indicates there was some question about the term's inclusivity. For
    a modern critique of the notion of the 'Universal Man' see S. Harding, 'The
    Instability of the Analytical Categories of Feminist Theory', Signs 11 (1986), 645–64
    (pp. 646–7).
7   K. E. Børresen, Subordination and Equivalence. The Nature and Rôle of Woman in
    Augustine and Thomas Aquinas, trans. C. H. Talbot (Washington, 1981), p. 29.
8   E. Gössman, 'The Construction of Women's Difference in the Christian Theological
    Tradition', Concilium 6 (1991), 50–9 (p. 52).
9   Børresen (Subordination and Equivalence, pp. 339–41) notes that by the thirteenth
    century this male-centred conceptual framework was so entrenched that it is
    amazing Thomas Aquinas was able to maintain the theoretical spiritual equivalence
    of women at all.

forgiving God, confession took as its particular focus the presumably sexless soul. Yet confession had also evolved in the peculiarly masculine monastic environment of the early Middle Ages.[10] Not surprisingly, then, in the literature associated with the *cura animarum* in general, and confession in particular, the male is taken as paradigmatic. Whenever women enter the discussion it is as a marked category, a signal of difference, exception or emphasis. The gendered nature of sin, and the role of pastoral literature in the construction of notions of gender, has increasingly attracted the attention of scholars seeking to expose medieval assumptions about male and female nature.[11]

Pastoral literature was immensely important in disseminating the Church's various moral teachings. This was particularly true for the manuals which appeared to teach priests how to hear confession. The parish priest gained a new significance in the wake of the Fourth Lateran Council's reforming programme. The legislation of mandatory annual confession for every adult Christian especially expanded his duties as confessor.[12] With these enhanced responsibilities, priests also needed more specialized training. In the first half of the thirteenth century a flood of manuals were written, particularly in England and northern France, to prepare the parish clergy to exercise the *cura animarum*, in general and to hear confession, assess sins and enjoin appropriate penances, in particular.[13]

These confessors' manuals provide us with a window onto the moral universe of the Middle Ages and present the values and behaviours that the Church was trying to promote as normative. Thus, they present values and ideas in the midst of inculcation, at the very point at which they were being disseminated to the laity through the mediation of the confessor. These

[10] E. Amann, 'Pénitence privée; son organisation, première spéculations à son sujet', *Dictionnaire de théologie catholique* XII.1, 845–948 (cols. 851–3) and Murray, '1215', p. 79.

[11] On the gendering of sin see in particular J. Murray, 'The Absent Penitent: The Cure of Women's Souls and Confessors' Manuals in Thirteenth-Century England', in *Women, the Book and the Godly*, ed. L. Smith and J. H. M. Taylor (Cambridge, 1995), pp. 13–25; R. M. Karras, 'Gendered Sin and Misogyny in John of Bromyard's *Summa Predicantium*', *Traditio* 47 (1992), 233–57; Biller, 'Pastoral Geography'; J. Longère, 'La femme dans la théologie pastorale', in *La femme dans la vie religieuse du Languedoc (xiiie–xive s.)*, CaF 23 (1988), pp. 127–52; and M. F. Braswell, 'Sin, the Lady and the Law. The English Noblewoman in the Later Middle Ages', *Medievalia et Humanistica* n.s. 14 (1986), 81–101. A more recent analysis of theological and pastoral literature, pertaining to human sexuality specifically but which does not problematize gender, is P. J. Payer, *The Bridling of Desire: Views of Sex in the Later Middle Ages* (Toronto, 1993).

[12] Fourth Lateran Council (1215), c. 21, *Omnis utriusque sexus*, in *COD*, p. 221.

[13] Among the numerous studies on the development of a literature focussing on pastoral care and confession see Boyle, '*Summae confessorum*'; P. Michaud-Quantin, 'Les méthodes de la pastorale du XIIIe au XVe siècle', in *Methoden in Wissenschaft und Kunst des Mittelalters*, ed. A. Zimmermann, Miscellanea Medievalia 7 (Berlin, 1970), pp. 76–91; Murray, 'Confession'; Tentler, *Sin*.

manuals make the modern reader privy to what the confessor was expected to teach to the laity: how he was supposed to construct their social and spiritual values so that they would be in harmony with the official doctrines of the Church. Because they had this practical intent, the manuals also take into account and, to an extent, reflect the values of lay society as well. Consequently, they present both the spiritual norms of sex and gender that the Church sought to impose and the secular norms of sex and gender that it expected to encounter.[14] For women these two threads converged and served to reinforce their ancient pre-Christian evaluation of inferiority within a uniquely Christian framework of sin and salvation. By the time these confessors' manuals appeared in the early thirteenth century, Paul's notion of a sexless soul had been obscured by layers of patriarchal social and theological expectations. Not only were women's souls now the marked category but the manuals went further and constructed women as sexual by definition.

Numerous scholars have already noted that by the end of the twelfth century the traditional division of medieval society into three orders, those who work, pray and rule, was breaking down. How and if women had ever fitted into the three orders remains a subject of discussion.[15] There was, however, an ancient tripartite division into which women had been divided traditionally, according to their sexual status as virgin, matron or widow. The breakdown of the three traditional social orders is widely reflected in the confessional literature of the period. In discussions of circumstance and status the moralists proposed many fine and nuanced categories of men: serf or free, cleric or lay, rich or poor, young or old, farmer or merchant, learned or simple.[16] Men, then, were assessed and distinguished according to their social status and their economic activities. Women, however, remained constrained by purely ideological criteria and limited to sexual categories.[17] In fact, in confessors' manuals, women's traditional tripartite sexual division almost

---

[14] For an interesting discussion of how the literature of penance and confession is located at the intersection of ecclesiastical and secular cultures see A. J. Frantzen, 'Préface à la Traduction de 1990', in *La Littérature de la pénitence dans l'Angleterre anglo-saxonne*, trans. M. Lejeune, Studia Friburgensia 75 (Fribourg, 1991), pp. xiii–xxx.

[15] The implication that women did not fit this ideological framework is seen in the title of S. Shahar's study of medieval women, *The Fourth Estate. A History of Women in the Middle Ages*, trans. C. Galai (London, 1983). On the other hand, another study of medieval women, by M. W. Labarge, seems to adopt and parallel the traditional orders of society: *Women in the Middle Ages. A Small Sound of the Trumpet* (London, 1986).

[16] For example, Robert of Flamborough advised confessors to consider a variety of circumstances including age, clerical or lay status, wealth or poverty and health. He did not even mention gender as a circumstance which ought to be considered. Flamborough, *Liber*, IV.viii; p. 200.

[17] G. Hasenohr, 'La vie quotidienne de la femme vue par l'église: l'enseignement des "Journées chrétiennes" de la fin du Moyen-Age', in *Frau und spätmittelalterlicher Alltag. Internationaler Kongress, Krems an der Donau, 2–5 Oktober 1984* (Vienna, 1986), pp. 19–101 (pp. 21–25).

disappeared and they were mentioned almost exclusively as matrons, discussed in connection with sexual intercourse and childbirth. In these manuals women were defined by their sexual and reproductive functions. They were not considered to have an independent or individual social, economic or spiritual identity. Nor were their souls seen as truly sexless because their whole spiritual identity was inextricably tied to their sexed bodies. This had an important influence on how writers constructed both male and female sexuality in confessors' manuals and the values that confessors subsequently conveyed to the laity. These points will be demonstrated by an analysis of some fifteen manuals, primarily from England and northern France, from the first half of the thirteenth century.

Where women appear in the manuals is instructive and indicates something of how the authors evaluated them. The Seven Deadly Sins was the principle of organization most commonly employed, although the Decalogue and the Seven Sacraments were also used early on. An author might also employ two or more schemata in a single manual.[18] Women appear almost exclusively in discussions of the sin of *luxuria*, the sacrament of marriage or the sixth and ninth commandments.[19] For example, the term *mulier* appears only eleven times in Peter of Poitiers' *Summa de confessione*, six of those times in one chapter on sins of the flesh.[20] Women's absence from discussions of other sins, sacraments or commandments is so complete that it is difficult to proffer exceptions from the thirteenth-century manuals under consideration. Confessors were not reminded to ask women about their economic activities nor their pride or vanity, a surprising omission given the misogynistic attitudes expressed in other kinds of literature. Alexander Stavensby did not even include the male/female distinction in a list of circumstances that effected qualitatively the nature of a sin, although he did mention such criteria as lay/cleric, young/old and free/serf.[21] The very structure of confessors' manuals reinforced the notion of women as primarily, even exclusively, sexual. In the process, therefore, the salvation of women's souls was linked to their sexuality and to their sexuality alone.

The narrowing of the sexual categories for women is also reflected in their

---

18 See, for example, Robert of Flamborough's *Liber Poenitentialis*, which employs the sacraments as an organizing principle, or the *Cum ad sacerdotem* which employs the Commandments, or Robert Grosseteste's *Deus est* which uses the virtues and their complementary vices. John Bossy, 'Moral Arithmetic', has argued that the Seven Deadly Sins was the preferred system of organization for confessors' manuals prior to the Reformation because of its social and flexible nature.

19 These are the same contexts that have been identified as containing the discussions of sexual sins in post-Reformation confessors' manuals. See M. Bernos, 'La sexualité et les confesseurs à l'époque moderne', *Revue de l'histoire des religions* 209 (1992), 413–26 (p. 414). Bernos does not discuss the gendered nature of sin, particularly sexual sin, in these later manuals.

20 Chapter 12, 'De modo inquirendi modos et personas circa lubricum carnis': Peter, *Summa* XII; pp. 13–17.

21 Stavensby, *Tractatus*, p. 222.

overall treatment in these confessors' manuals. The virgin/matron/widow distinction was modified significantly and virgins and widows virtually disappeared as categories of women.[22] The only situation in which these categories of women were discussed regularly had nothing to do with assessing the sins of a female penitent. Rather, whether a woman was a virgin, matron or widow was important in assessing the relative seriousness of a man's sexual sins. Virtually every author required a confessor to ask a man if his partner in illicit sexual activity was a nun, a virgin, a married woman or a relative because the woman's status exacerbated the seriousness of the man's sin. Thus, fornication with a nun was sacrilege, with a relative, incest, with a married woman, adultery, and each more serious than simple fornication. The concern in the manuals, however, is solely to ensure that the exact nature of the man's sin is identified. His partner remained in the background, the passive vehicle which exacerbated or diminished his sin.[23]

One of the only deviations from this formula is found in Magister Serlo's treatise, which advised that a man's fornication be judged according to 'the excellence of his status or office or according to the type of prostitute (*meretrix*) or according to the manner of his deed'. In this form of assessment of circumstance, the man's status was evaluated while his partner in fornication was automatically termed a *meretrix*.[24] Other authors said less about the man's circumstances and avoided such a blanket condemnation of the woman.

The manualists agreed that fornication with a virign was especially serious because the girl was 'irrecoverably damaged'.[25] Peter of Poitiers insisted that a man who violated a virgin ought to marry her if he were able or else procure her entry into religious life. This advice reflects the values of patriarchal society that considered a woman's whole identity to be bound up in her sexual status. No longer a virgin, her one redeeming feature irrevocably destroyed, such a woman could not expect a legitimate marriage. Her despoiler, therefore, was required to marry her or otherwise compensate for her damaged state. The implication is that the virgin's whole identity and social existence rested in the intact state of her hymen. Once that was gone, she ceased to have a place in the world. Since no one else would, her despoiler should marry her or procure

---

[22] One significant exception to this is Robert Grosseteste's division of the virtue of continence according to the subject of continence: virgins, the married or widows; Grosseteste, *Deus est*, p. 281.

[23] See, for example, Richard Wetheringsette, *Qui bene presunt*, Oxford, New College, MS 94, fol. 59r; Stavensby, *Tractatus*, p. 222; Serlo, *Summa*, p. 34; Grosseteste, *Deus est*, p. 281; and Walter de Cantilupe, *Omnis etas*, in '*Summula of Peter Quinel*', *Councils & Synods*, II, 1059–1077 (pp. 1068–69). For the attribution of this treatise to Walter de Cantilupe see J. Goering and D. S. Taylor, 'The *Summulae* of Bishops Walter de Cantilupe (1240) and Peter Quinel (1287)', *MS* 67 (1992), 575–94.

[24] 'quia in ipsius vicii executione oportet eum penitere fornicantem secundum excellentiam sui status vel officii vel secundum modum meretricis et secundum modum operis sui'; Serlo, *Summa*, p. 5.

[25] For example, Wetheringsette states 'Cum virgine incorrupta quod est dampnum irrecuperabile'; New College, MS 94, fol. 73r.

her a place in a convent.[26] What distinguishes this pastoral perspective from a secular one is the focus on the victim herself. Secular law would have required that her father or another male relative or guardian receive compensation.

In the Middle Ages women's role in sexual sins was perceived to be inherent and definitional but also minor and passive. For example, Guido Ruggiero has discussed how Venetian court records, which recorded in Latin testimony presented in the vernacular, constructed female sexuality as passive in conformity with the expectations of the scribe.[27] Similarly, the words used to denote sexual intercourse in the confessors' manuals all reinforce the passive role of women. Men know women,[28] have them,[29] deflower them,[30] use them[31] or abuse them.[32] Occasionally they even deviate against nature with women.[33] Men join with women[34] but women are known by men[35] or are approached by men.[36] One of the rare active verbs used to denote women's sexual activity is Serlo's statement that women corrupt the men if they seduce them by means of sorcery.[37]

Peter of Poitiers provided an unambiguous statement about the natural hierarchical order of sexual relations between men and women. In a discussion of sexual activity 'against nature' (*contra naturam*) he not only censured the ejaculation of semen outside the 'due vessel' but also included sexual positions with the woman on top. This, he declared, was so unnatural that the martyr Methodius identified it as one of the causes of the flood.[38] *Cum ad sacerdotem* similarly advised that the natural means for a man and woman to have

26 'Item si cum uirginibus. Quot autem deflorauit non sibi coniugatas tot maritet, si potest, alias pauperes uirgines. Si uult, uel aliter compenset, uel ipsas a se corruptas, si indigeant, sustentet uel procuret eis ingressum religionis, si maluerint'; Peter, *Summa* XII, p. 15. John of Kent was of the same opinion in his *Summa de penitentia*; London, British Library, MS Royal 9.A.XIV, fol. 226va.

27 G. Ruggiero, *The Boundaries of Eros. Sex Crime and Sexuality in Renaissance Venice* (New York, 1985), p. 47.

28 For example, 'Fornicatio est quando vir congnoscit mulierem que sibi non est desponsata'; Stavensby, *Quidam tractatus de vii criminalibus*, in *Councils & Synods*, I, 219.

29 'Hic querat utrum uxorem proximi habuerit'; *Cum ad sacerdotem*, p. 36.

30 'Quot autem deflorauit'; Peter, *Summa* XII, p. 15.

31 'et sciendum est quod secundum debitum nature debent propriis uti uxoribus . . .'; Stavensby, *Tractatus*, p. 222.

32 'et ideo gravior quia uxoribus quas possunt habere ad necessitatem abuntur ad voluptatem'; Chobham, *Summa* VII.2.IIa.iii, pp. 335–6.

33 'Item an umquam cum mulieribus exorbitauerit contra naturam'; Peter, *Summa* XII, p. 16.

34 'uir coheat cum muliere'; *Cum ad sacerdotem*, p. 34.

35 'Si uero dicat mulier a uiro se non posse cognosci . . .'; *Quia non pigris* 70, in *Trois sommes*, II, 135–332 (p. 324).

36 'An confitens accesserit ad mulieres elocati corporis'; Peter, *Summa* XII, pp. 13–14. 'Aut scivisti illam ad quam accessisti esse solutam'; Stavensby, *Tractatus*, p. 222.

37 'ut arte sortilega eum corrumpere . . .'; Serlo, *Summa*, p. 26.

38 'Item an umquam cum mulieribus exorbitauerit contra naturam . . . id est, extra uas deputatum a natura, et an mulier supergressa sit ei. Nam, ut dicit Methodius martyr,

intercourse always had the man superior and the woman lying inferior.[39] Elsewhere, the author described sexual activity as something men 'do' to women. Confessors should inquire 'Concerning touch, whether he touched a women disgracefully, that is whether he touched her nipples, breasts or genitals'.[40] Thus, women's nature, while inherently sexual, was also perceived to be sexually passive.

This understanding of female sexuality as essentially passive is also reflected in the standard definition of adultery as 'the violation of another man's bed', a definition that also shows the influence of the secular ideology of marriage.[41] Highly unusual, however, is the statement in *Cum ad sacerdotem*, that adds 'as when a married woman approaches another man or vice-versa'.[42] Lest, however, this sound perilously close to attributing sexual agency to an adulterous woman, the author elaborated elsewhere saying, 'Let [the confessor] ask this, whether he had his neighbour's wife or if he kissed her, or dishonestly approached her, and did whatever he was able so that he would have her.'[43] Finally, since a woman is sexually passive by nature, she could not be considered equally responsible for adultery. Magister Serlo advised that women be punished more leniently than men.[44] The *Summula Conradi* stated that a woman could not be held responsible for her adultery if she were ignorant that another man had entered her bedroom under the pretext of being her husband.[45] In a similar vein, sexual activity with women could lend a man a certain prestige. *Cum ad sacerdotem* censured men who gloried in sin by boasting about their sexual conquests, saying 'I knew this woman or that one.'[46] Thus, women were perceived to be so passive as to be unable to distinguish between sexual partners. In addition, they were objectified and were individuals only in so far as they enhanced a man's reputation for sexual

---

haec fuit una causa diluuii, scilicet quod mulieres uiris supergressae ferebantur'; Peter, *Summa* XII, p. 16.

[39] 'Modus <naturalis> est ut uir coheat cum muliere semper <sit superior, mulier> iacendo inferior'; *Cum ad sacerdotem*, p. 34.

[40] 'De tactu, utrum tetigerit mulierem inhoneste, scilicet utrum tractando eius mamillas, pectus, uel eius pudibunda'; *Cum ad sacerdotem*, p. 38.

[41] 'Item adulterium proprie est alterius thori violacio'; Wetheringsette, *Qui bene presunt*, in London, British Library, MS Royal 9.A.XIV, fol. 62v. Similar terms are used in the *Cum ad sacerdotem*, p. 31.

[42] 'adulterium, quod est alicuius thori uiolatio, ut cum coniugata mulier <accedit> ad alium uirum uel e conuerso'; *Cum ad sacerdotem*, p. 31.

[43] 'Hic querat utrum uxorem proximi habuerit, uel si eam osculatus fuerit, uel inhoneste ad eam accesserit, et ut eam haberet quicquid potuit fecit'; *Cum ad sacerdotem*, p. 36. Walter de Cantilupe said much the same in *Omnis etas*, in *Councils & Synods*, II, 1064–5.

[44] 'Mulier tamen lenius puniatur'; Serlo, *Summa*, p. 33.

[45] 'Item, si, ignorante uxore, alius sub pretextu uiri intrat cubiculum eius'; *Summula magistri Conradi* 2.18.2, in *Trois sommes*, II, 1–133 (p. 33). The same sentiment is expressed in the *Quia non pigris* 41, in *Trois sommes*, II, 252.

[46] 'Vel querat utrum gloriatus fuerit de peccato, sicut faciunt quidam dicentes, "Ego cognoui istam uel illam", uel huiusmodi'; *Cum ad sacerdotem*, p. 36.

prowess. In these discussions women are portrayed as the passive objects of men's sexuality, while at the same time they are also defined only in relation to their own sexed bodies.

This tendency to render women inherently and exclusively sexed can also be observed when women enter into discussions of sins not conventionally considered sexual in nature. These sins are suddenly imbued with sexual meaning when they pertain to women. For example, women occasionally appear in discussions of homicide, but only in the light of their sexual and reproductive functions. Serlo alleged that fornicating women kill their foetuses and teach other women how to procure abortions. Women were regularly accused of overlaying their infants either through accident or negligence.[47] Other manuals similarly incorporated discussions of abortion, contraception and infanticide under the rubric 'Homicide'. Consequently, in their rare appearances as subjects of discussions not devoted primarily to sexual matters, women, nevertheless, remain entwined with their sexual and reproductive functions.[48]

Not only was women's nature understood to be essentially sexual, but women's sexuality was also constructed as disgusting or inherently dangerous to men. Odo of Cheriton likened kissing a woman to biting an apple. As soon as a man realizes there is a worm inside he will spit it out. He construes the devil or sin to be the worm hiding inside and so, after kissing a woman, he ought to spit out the sin in confession.[49] Peter of Poitiers wanted confessors to ask if a man had had sexual relations with women who sell their bodies or with public prostitutes. The woman's sexual status not only affected the seriousness of the man's sin, but he faced physical dangers, as well. Women who sold their bodies might have had sexual relations with lepers or other unclean men. Consequently, their other clients risked infection from these prostitutes. In this discussion of the possible health risks associated with sexual relations with prostitutes, Peter of Poitiers wrote that prostitutes 'place themselves under lepers (*supponunt se leprosis*)'.[50] Thus, this language of sexual encounter was able to construct women's sexuality as at once both passive and dangerous.

For many moralists leprosy and menstruation were conceptually related. In the process, they linked female sexuality with the most frightening illness of the period. The *Summula Conradi* advised that, although a healthy man should

---

47 Serlo, *Summa*, p. 19. See similar views in John of Kent, *Summa de penitentia*, in BL MS Royal 9.A.XIV, fol. 231r.

48 See, for example, *Cum ad sacerdotem*, p. 36.

49 'Si quis pomum pulcherrimum morderet et uermem intus iuenerit, statim expueret. Pomum sapidum est pulcra mulier. Hoc pomum gustat qui hanc amplectitur. Set consideret uermen, id est, diabolum, siue peccatum, in tali pomo latitare, et statim per confessionem expuere festinet'; Odo of Cheriton, *Summa de poenitentia*, in Cambridge, Trinity College, MS 356, fol. 4rb.

50 'An confitens accesserit ad mulieres elocati corporis, seu ad publice prostitutas. . . . Est etiam ibi periculum corporis, quia supponunt se leprosis et huiusmodi'; Peter, *Summa* XII, pp. 13–14.

render the conjugal debt to his leprous wife, he 'is excused on account of the horror' of the disease. The author then linked this exception to the requirement that a menstruating woman refuse to render the conjugal debt to her husband because a foetus so conceived would be leprous.[51] Peter of Poitiers was more explicit and suggested that a menstruating woman could infect a man with leprosy and so forbade completely intercourse during menstruation. 'The Jews', he wrote, 'are rarely defiled by the stain of leprosy because they do not approach menstruating women.'[52] Thus, the ancient blood taboos and pre-Christian notions of ritual purity, which silently underlay so many of the theological and canonical rules governing human sexuality,[53] took on a sinister and life-threatening tone when paired with the most frightening disease of the day. Female sexuality was the mechanism of this threat.

Similarly, the link between women, witchcraft and sorcery had a specifically sexual connotation and perpetuated the construction of female sexuality as being dangerous to men. Serlo postulated that a woman might so delight in fornication that she would resort to sorcery and bewitch her partner with a love potion made from her menstrual blood.[54] Conversely, Robert of Flamborough censured women who mixed a man's semen into a love potion,[55] thus turning his own masculine potency against him.

Women, however, did not always have to resort to sorcery to elicit sexual attentions or awaken desire in men – their very presence could engender lust. Talking with a woman could, in itself, prove sexually dangerous to a man. Richard Wetheringsette stated that sexual desire was a heat that coursed through those who were defiled, causing them to experience movements of the flesh from the contact and society of women.[56] Odo of Cheriton cautioned that

---

51 'Vnde, notandum quod sanus tenetur reddere debitum leprose, set propter horrorem excusatur; perfectius tamen esset si redderet debitum. . . . Vel sic dic quod, si mulier patitur menstruum naturaliter, non debet reddere debitum uiro; nam, si ex tali coitu concipitur, . . . fetus est leprosus'; *Summula magistri Conradi* 2.11, in *Trois sommes*, II, 25. Other manualists also highlighted the dangers of intercourse during menstruation. John of Kent noted a long list of possible consequences and advised menstruating women to take extraordinary measures to avoid intercourse with their husbands; *Summa de penitentia*, in BL MS 9.A.XIV, fols. 226vb–7ra. Robert of Flamborough linked a leprous foetus with intercourse during menstruation, *Liber* IV.226, pp. 197–8. So, too, did Chobham, *Summa* VII.2.Xa, pp. 365–6.

52 'Iudaei, quoniam ad menstruatam non accedunt, leprae macula rarius resperguntur'; Peter, *Summa* XII, p. 17.

53 J. A. Brundage, *Law, Sex, and Christian Society in Medieval Europe* (Chicago, 1987), pp. 2–3.

54 'Item si qua fornicaria mulier in tantum fornicatorem dilexerit ut arte sortilega eum corrumpere . . . Si qua mulier misceat sanguinem suum menstruum in cibo vel potu et dat viro ut plus diligatur ab eo . . .'; Serlo, *Summa*, p. 26.

55 'Sic et illa quae semen viri sui cibo miscet ut inde plus ejus accipiat amorem poeniteat'; Flamborough, *Liber* V.iii.272, p. 229.

56 'Libido est ardor per quaslibet turpitudines discurrens ut hiis qui procurant motus carnis ex contactu et societate mulierum et ex inde in sompnis inquinantur et frequenter in vigilando'; Wetheringsette, *Qui bene presunt*, in BL MS Royal 9.A.XIV, fol. 62r.

the fires of lust were ignited in a man when he associated with a woman.[57] Robert Grosseteste discussed women who used bath oils to soften their skin and make themselves more delicate and attractive to men.[58] His criticism is linked to more traditional and commonplace denunciations of women who used cosmetics to trick and seduce men.

Thomas of Chobham thought the mere presence of women held potential danger for men. He warned men to avoid the company of lascivious women and prostitutes who might incite their sexual desire. He posited the case of a husband who constantly sought sexual relations with his wife because he was consumed by lust, either because of her beauty or because he had been solicited by prostitutes.[59] Although such a man sinned, in fact his sin was incited by women, either passively, by his wife's beauty, or actively, by the imprecations of prostitutes. John of Kent and Odo of Cheriton extended this fear of women's sexual attractions and warned confessors not to become aroused while hearing the confession of women. This was especially dangerous when the women were young or confessing to sins of the flesh.[60]

The author of *Cum ad sacerdotem* pushed this fear of the very sight of women to its logical conclusion. He suggested that a man could experience nocturnal emissions as a result of merely speaking with a woman, as well as from more direct contact such as a touch or a kiss.[61] The author similarly attributed seminal emissions while awake to conversation with a woman, or a kiss or a touch and then, in the same sentence, asked if the penitent had ever had sex with a woman.[62] He therefore linked conversation with a woman directly to

---

57 'Sic ignis luxurie est ex lapideo homine cum mulieri associatur'; Odo of Cheriton, *Summa de poenitentia*, in Cambridge, University Library, MS Peterhouse 109, fol. 245v.

58 'Quaerendum etiam de superfluitate, quae maxime mulierum est. Fruuntur enim talibus frequenter et nimium ut cutis tenerior et perspicabilior sit et subtilior, hoc est peccato carnis aptior et appetibilior'; Grosseteste, *Deus est*, p. 285.

59 'Unde qui ita delectantur vel in pulchritudine uxoris sue vel in suavitate carnis vel in blanditiis meretriciis vel adulterinis quod effundunt se in libidinem et tota nocte et die utuntur uxoribus suis quasi pro culcitra per oscula lasciva et per turpes amplexus peccant mortaliter'; Chobham, *Summa* VII.2.IIa.iii, p. 335. See a similar discussion in Flamborough, *Liber* II.71, pp. 97–98.

60 'Consulo tamen si sit mulier que confitetur et maxime si iuuenis et ipse sacerdos timeat ne per audita uerba carnalia sui uel illius fragilis sensualitas moueatur'; John of Kent, *Summa de penitentia*, in BL MS Royal 9.A.XIV, fol. 225vb. 'Item si fuerit <in>continens iniungatur ei sacerdos ut visum et colloquium mulierum summo studio devitet'; Odo of Cheriton, *Summa de poenitentia*, in Cambridge, MS Peterhouse 109, fol. 245r.

61 'Accidit tibi pollutio nocturna? . . . ex confabulatione mulierum, tactu, uel osculatione'? *Cum ad sacerdotem*, p. 31. This view is expressed by others as well. For example, Thomas of Chobham advised that if a man thought about a woman or conversed with her for a long time, the residual thoughts left in his mind could excite his body while he was asleep; *Summa* VII.2.Ia.iii, pp. 331–2.

62 'Accidit tibi pollutio uigilando aliquando ex mutuo colloquio mulierum uel osculatione uel etiam tactu, uel mulierem cognouisti unquam?'; *Cum ad sacerdotem*, p. 32.

sexual intercourse, implying that the one led inexorably to the other. These examples are extreme points of a continuum that defined all contact with women as inherently sexual in nature.

Similarly, in other areas in which men were judged according to social concerns, women were judged according to sexual ones. An example is found in the cases in which spouses could separate. A man could separate 'from bed and board' (*a mensa et thoro*) if his wife had fornicated (although perhaps this should be more accurately termed adultery), but a woman could not initiate a separation on the grounds of her husband's sexual misbehaviour. According to the *Summula Conradi*, however, a woman could separate if her husband was a thief, a robber or an actor or engaged in similar antisocial activities.[63] For women, sexual behaviour was the crucial factor in establishing their unworthiness and giving their spouse grounds for separation. For men, however, social considerations dictated whether or not they were considered to be unsuitable husbands. The one exception to this pattern is noted by John of Kent, who urged a wife to separate from her sodomite husband if she feared he would corrupt her.[64] Clearly, in this case, the sodomite husband has so overturned the natural order that he, too, could be judged on purely sexual criteria.

The social grounds for marital separation also highlight the role of women in marriage, as sexual outlets for their husbands and agents of procreation. Thomas of Chobham thought a woman's sexual function in marriage was so great that, after childbirth, she should be churched early lest her husband seek a sexual outlet elsewhere.[65] Thomas thought that wives should function as safety-valves for their husband's libido. For example, if a man was going to be in the company of a lascivious woman, and he feared his own weakness, he could legitimately seek the conjugal debt from his wife to ensure he would avoid committing the serious sin of adultery.[66] Ironically, in this passage, Thomas managed to highlight not only a wife's essentially sexual function, but

---

63 'Duobus modis fit diuortium inter coniuges. Primo, quantum ad thorum, ut cum mulier fornicatur, potest eam uir dimittere quantum ad thorum tantum, . . . Scias etiam quod, si uir sit fur uel latro uel hystrio, uel aliquid huius<modi> fuerit et nolit cessare, uel uxorem ad maleficium trahat, potest uxor ab eo separari'; *Summula magistri Conradi* 2.18.2, in *Trois sommes*, II, 33–34. See also *Quia non pigris* 75.4, in *Trois sommes*, II, 330, for a virtually identical statement.

64 'Idem de uicio sodomitico. Si autem in tali casu uelit uxor tenere maritum reum uel econuerso cohabitare permittuntur si sit spes de correctione, alioquin precepti est dimittere cum sibi ipsi de corrupcione timeat'; John of Kent, *Summa de penitentia*, in BL MS Royal 9.A.XIV, fol. 217va–vb.

65 'Item, prohibendum est ne quis cognoscat uxorem suam in puerperio, sed si vir instanter petat debitum et illa timeat de lapsu eius, statim accedat ad purificationem et sic debitum reddat'; Chobham, *Summa* VII.2.Xa, p. 366.

66 'Licitus est secundum quosdam triplex, scilicet causa suscitande prolis ad cultum dei unius, vel causa reddendi debitum exigenti, ut si aliquis accessurus sit ad consortium lascivarum mulierum et timeat sibi de lapsu et propter hoc prius refrigerat se in propria uxore per hoc meretur'; Chobham, *Summa* VII.2.IIa.i, pp. 333-4.

also the dangerous lasciviousness of all women. While Robert Grosseteste was critical of women who bathed to enhance their beauty, John of Kent noted that it was quite permissible for women to adorn themselves for their husbands.[67] Thus, while the presence of women could be the source of sin for men outside marriage, within the marital relationship wives could and indeed should make themselves sexually attractive and available to ensure their husbands did not stray.

While the theological values of the time would lead us to expect to find women's sexual nature being harshly evaluated in confessors' manuals, it comes as more of a surprise to find that their reproductive functions fared little better. Not only were menstruating women considered to be responsible for the birth of children with leprosy, elephantitis and all manner of birth defects, but childbirth itself had a negative connotation. John of Kent likened the confessor to a midwife, observing that 'a tortuous snake is brought forth by the midwife's hand'.[68] This underscores the sinful origins of conception and childbirth and how women were tainted by their association with it.

How women *were* their bodies is also seen in the case where a man disputed his wife's claim that he was impotent. Following canon law, moralists advised that in the event of a disagreement the man was to be believed rather than the woman, unless she could prove herself a virgin.[69] Although women's testimony was not to be given credence and it was assumed that women might lie and unjustly accuse a man of impotence, women's bodies did not lie. The evidence of the woman's body, her intact hymen, carried a voice of authority that her words, her oath, were never accorded. Interesting, as well, is Guy of Orchelles' distinction between frigidity or impotence in men and women. In women, arctation that would inhibit intercourse was considered to occur naturally and could be cured by frequent attempts at intercourse or by medical intervention.[70] On the other hand, men were presumed to be naturally potent and able to have intercourse. In them, impotence was understood to be the

---

67 'Feminis enim se ornari permittitur propter maritos'; John of Kent, *Summa de penitentia*, in BL MS 9.A.XIV, fol. 219v.
68 'Obstetricante manu educendus est coluber tortuosus'; John of Kent, *Summa de penitentia*, in BL MS 9.A.XIV, fol. 225r.
69 For example, 'Si autem mulier dicat se non posse a uiro cognosci, uir autem contrarium asseueret, standum est uerbo uiri, nisi mulier uirgo fuerit; tunc enim potest probare per aspectum corporis se integram euasisse'; *Summula magistri Conradi* 2.16.1, in *Trois sommes*, p. 31. The same sentiment is expressed in the *Quia non pigris* 70, ibid., p. 324 and by Guy of Orchelles, *Tractatus de sacramentis* IX.3.5.244, in *Guidonis de Orchellis. Tractatus de sacramentis et officiis ecclesiae*, ed. D. and O. Van den Eynde, Franciscan Institute Publications Text Series 4 (St Bonaventure, N.Y., 1953), p. 213.
70 'Si autem artatio talis sit quod ei subveniri possit per frequentem accessum hominis convenientis staturae vel beneficio medicinae . . .'; Guy of Orchelles, *Tractatus de sacramentis* IX.3.5.241, p. 212. Thomas of Chobham also recommended surgery for the woman; *Summa* 4.VIIa.xxii, p. 183.

result of witchcraft.[71] Consequently, whereas men's bodies were presumed to be created potent and any problem like impotence attributable to supernatural intervention, women's bodies were considered to be weaker and to have natural defects.

The centrality of the female body in defining women's identity and their place in marriage and in the world at large is also clearly presented in John of Kent's discussion of how the impediment of affinity was established. John reiterated the standard definitions that affinity was contracted by sexual intercourse between a man and a woman, either legitimately, in marriage, or illicitly, in extramarital intercourse. He extended the discussion in a unique direction, however, to consider 'extraordinary pollution'. No matter what the sexual activities in which the man and woman engaged, no affinity resulted if the so-called 'natural vessel' was not used.[72] While this discussion is in harmony with that of the canonists, who argued that neither unnatural intercourse nor *coitus interruptus* created a relationship of affinity, it is unique among these confessors' manuals.[73] It also highlights the deciding factor in what constituted intercourse: the ejaculation of semen inside the vagina. There are many troubling aspects to this passage, not the least of which is the reduction of women and female sexual identity to specific genital organs. Human sexuality was completely genitally defined. Vaginal penetration by the penis was the only recognized sexual act, and in the process women were reduced to the organ to be penetrated. It is no wonder, then, that the language of sexuality in the confessors' manuals placed women in the passive and inferior position.[74]

This reduction of women to their sexual and reproductive functions is not unique to confessors' manuals.[75] It reflects a complex interweaving of the values of theology and canon law, informed by ancient misogyny, both popular and philosophical. It also reflects many of the concerns and

---

71 'A principio quodlibet maleficium intelligitur temporale, quia naturaliter praesumitur omnis homo potens esse ad coeundum'; Guy of Orchelles, *Tractatus de sacramentis* IX.3.5.242, p. 212.

72 'Extraordinaria autem pollucio qualitercumque facta si non est facta infra uas aptum nature non inducit affinitatem nec impedit matrimonium, dummodo uterque pollutorum iuret pollucionem illam naturaliter non esse factum'; John of Kent, *Summa de penitentia*, in BL MS Royal 9.A.XIV, fol. 215va.

73 See Brundage, *Law, Sex, and Christian Society*, p. 356 and note 156, which includes a telling quotation from Bernard of Pavia.

74 Ironically, although men are construed formally as superior, active and rational, the cumulative message of these manuals is quite different. Men are presented as prey to their passions, unable to control their desires even at the sight of a woman. Women are discussed in relation to their influence on men's bodies. Thus, there is an inherent contradiction between the unexamined ideology of male superiority and the underlying message which highlights the tenuousness and instability of reason in the face of the insistent demands of the male body and its sexual urges.

75 Eleanor Commo McLaughlin has observed that, for medieval theology in general, 'the female, although possessing a rational soul, was created solely with respect to her sexuality, her body, as an aid in reproduction for the preservation of the species':

preoccupations of secular society, which subordinated women to the land and lineage and stressed the necessity for legitimate heirs. Reflecting the values of their times and the interests of their male authors, confessors' manuals served to reinforce women's inferior and subject social position. They went even further, however, in marginalizing women within the community of the faithful. By confining women to their sexual functions, the authors of confessors' manuals chose to ignore women's broad social and economic functions. By reductively reinforcing stereotypes of women's sexual passivity and women as a source of sexual temptation, they rendered invisible women's place in the community of the faithful. The androcentric perspective of medieval theology restricted women within the order of salvation and in the process contributed to the gendering of women's souls.[76] Paul's admonition to spiritual equality faded in the face of a hostile, male-defined view of women as so thoroughly defined by their sex that they in essence became their sex. Numerous scholars have already noted the androcentric and misogynistic nature of medieval theology but they reiterate the church's claim to envisage equal rational souls for women and men.[77] An examination of the literature which served to disseminate this theology, however, suggests that the equality of souls was overshadowed by the patriarchal ideology embraced by the clergy. Theoretical notions of the sexless soul and the spiritual equality of men and women disappeared when theological doctrines were condensed in the practical manuals written for confessors. These manuals convey an ideology in which the sexless souls belong to men. Women's souls were assigned qualities based on earthly categories; in effect, women's souls were gendered female.

'Equality of Souls, Inequality of Sexes: Woman in Medieval Theology', in *Religion and Sexism. Images of Woman in the Jewish and Christian Traditions*, ed. R. R. Ruether (New York, 1974), pp. 213–66 (p. 217).

76 McLaughlin has argued that the sexual essence that defined women rendered them morally inferior; 'Equality of Souls, Inequality of Sexes', p. 218. If this is the case, then gender in fact influenced women's spiritual perfectability and arguably female souls were inferior to male souls.

77 Børresen, *Subordination and Equivalence*, and McLaughlin, 'Equality of Souls, Inequality of Sexes'.

William of Auvergne and Confession

Lesley Smith

Vomit, literally speaking, is the emptying of the belly, either partly or fully, via the mouth or by the agency of the mouth; I repeat, the emptying of the belly partly or wholly, which an upset of the stomach or belly or something inimical to them inside the belly usually induces. In the same way, the belly of heart, or conscience, is emptied or relieved from vices or sins, by the agency of the mouth, by speaking or revealing these things to a priest. Therefore, just as someone with an upset stomach [*indignatio ventris*], straining to expel what is harmful or unsuitable to it, distends his belly and opens his mouth wide to get rid of it, so too someone with an upset to a noble and holy conscience strains and searches the belly of his heart to throw out and expel detestable and filthy vices and sins, opening his mouth wide for them to leave via the words of confession. Therefore, since the noxious humour of vices and detestable sins is pushed towards the mouth, because of this upset and disturbance of the spiritual belly or conscience, and leaves via confession, this confession is rightly called spiritual vomit, because of the similitude with bodily vomit.

You, however, already know that vomit is sometimes one of the bodily purgations, and it happens in the belly when fever-inducing material is at the opening of the stomach, or near it; for at that point the awfulness of this material comes to the palate [*virtus gustabilis*], and on account of this the mouth of the stomach distends, together with a forceful widening all the way to the throat, so that it may be expelled. But when such material has sunk deep into the stomach or into the intestines, vomiting like this is rare or doesn't happen at all; and in this case it is clear for the healthy to see that since the faeces of vices and sin will have sunk deep by habit, or through ignorance, or simply because of the passage of time, that the vomit of confession rarely or never happens. Similarly, when the appetite or the digestive system have been mortified or weakened so that they are unable to sense detestable flavours or unhealthy liquids, vomit is reduced or stopped altogether. However, when these functions are stong and healthy, vomit increases and is more frequent. . . .[1]

---

[1] *Guilelmi Alverni Episcopi Parisiensis Opera omnia*, 2 vols., ed. F. Hotot, and *Supplementum*, ed. B. Le Feron (Orléans and Paris, 1674; repr. Frankfurt a. M., 1963), I, 487aB–D. Hereafter referred to as *Opera*.

It must indeed be declared that making confession is a necessity: I repeat, that this is a vomiting of necessary and healthy purgation, and spiritual emptying. If anyone asks why this vomiting should happen, I answer that it comes from the filth in which you wallow. For unless you are in fact a pig, to whom the foulest wallowing is like a chemist's shop or an aromatic room; for whom a great dung-heap becomes a cloud of cinnamon and a treasure-chest; then, by a miracle of devilish transformation, we can see such men have degenerated from the nobility of the human species (since they are already not men, if they have the filthiest habits and manner of life), but rather they seem to be changed into pigs. Indeed, they will be counted pigs rather than men if they cannot throw out as great a cloud of filthy life-giving spiritual vomit, as they wallow in abomination.[2]

Long though they are, I could not resist beginning with those extracts from William of Auvergne on confession. It will give readers some idea of why I considered calling this paper 'Better Out Than In', and why I *did* resist reading his section on lavatories. William has a gift for the memorable phrase and pithy description: at another point in this treatise, he brings to mind Franklin Delano Roosevelt when he says, 'we have nothing to fear but the lack of fear'.[3] This masterly use of colourful and, as he might say, adhesive language is one of William's great characteristics, along with his independence of mind. And yet, for reasons which I will suggest later, this man highly-regarded in his own day remains relatively unknown in ours. I will begin, then, by explaining who he was, and then go on to look at more of his treatment of confession.

William was a Frenchman, born in or around Aurillac in the Auvergne, probably about 1180.[4] His southern background left its mark, for he is ever-conscious of the varieties of religious experience, whether it be unorthodox, like that of the Cathars, or non-Christian, like the Jews or even Muslims whom he discusses with an unusual sensitivity and knowledge. As with so many schoolmen, we know little of the early part of his life; but it is presumed that he studied arts and then theology in Paris, where he became a teaching master of theology and a canon of Notre Dame. He appears to have

---

2   *Opera* I, 488aH. Prof. David Ganz and I searched the *Patrologia Latina* CD database for any similar uses of the metaphor of vomit, but we found none. I am very grateful to Prof. Ganz for his painstaking help.

3   *Opera* I, 482aA.

4   The most comprehensive work on William is still N. Valois, *Guillaume d'Auvergne, évêque de Paris, sa vie et ses ouvrages* (Paris, 1880), which enjoyably combines the use of William for patriotic purposes with some careful scholarship. J. Kramp, 'Des Wilhelm von Auvergne "Magisterium Divinale" ', *Gregorianum* 1 (1920), 538–616; 2 (1921), 42–103 and 174–95 attempts with thoroughness to put the *opera* into order. B. Switalski, *William of Auvergne: De trinitate* (Toronto, 1976) edits one important text and has an extensive bibliography. Accessible encyclopedia articles on William appear in *The Encyclopedia of Philosophy* (by D. Knowles), *Lexikon für Theologie und Kirche* (by R. Heinzmann), and *The New Catholic Encyclopedia* (by J. R. O'Donnell). I hope to complete a larger study of William and his work in the near future.

been known for his good sense and fairness, acting throughout his life as an arbitrator in disputes; so that when, in 1227, Bartholomew, bishop of Paris, died, it was not surprising that William was sent to Rome by a group of canons and theologians who felt that the election of Bartholomew's successor had not been carried out according to the (relatively new) rules of the Fourth Lateran Council. He appeared before Gregory IX a deacon; he came back bishop of Paris. Gregory's letter of appointment describes William as 'a man of highest learning and spotless virtue'; nor need this be dismissed simply as a piece of self-justificatory rhetoric on Gregory's part, for no contemporary Christian source speaks of William with anything other than the highest respect. Indeed, Gregory soon had cause to realise just how independent his bishop's learning and virtue were when, during the Great University Strike of 1229–31, William opposed Gregory's wishes by refusing to overlook the murder of a townsman by a university student. Gregory felt William was taking things much too seriously and ordered him to stop; but William insisted on proper judicial proceedings, to the dismay of the University which had thought that, as a master himself, he would be on their side.

The University strike provoked, or at least highlighted, another conflict – that between the secular students and masters and the Mendicants. The Franciscans and Dominicans had come to Paris, to the Schools, almost as soon as they gained official papal status. The 'defections' of masters Roland of Cremona and Alexander of Hales to the Dominicans and Franciscans respectively, taking their chairs with them, were *causes célèbres*. Opinions ran high over whether or not this should be allowed, although the issue was soon settled by events: the Mendicants swiftly became such a force in the University that secular masters became almost a thing of the past. Although always a secular himself, William was firmly in favour of the Mendicants and lent the weight of his episcopal office to their support. This is, I think, for two linked reasons. Firstly, William is, even as an academic, never merely a theoretician. He is constantly aware of his audience, both in terms of the direct readers or hearers of his work, and those in the wider world outside, where most of his students will go to minister. Thus, even in the most academic of his works, William retains a sense of the wider context and he attempts to address it. Secondly, as we saw with the case of the election of the bishop of Paris, William was a man of unimpeachable orthodoxy, who believed totally in the Church as an institution (for him, as for Augustine, there could be no salvation outside it[5]), who kept up-to-date with its pronouncements and decrees, and who realised that the canons of the recent Lateran Council needed structures, if they were to take effect. For both of these reasons, William must have recognized the Mendicants for what they were – an educable link with the lives of ordinary people, a way of getting what happened in the Schools out to what was happening in the parishes. Much like his contemporary, Robert

---

5   Cf. *Opera* I, 503aB, 'Locus gratiae et remissionis peccatorum Ecclesia Dei est: certum enim est quia extra illam, nec gratia, nec remissio peccatorum.'

Grosseteste, whom he knew, William was a reforming bishop; the two men share a number of characteristics.

From this brief description, I hope it will have become clear that penance and confession were important to William of Auvergne. Let us now move on to look directly at his treatment of them. William has two works on penance. There is a short, single *New Treatise on Penance* (*Tractatus novus de penitentia*) and a much longer discussion which forms part of his treatise on the seven sacraments, *De sacramentis*, in which he refers to his earlier work. (In order to distinguish them easily here, I shall refer to them as the *Treatise* and the *Sacrament* respectively.) Dating William's works can be little more than guesswork, and I shall follow Glorieux in saying that the *Treatise* dates from about 1223 and the *Sacrament* from about 1228, that is, both were written whilst he was a teaching master but probably before he became a bishop.[6] Many of William's works are easily available in a facsimile reprint of the 1674 Paris edition of his *Opera omnia*; both these treatises are included in that edition, and I have used it here for ease of access.[7] The authenticity of his writing on the seven sacraments has never been questioned, but the treatise on penance has a more chequered history. In the edition, it is divided in two: a first section of seventeen chapters on penance itself, followed by a second section of nine further chapters, which form a sort of practical confessor's manual, and which claim to be a supplement to the first part. The genuineness of this second section is suspect. Certainly, the manuscript history of this part of the work is sketchy: I have only been able to find five copies of the 'whole' work, as opposed to twenty-five copies of the prior part. For our present purposes, I propose not to consider the supplement here, and, in fact, I shall concentrate on the treatment of penance in the *De sacramentis*, which draws heavily on and expands the earlier work. To date, I have found twenty-six manuscripts of William on the sacraments, and coupled with the twenty-seven manuscripts of *Treatise* (at least twelve of which contain only the first section of seventeen chapters on penance and confession) this total of about fifty manuscripts adds up to a picture of some influence.[8]

---

6 P. Glorieux, *Répertoire des maîtres en théologie de Paris au XIIIe siècle*, 2 vols. (Paris, 1933), I, 317.

7 *Treatise* = *Opera* I, 570b–592b.
   Sacrament = *Opera* I, 451b–512b.

8 I have not yet seen all of these manuscripts and so cannot vouch completely for the accuracy of this list; I draw on basic information given in Glorieux, *Répertoire*, and searches in published manuscript library catalogues.
   MSS of the *Sacrament*: Barcelona, Bib. Cent., MS 1763; Brussels, Bib. Roy., MS 1660; Cambrai, Bib. mun., MS 434; MS 483; Chartres, Bib. mun., MS 470; Melk, Stiftsbib., MS 35; Munich, Clm 1851a; Clm 2734; Oxford, BL, MS Bodl. 281; Oxford, Balliol College, MS 174; Oxford, Lincoln College, MS 8; MS 11; MS 70; Oxford, Merton College, MS 136; MS 155; Oxford, New College, MS 114; Paris, BNF, MS lat. 14842; MS Nouv. acq. 660; Philadelphia, Univ. of Penn. Libr., MS Lea 22; Rein, Stiftsbib., MS 90; Rome, BAV, MS Vat. lat. 849; Stockholm, Kungl. Bib., MS F. min. 597; Toulouse, Bib. mun., MS 210; Vienna, ÖN, MS 3157; MS 4568; Worcester, Cath. Libr., MS F. 44.

Penance gets about forty percent of the space devoted to the sacraments, and is almost three times as long as its nearest rivals, the Eucharist and Orders. It fills, in the seventeenth-century edition, about sixty-three folio pages. William is not an especially verbose writer, as medieval authors go, and the length is not the result of repetition; rather, the treatment is comprehensive in a number of ways. He begins by asking why God established penance, and he is anxious to show that it was not for God's own gratification but for our own good (God, in many of William's descriptions, has a psychology as much as do humans). He then argues that penitence is natural to us, since we are always, at some deep level, seeking to turn away from sin and return to our pristine state of innocence; therefore it is merely just that God allows us a means of repentance. Finally, he asks why priests are necessary to this process, and he gives a host of reasons, including the need for a mediator between God and penitent and the impossibility of self-judgement. This was obviously a contemporary disputed question, and he wants to be convincing: he returns to it several times.

After his introduction, William addresses separately the three main divisions of penance: contrition, confession and restitution. The triad follows the familiar Augustinian threesome of movement from the heart (contrition) to the word (confession) then the whole body in deeds (satisfaction).[9] Contrition focuses on what motivates our sense of guilt, showing the ways in which contrition both demands that we be co-operators (co-workers) with God, and illustrates how we are. Confession is the longest section of the work. William shows why confession is useful and necessary by giving it a series of alternative names, such as calculation of our debt to God, or spiritual vomit, as we have heard already. After considering the fruits of confession, he asks four more questions which, though practical in tone (for instance, how soon after a sin should one confess it?), are given theological answers; and he ends with an exhortation to keep busy with good works. Finally, William looks briefly at restitution, insisting that it is spiritual and not temporal. This allows him to argue that any apparent arbitrariness on the part of priests who give varying penances is both unimportant and untrue, since no outsider can know all the circumstances of a situation; and we simply must, in any case, trust the clergy. He finishes with a very short section on how a confessor should behave.

Let us then look at some of the issues he addresses, and consider how he

---

MSS of the *Treatise*: Avignon, Bib. pub., MS 38; Cambrai, Bib. mun., MS 434; Cambridge, Univ. Libr., MS Ee. 11. 29; Chartres, Bib. mun., MS 377; MS 389; Innsbruck, Universitätsbib., MS 229; Klosterneuburg, Stiftsbib., MS 205; [?Michigan Univ., MS 199]; Munich, Clm 3798; Oxford, BL, MS Laud 146; Paris, Bibl. Mazarine, MS 991; Paris, BNF, MS lat. 8433; MS lat. 14891; MS lat. 15988; Philadelphia, Univ. of Penn. Libr. MS Lea 22; Prague, Metro. Kap., MS c. 110; Prague, Univ. Libr., MS 1862; MS 2138 and MS 2343; Rome, BAV, Pal. lat. 602; MS Reg. lat. 444; MS Vat. lat. 849; St Omer, Bib. mun., MS 316; Stockholm, Kungl. Bib., MS F. min. 597; Toulouse, Bib. mun., MS 210; Tours, Bib. mun., MS 406; Vienna, Schottenst., MS 311; MS 413.

9   *Opera* I, 489b.

goes about tackling them. Overall he relates penance to three processes: to the
metaphor of medicine; to its likeness to the actions of civil courts; and to the
stewardship of the talents God has given us. (Most of the examples in this
essay deal with the first and second of these, but that is accident rather than
design.) All of William's writing has a feeling of directness and purpose, but
the *Sacrament*, especially the section on confession, is one of the strongest
examples of this. As is his usual practice, he consistently uses the first person of
verbs, such as *ego, respondeo, dico*, and he refers to his reader familiarly as *tu*.
But the works on penance show an even greater directness and urgency than
elsewhere. He uses immediate forms of address such as, *O peccator, O penitens,
O villice*; he gives commands in the singular form: *dic! fac!*; and he makes direct
demands: *interroga teipsum, memento igitur*. His tone is urgent and compelling:
'Do you think you have sins to confess? There's no blame in that. Do you fear
the shame which you run from at such speed? Are you ashamed? Have no sins,
then; but, as far as I am able, I especially wish, I ask, I warn, I commend, I beg
you to have shame: for shame over sins is healthy and should be praised and
richly accepted, from the most gracious God.'[10] In the *Sacrament*, these forms of
language are even more marked than in the section on the Eucharist, and it
seems clear that William is building on his earlier work in the *Treatise* and
adopting much the same tone.

He is a pious writer, by which I do not mean pietistic or simperingly
religious, but rather that he is always clear in his mind that he is writing, even
as an academic, in order to build up the body of Christ. As has been noted, he is
always aware of audience in the widest sense. This attention to the wider
world has a tendency to give his work a slightly less-than-scholarly feel, which
is part of the pleasure of reading him. By this I do not wish to suggest that he is
not serious, nor that he is unlearned. On the contrary, William's biblical
knowledge matches that of any medieval academic; and his list of sources
outstrips almost all his contemporaries, embracing alongside Christians,
pagans (including Aristotle), Arabic writers such as Avicenna and Avicebrol,
and the rabbi Maimonides: he is the first or amongst the first to use many of
their works in a theological setting. Moreover, he has as sharp a sense as any
medieval theologian of the pains of eternal punishment and the learned man's
responsibility to advise and warn those who know no better. Constantly he
refers to the 'dangers' of certain courses of action, and the 'miracles' to be
achieved by turning to God. Hell is tangible to him, an icy wilderness where
the warming heat of the Holy Spirit will not reach the desperate soul: 'there,
your heart is not only chilled, but rather turned to ice; and the warm winds of
grace are made stone cold'.[11] He makes the results of impenitence quite clear.

Yet this all-inclusive, rounded approach marks him out from
contemporaries and is, perhaps, part of the reason for his later neglect. An
exhortatory tone combined with strong theological content was commonplace

[10] *Opera* I, 578a.
[11] *Opera* I, 472bA.

in earlier writers such as Gregory the Great or Bernard of Clairvaux: William does indeed resemble his patristic or monastic predecessors. But the work of fellow academics of his own day was moving in another direction, towards greater divisions between the roles of pastor, scholar, and contemplative – at least in the ways in which these roles were written about. The development of the Schools shifted the cutting edge of theology from monastic to secular establishments, and broadened the student body from being overwhelmingly made up of men who were to be 'religious professionals' to a wider mix of some who would work in the Church and others who simply wished to use their university training to get a good job. These changes acted to define theology as an academic discipline and to divide it into constituent parts. William defies such pigeon-holing in his work, always aiming for a complete picture. This means that, notwithstanding his extraordinary and pioneering use of Aristotle, Maimonides and the rest, the overall tenor of his writing may have seemed conservative and old-fashioned to the young Turks who succeeded him. They are deceived by the form and overlook the content. His originality of mind is clothed in a soft-edged style at a time when theologians were moving towards a more legalistic formulation of their science: it made him something of an odd-man-out; he did not subsequently secure a large following of disciples. Nevertheless, his ideas find their way into the works of the most brilliant of his successors. These writings on confession throw up a number of examples of his illuminating and incisive thinking.

As is common in his work, William is deeply concerned with the question of motive, or rather, with the many and varied motivations of the penitent. In the *Treatise*, he notes four motivations, but by the *Sacrament* these have expanded to ten and become more subtle. The first of the motives in the *Treatise* – compunction – becomes in the *Sacrament* something wider. By 'compunction' he defines the first stirrings of sin in the heart as the heart attempts to be cleansed of evil – hence the word *compunctio*, since the sins pierce the heart of the penitent like spiny thorns, before the Holy Spirit can enter and heal it. In a lovely image, William compares compunction to the piercing of the bark of certain trees which, when wounded, send out incense or myrrh, as though they were shedding tears.[12]

Compunction is part of a complex series of movements in which the sinner turns to to the good, from an initial motion away from sin to the making of full satisfaction. They begin with attrition, which is a generalised wearing away of, as it were, non-specific sin, inside the sinner, by good works, prayer, sorrow for one's sins and so forth. Contrition, which is the next level up, refers to specific evil-doings and turning from them. Penitents go from contrition, with its ten possible motivations, to confession, then on to restitution or satisfaction.[13]

12 *Sacrament*, c. 5: *Opera* I, 462bG–5aD.
13 *Opera* I, 465aD–bD.

These ten motives are somewhat similar to modern psychiatric charting of the stages of healing in situations such as bereavement. The sinner begins in fear, recognising what he has done, then moves to shame. Both of these are multi-faceted motivations and William realises that, if not handled properly, they can be as much a hindrance to confession as a help. Shame in particular is, he knows, the reason why many people do not wish to confess in front of a priest: they fear for what the priest, their neighbour, will think of them. William will have none of it. In a chapter[14] which moves from the solemn to the everyday, to the burlesque, and finally to the exhortatory, he shows that allowing shame and fear to blight your chances of wholeness and life is absolutely ridiculous. He begins by asking whether you would allow the devil victory simply out of fear of one man's face – i.e., your confessor. But this is foolish, because shame can only have power over you if you stay silent about the offences. Once they are out in the open, they have no more strength. However great is your shame for what you have done, when you overcome that shame and confess, you will be victorious to the same degree. How can anyone be ashamed of something so glorious?

William continues with a metaphor everyone can understand. Are you ashamed to wash your dirty linen, or have people know you need to? Are you ashamed to spring clean your house and throw out the unwanted and useless? Of course not! Moreover, it could not be simpler; even the speaking of the evil deed in some sense overcomes it, and is a victory. This is again reminiscent of modern counselling theory – the sense that simply speaking problems or difficulties out loud in front of another person is a step to healing. Here again (in a separate passage from that with which I began) he uses the image of vomit – since vomiting both does good of itself and indicates that something medicinal is going on inside. This is a small example of a point William makes many times, that the impulse to go to confession is in itself a grace, as well as a sign of further grace, whether received or to come.

Neither should you worry about the size of the sins. On the contrary, the bigger the sin, the bigger the success when you've destroyed it. A penitent, dutifully and sincerely making his confession, is not so much a penitent as a victorious warrior, welcomed by his confessor with the greatest triumphant applause. But for those people who confess only their least and most trivial sins, it is as if they assert a victory only over dead fleas or flies. Ancient Rome had a ruling that victory celebrations could only be held if you had killed more than seven thousand of the enemy. Similarly, you should want to show your success by confessing huge monsters of sin: elephants of pride, whales of avarice, lions of anger, wolves of rapacity and bulls of indiscipline. Quoting the most famous gospel passage on repentance ('There will be more joy in heaven over one sinner who repents . . .', Luke 15.7), he adds 'Pity the poor priest who doesn't get the chance to hear such sins!'[15]

14 *Sacrament*, c. 14: *Opera* I, 489bD–91aC.
15 Spring-cleaning: *Opera* I, 490aG; speaking of the evil deed, I, 490aH; vomit, I, 490aH; beasts as sins, I, 490bF–G.

Rather than fear one flea, the sinner should worry about lions waiting in the world to come, if he does not confess them now. 'I wish' (*Utinam*), he says several times, I wish I could show you the rejoicing in heaven over your sincere confession. 'Open your mouth so that God may fill it. Be freed from the tyranny of the devil to the freedom of the glory of God.'[16]

William's concern that the penitent confess to a *priest* is repeated several times in the *Sacrament*, and is drawn closely from the *Treatise*. It reflects his recognition and knowledge of questions that 'ordinary people' ask, and his concern to answer them. He is also acute in knowing how people try to get away with things by clever argument. His response to this sort of 'but what about' wheedling is usually in the most everyday terms. He gives the most concrete example he can think of as a sort of unanswerable simile. In the earlier discussion about the shame of confession, for instance, William used the images of spring cleaning and doing-your-laundry. Such 'arguments' are straightforward, understandable by everyone, and yet very compelling. They do not come wrapped in the specialised language of the theology classroom, but their simplicity is wholly deceptive of their power.

However, William is not tied down to this everyday level of objection, nor does he think that all such complaints are simply sham arguments to get out of something distasteful. Let us look in detail at a question which shows his interplay between theological complexity and pastoral reality. William addresses the question of whether it can ever be right to confess to a priest other than your own parish priest (*proprius sacerdos*).[17] Although he assumes that confessing to your own priest should be the norm, he recognises that there may be occasions on which this would not be wise. These must include, as he has earlier noted, occasions when women feel threatened by their priest, or when the priest feels threatened by a woman parishioner.[18] If either party would suffer, bodily or spiritually, from such a confession to the parish priest, then with permission from the priest or bishop, the penitent may go elsewhere. If this were a straightforward manual of confession, that might be the end of the matter; but one of the things that makes this work so interesting is the theological questions that it goes on to ask. William never divorces the theology from the everyday, nor the 'ignorant' questions from the theology. Having looked at the practical question of 'which priest', he follows up by wondering about the nature of absolution. If you confess half your sins to your own priest and half to an outsider, does each give you semi-absolution?[19] Clearly, this might not be sufficient, since two halves of a story do not make a whole: 'I got married secretly to Peter', told to one priest, and 'I got married secretly to John' to another, is a case in point! Furthermore, surely grace, like marriage, cannot be partial. One cannot be in part a sinner and in part a saint, or else you would be able to leave your legs in hell when your arms are in heaven. If the soul is indivisible – and it is – so too must be its final reward. So,

---

16 *Opera* I, 491aA–C.
17 *Opera* I, 499aC.

18 *Opera* I, 457bC–D.
19 *Opera* I, 499bB–D.

from which priest does the penitent get absolution and blessing? In theory, he could get it from both or neither; yet the answer cannot be 'neither', since this would defeat the purpose of confessing. But how, on the other hand, could the answer be both? Equally clearly, just as a judge cannot sentence you for crimes he does not know you have committed, so a priest cannot absolve you from sins he has not heard. Or can he? The solution comes in the space between an external court and an internal judgement. For, unlike a civil court, the priest/judge does not acquit or condemn; but rather, when he says 'We absolve you' he is using a shorthand form of saying that he is praying to God on the penitent's behalf for absolution and the grace of sanctification. So, of course (and not just in cases like this), the priest must pray that the penitent be remitted from sins which he may not even have recognised in himself, nor admitted to the confessor. Hence, the priest does *not* say to the penitent, 'May the Lord remit those sins you have confessed to me' but 'May the Lord remit all your sins.' William must take care not to find himself in something of a corner here, since he must nevertheless adhere to the theory that sins unconfessed will go on festering.

A further problem remains. If the penitent receives full grace from the first priest, what is left to be gained from the second? The answer to this is somewhat tricky. Sins are remitted through the grace of contrition. It is the contrition, which appears only from an influx of grace, that leads one to confess. The contrition is the crucial point, for it leads one to make the outward sign of the inward grace (the definition, after all, of a sacrament). Nevertheless, confession can be divided because one priest can hear you in order to give counsel and enjoin penance; and the other gives a priestly blessing and absolution. Note that this implies that the two priests will know their respective roles: hole-in-the-corner, furtive division of confession is not on.

So far so good. But William takes his exploration slightly further. This division of labour in confessors is also possible when you have an uneducated or simple priest (*simplex et sacrarum litterarum ignarus*[20]). Such a priest can summon help to advise or counsel on the judicial position. After all, this happens in civil courts where the penalties are much less important; clearly it must be possible in matters of real life and death.

But this leads to dangerous inferences: if a deacon who does not yet have the power to absolve is nevertheless full of sense, knows his law, and understands human sin – in William's phrase, is full of the knowledge of heavenly medicine[21] – he can supplement the work of an ignorant priest. Similarly, a foreigner may need to confess entirely through an interpeter. If the priest is, perhaps, ignorant, he may need to do the whole thing, except the absolution and blessing, through a mediator. And more, he says, some people agree that, for venial sins, or in cases of extreme necessity, a lay person may absolve you.

---

[20] *Opera* I, 499bD.
[21] *Opera* I, 499bD.

It is no wonder that a later reader has written in the margin here, *Caute haec omnia!*[22]

William goes on from this to more completely theological questions, such as whether recidivism is possible and how; and whether a second absolution is possible in such cases of relapse.[23] The issues are complex; he treats them seriously and at length. As we have seen in the previous examples, William rarely uses a single position, pro or con, to argue for one line, in the classic scholastic manner. Rather, he uses a series of reasons or similitudes pertaining to the topic, like planets in orbit round the sun, so that weight of evidence and comprehensive coverage as much as anything are meant to convince. In the case of backsliding,[24] he believes that it is possible because sin is ineradicable in this life. (Nor does God expect us not to sin: God would never ask the impossible.[25]) *We* feel that repeated absolution is wrong because we wish God to be bound by what we see as fair. It is wrong for bad men who repent to be treated better than good men who do not need so much! But this is to limit God with our boundaries; God, however, is limitless goodness.[26] Is this a direct argument against the Cathars? I think so. William says at the beginning of the *Sacrament* that it is only heretics who say there is no going back for sinning souls, nor any hope of pardon after falling from grace.[27] He specifically argues against that line of thought.

Neither of William's works on penance is a straightforward *Sic et non* type of treatise, with linear questions and answers, but a richer and more discursive blend of theology and practical examples. In saying that, I do not want to make a value judgement for his work over that of other, more theologically rigorous, academics. Nor do I wish to imply that William is unable to use logic. He does, in fact, use logic, sometimes even symbolic logic; and if we believe, as seems likely from his list of sources, that he had studied arts to a high level before turning to theology, this would have included a training in logic. But logic is not given a privileged place in any particular solution to a problem, but only as and when he feels it to be useful; it is part, but not the whole picture, of what people need to be convinced. William does this, I believe, not because he is unable to follow or copy the normal run of scholastic treatises – he simply prefers not to, thinking that he can achieve his aims better in other ways.

For William is always looking to the audience and the long-term purpose behind his task, which is to build up the faith of the Church. His own sense of complete belief in the Church, outside of which there can be no salvation, is palpable. He propounds high moral standards, but he is always aware of

---

22 It was written in the margin of the manuscript (identity not clear) used to produce the 1674 printed edition.
23 *Opera* I, 500–505.
24 *Opera* I, 502aE–F.
25 *Opera* I, 452bE.
26 *Opera* I, 504aE.
27 *Opera* I, 451bD–2aE.

human frailty, thinks sin is inevitable, and does not believe that God asks us to do the impossible. Added to this, he believes strongly in the goodness of creation; this means that his thoughts are always based in the temporal world, and it leads him constantly to make the link between our physical and spiritual lives. His writing, as we have seen, is very vivid and personal, even in an age when personality stands out strongly in theology. And he was an individualist who was never afraid to make his own way through a problem and give his own solutions, though his aim is always to maintain the orthodox faith.

We can see this heady mixture if we look back at the first quotation, returning as it were, to our vomit. The passage reflects the overarching metaphor of medicine: penance is the remedy and the priest the doctor. This was, of course, a common metaphor for sacraments in general, but William's treatment of it is particularly startling. From medicine we move easily to his use of whole body images. He is particularly good at conjuring up the feeling of *being bodily*, and the experiences that gives us. The small details, such as tasting bile in the mouth, which makes us want to vomit, are very telling. This is a man who wants to move both minds and hearts. The vomit example is not, of course, 'an argument', in the classical sense, but it does carry forward the point he wants to make in a very strong way. Finally, he makes much of the difference between the human and the animal. This difference is very important for William, since becoming fully human is the first step on the road to salvation.

I would like to end with a question that intrigues me: for whom was this text written? William never writes without a purpose and, as we saw earlier, he addresses the putative penitent specifically and repeatedly. This penitent is not a priest. Priests are not, obviously, excluded, and there are a couple of short passages addressing the matter of clerical conduct, but the work as a whole is for lay consumption. Yet what sort of layman or woman can this be? These treatises are not simple advice books to laypeople telling what to confess and how. Indeed, very little of that sort of issue is addressed at all. Theological questions on the motivation of God, as well as the state of mind of the parishioner, are equally considered. William uses an allegory of confession as a spiritual form of bodily resurrection right next to a vivid image of the heat of the holy spirit melting the Old Adam like a child's snowman left in the sun.[28] But these are not treatises over the heads of their readers, or certainly they were not meant as such, for he means us to understand and apply their theological ideas. For instance, William asks how we are to get the gift of the grace of contrition that is the beginning of repentence.[29] There are three ways: firstly, it just happens – a donation from God; secondly, through the intercession of the saints; and thirdly by co-operating with God. Now there are seven types of co-operation, beginning with simply turning ourselves from darkness to light. William does not say, with this or any of the other types, how

[28] *Opera* I, 471bD.
[29] *Opera* I, 472aA–3aC.

we might do this; he leaves the circumstances to us to work out. But he does expect it. So the reader is left to do quite a lot of work, sophisticated consideration of the text and its implications, for him or herself.

These treatises, written for a literate layperson, who seems to be thought to be reading the work to him or herself (and surely if the work was to be read aloud to a group of hearers, the penitent would not be addressed so consistently in the singular?), strike me as important for this reason alone. They assume the existence of an audience which lies between the parish clod and the Paris theologian. They suggest an educated, interested, devout reading public which, though not theologically trained, nevertheless wishes to know more of the Why, and not simply the How or What.

Did William know such people? Indeed he did, for he was an esteemed friend to Louis IX – St Louis – and confessor to Blanche of Castille, Louis' mother. I make no claims that either was the recipient of William's work; indeed, in one sense I wish to argue that such a work suggests the existence of a much wider audience than this limited royal milieu. But it allows me to point, at least, to two educated and devout readers, who might have found this sort of work more than a good read. As for William, no doubt confessing Blanche gave him a rich sense of life as she is lived!

Confession, Social Ethics and Social Discipline in the *Memoriale presbiterorum*

Michael Haren

The *Memoriale presbiterorum*, a fourteenth-century pastoral manual of English production, is preserved in whole or in part in five known manuscripts. Of these, Cambridge, Corpus Christi College, MS 148 (referred to below as C) – a manuscript dated palaeographically as of the first half of the fourteenth century – is the earliest and offers generally the best text. A fifteenth-century manuscript in Westminster Diocesan Archives[1] derives at a remove from this manuscript, and Cambridge University Library, MS Mm. v. 33, which contains a small part of the text in a late fourteenth or early fifteenth century hand, may be descended from a parent of C, though since there are few crucial readings the latter judgement is tentative. London, British Library, MS Harley 3120, of the early fifteenth century, is of peculiar interest for its unique colophon, attributing the 'composition' of the treatise to 'a certain doctor of decrees at Avignon in 1344'.[2] There is no other indication, from the transmission, from early bibliographers or from elsewhere, of the identity of the author. I am satisfied that it can be shown, with as complete certainty as may attach to an accumulation of circumstances, there being no direct statement to that effect in any source, both that the treatise comes from the circle of Bishop Grandisson of Exeter and that its author is in fact Mr William Doune. Doune was a functionary in the Exeter administration from the mid-1330s and Grandisson's registrar from the late 1330s to about the mid 1340s. Subsequently, from about 1352, he served as official of Lincoln under Bishop Gynwell and from 1354 as official of Worcester under Bishop Brian. In 1354 he became archdeacon of Leicester. He died, still official of both dioceses and archdeacon of Leicester, in 1361, leaving the remarkable will edited in its extant part by Professor Hamilton Thompson.[3] The argument for authorship, which is complex and detailed, cannot be presented here.[4] In what I say therefore of the treatise's

---

1 See N. R. Ker, *Medieval Manuscripts in British Libraries*, I (Oxford, 1969), pp. 419–21.
2 See Pantin, *English Church*, p. 274.
3 See A. H. Thompson, 'The Will of Master William Doune, Archdeacon of Leicester', *The Archaeological Journal* 72 (1915), 233–84.
4 It will be presented in a forthcoming monograph, to be entitled *Confession, Social Discipline and Diocesan Government in Fourteenth-Century England: a Study of the 'Memoriale presbiterorum'*, currently in preparation.

context, I must rely by anticipation on my case for authorship. My purpose here is to tease out some of the implications of the particular historical setting in which I locate the treatise and to indicate some wider implications that arise from William Doune's authorship.

The *Memoriale presbiterorum* is a part of that great body of writing for the instruction of parish clergy which is so prominent a feature of the intellectual life of the English church in the thirteenth and fourteenth centuries. Some of these manuals, such as the enormously influential *Oculus sacerdotis*,[5] range widely over the pastoral cure. In contrast, the *Memoriale presbiterorum*, which consists of 218 chapters and runs to ninety-six folios in C, is exclusively devoted to confessional technique. It purports to have been written for a friend in the first instance. That the address 'amice karissime' – which occurs internally at various junctures – is more than a convention, has powerful support in the manuscript tradition, where the final chapter is an addendum, an edited letter on the law governing the burial of a pregnant woman, in response to a scruple raised by the original recipient (unnamed, but now also identifiable). This chapter, tacked on after the concluding formula of the treatise proper, is an evident and unique departure from the main subject. Apart from this ultimate digression, the structure of the treatise may be briefly outlined as comprising some seven sections, which are not, however, explicitly distinguished in the work. There is an opening section on the reception of the penitent, followed by a dogmatic section based partly on Archbishop Pecham's statute 'Ignorantia sacerdotum'. A general account of the importance of the circumstances and of the manner of confession precedes the programme of interrogation. The interrogation consists of inquiry into the seven deadly sins and on the circumstances, leading to examination of the penitent on the basis of his station in life. The general inspiration for this latter is the corresponding section of the *Summa aurea* by the great thirteenth-century canonist, Henry of Susa, Hostiensis,[6] but the author of the *Memoriale presbiterorum* modifies Hostiensis's programme to suit his purpose, adding material to the questionnaires on several of the classes considered by Hostiensis, inserting a number of groups not found in Hostiensis's schema and omitting a number of persons and types – such as the higher ecclesiastical and secular dignitaries – traditionally included in the programme, presumably on the grounds that they are outside the scope of the parish confessor. The central portion of the work is devoted to canonical material, including reserved sins and the penitential canons. The author next proceeds to the subject of restitution. First are discussed a number of general legal points of difficulty in this connection, such as the nature of a prelate's obligations in respect of the goods of his church, the salaries of the harlot and actor, claim to wreck, unjust tallage and the spoils of war. Then are considered the obligations of various classes and persons, notably administrative officials, to make restitution of

---

5 See Boyle, '*Oculus*', and Boyle, 'Study'.
6 Henry de Susa (Hostiensis), *Summa aurea* (Basle, 1573).

unjust gains. This section is therefore, in one respect, the obverse of the examination of the classes in the earlier part of the work and, like the interrogatories, owes its inspiration and much of its legal content to the relevant sections of Hostiensis's *Summa aurea*. However, the author's own contribution is considerable and he reveals a marked zeal for his subject. The remaining sections of the treatise consider the demeanour of the penitent and the relationship set up between himself and his confessor, and supply information relating to excommunication, including papal and Canterbury provincial sentences of excommunication.

As a manual for confessors, the treatise is a thoughtful application of the continental canonical tradition to the mid fourteenth century English scene by a puritanical though sensitive observer. Its historical interest is on a number of levels. First, it is noteworthy precisely as the work of a writer of wholly orthodox bent, whose denunciation is as severe of abuse in ecclesiastical structures as in secular. If the primary import of this point needs less emphasis now than formerly, this is partly the effect of the uncovering of sources of a similar kind and of the consequent perception that the pre-Wycliffite church contained, at its middle levels certainly, a ferment of self-criticism. The treatise fits perfectly within the interpretative view adopted by the late W. A. Pantin in his study of the fourteenth-century English church[7] as an outgrowth of the previous age rather than a transition to the succeeding, although there are engrossingly suggestive points at which my subject merges – as all historical movements must – with what follows. The historian's problem here is that of the novelist too, in E. M. Forster's injunction, 'Only connect'. To this, the historian's reply will often be 'If only I could', for the historian's connections must not just, as the novelist's, be plausible and satisfying but evidenced too. To this point, I will return in due course.

Then, as regards wider history, especially as its study is conducted under the pervasive influence of the *Annales* school, the *Memoriale presbiterorum* is a fertile source. It is sharply focussed on the social dimension of confession and from being a didactic manual it becomes, for the historian, in large part a vehicle of social comment. The author is a fierce critic of contemporary society which, in its middle and lower strata, he subjects to systematic review from the unusual perspective of penitential discipline. His strictures, when controlled by the documentary evidence and the views of other commentators, are valuable as the observations of someone who feels deeply about social abuses – most notably those which proceed from the malpractices of officialdom – and who has considerable experience of this latter aspect of his subject. The effect can be coherently, even if not comprehensively, illustrated by the extracted interrogatories that follow this paper.[8]

---

7 Pantin, *English Church*.
8 See below, pp. 126–163. The principal defect of the sample of the treatise's doctrine presented below is the omission of the powerful complementary sections on restitution.

I have elsewhere considered this line of implicit commentary and criticism within the tradition of social ethics stemming from the biblical-moral movement of the twelfth-century schools identified by Grabmann and explored subsequently by Beryl Smalley, in her study of the Bible, and Professor Baldwin, in his examination of the views of Peter the Chanter and his circle.[9] This was a tradition that made early and substantial contribution to the literature on penance, with crucial effect in the inter-conciliar period, 1179–1215, that Professor Leonard Boyle has shown to be so significant for the beginnings of pastoral manuals.[10] As I have argued, this tradition, which received its first major elaboration at the hands of theologians, rapidly became the inheritance of the canonists.[11] In articulating my views on the penitential manual as a medium of social ethics, I also toyed with the other model which is sometimes advanced, of its being regarded as an instrument of social control.[12] In reaction to some of the promptings that derive from the proposed identification of its particular historical context, I should like briefly to examine how it would relate to such a model, while suggesting an alternative nomenclature for the outlook into which the *Memoriale presbiterorum* fits.

There is in fact no universally accepted definition of the concept of 'social control'. The term has been used to embrace a broad reference which takes in 'all social forms that allow groups to achieve legitimate moral aims' and a narrow reference which would restrict it to 'a coercive process imposed upon individuals to enforce normative conformity'. As an alternative, one recent theorist has proposed a normative definition of 'social control' as 'purposive actions that define, respond to, and control deviant behavior', distinguishing the concept on the one hand from other 'processes that contribute to social order' and, on the other, extending it beyond solely coercive responses.[13] On these models, confession would have elements corresponding to both the broad and normative concepts. It is not formally coercive in that the proceedings of what canonists called the 'private forum' are protected by secrecy and its injunctions carry moral force only, though in medieval context the requirement to confess annually was itself enforceable by coercion. While confession is capable of transcending the focus of social control viewed as a response to wrongdoing, of serving as medium of what I would call 'social ethics' by raising moral horizons, it is certainly the case that a main thrust of the *Memoriale presbiterorum* is as a 'remedy of sin'. There is in fact substantial evidence from the context in which it was written that it forms part of the thinking of a circle bent on the direction of society along moral lines and that

---

[9] See Haren, 'Social Ideas'. Cf. below, p. 124.

[10] L. E. Boyle, 'The Inter-Conciliar Period 1179–1215 and the Beginnings of Pastoral Manuals', in *Miscellanea Rolando Bandinelli Papa Alessandro III*, ed. F. Liotta (Siena, 1986), pp. 45–56.

[11] Cf. below, p. 124.

[12] Haren, 'Social Ideas', p. 56.

[13] A. V. Horwitz, *The Logic of Social Control* (New York, 1990), p. 9, for this and the formulation of the alternative concepts cited.

confession was seen as a main instrument through which that direction could be exercised and maintained. I say here 'direction' rather than 'reform' in deference to an Augustinian strand within the thinking of Bishop Grandisson, though the temptation to talk more loosely of 'reform' is constant. In this respect there is the comfort that not even Augustine was consistently 'Augustinian'. For a programme in which the concern with society – though real and urgent – is secondary and subsidiary and in which the expectations of results seem strictly limited, I propose to use the diffidently neutral term 'social discipline'. It is evident a priori that since the prescriptions of the confessor were largely at his discretion, even on the level of theory, and on the level of practice were wholly so, the degree of expertise and the uniformity of outlook obtaining among confessors must be pivotal to the penitential system, viewed as a mechanism of social discipline. The writing of a manual for confessors was one approach to the question of expertise. It can be considered a partial response to that of uniformity too. However, as I will suggest, this latter dimension evoked more specific effort within the circles from which the *Memoriale Presbiterorum* emanated.

A complete presentation of the *Memoriale presbiterorum* within the programme of social morality in action of which I see it as a part at Exeter would require both a more detailed review of the character of Grandisson's episcopate and a closer exposition of the doctrine of the treatise than is possible here. It would also require some consideration, more or less detailed, of other and quite different works with which it has interests in common. One of these is the middle English poem, *Speculum vitae*, attributed to the York advocate, William of Nassington.[14] With some reservation, the *Speculum vitae* may be taken as another potential source for the views of the Grandisson circle. The reservation is two-fold. In the first place, there must at present be more residual doubt over the authorship of the *Speculum vitae* than over the authorship of the *Memoriale presbiterorum*. However, Nassington's authorship, which has a basis in manuscript attribution, is wholly probable and the probability is greatly strengthened by the case for the provenance of the *Memoriale presbiterorum* itself. The second reservation derives from the fact that the strong Northern affiliations of the *Speculum vitae*[15] mean that, if it is indeed

---

14 See Pantin, *English Church*, pp. 228–9; H. E. Allen, 'The *Speculum Vitae* – Addendum', *PMLA* 33 (n.s. 25) (1917), 133–62; I. J. Petersen, *William of Nassington, Canon, Mystic and Poet of the Speculum Vitae* (New York, Berne and Frankfurt-am-Main, 1986). The case for William of Nassington's authorship has also been addressed by Dr Jonathan Hughes in an unpublished paper of which he kindly provided me with a copy. For suggested links between Nassington's career and writings, see J. Hughes, 'The Administration of Confession in the Diocese of York in the Fourteenth Century', in *Studies in Clergy and Ministry in Medieval England*, ed. D. M. Smith, Borthwick Studies in History 1 (York, 1992), pp. 98–9.

15 See J. Hughes, *Pastors and Visionaries: Religion and Secular Life in Late Medieval Yorkshire* (Woodbridge, 1988), p. 148; V. Gillespie, 'The Literary Form of the Middle English Pastoral Manual with particular reference to the *Speculum Christiani* and some related Texts' (unpublished D.Phil. thesis, Oxford, 1981), p. 134.

by William of Nassington, it must more plausibly be deemed to have been written during the period *c*. 1343–55 when he was active both as an administrator in York diocese and as an auditor of causes of the court of York, than in the preceding period of his activity in Exeter. There he had been for many years, from near the beginning of Grandisson's episcopate, one of the most prominent members of the diocesan administration. However, it is reasonable to suppose, as regards the coincidence of concerns between the *Speculum vitae* and the *Memoriale presbiterorum*, that Nassington's views had been forming in the earlier period. The correspondences are most pronounced and the social dimension most overt in the poem's exposition of Rapine and Calumny – the third and fourth branches of the vice of Avarice. Under Rapine are grouped common robbers, false executors, false debtors, covetous lords, covetous prelates, and a miscellany of officials, deans, bedells, bailiffs and sheriffs, while under Calumny comes a concatenation of legal classes: false plaintiff, false defendant, false witness and juror, false advocate, false procurator and attorney, false notary and clerk, false judge and justice, false maintainer and counsellor.[16] This careful and specialised interest in legal officials and personages is particularly noteworthy. In the abstract, it might as well be associated with Nassington's experiences at York as at Exeter, but its resemblance to the preoccupation of the *Memoriale presbiterorum* with forensic abuses suggests that its genesis owes something to Exeter, where Nassington was closely involved with Grandisson's consistorial reforms.[17]

Another figure with whose outlook the *Memoriale presbiterorum* requires some lengthy comparison is Richard FitzRalph, the most egregious of Grandisson's protégés. I shall in fact say something of this connection, in pursuit of the theme of 'social discipline', though much less than could be said in terms of the intellectual biography of FitzRalph himself.

Short, then, of a full-scale examination of the *Memoriale presbiterorum*'s social doctrine, much less of its witness to the programme of the Grandisson circle, I will dwell briefly on three prominent aspects of the treatise: concern with ecclesiastical officials and administrators, sensitivity to lay incursions on ecclesiastical rights, and a pronounced hostility to the mendicant friars. My immediate object is to suggest how through the proposed identification of the author the treatise fits into an intellectual and administrative milieu.

It is worth noting at once that the concern of the *Memoriale presbiterorum* with legal officials is untypical of English confessional manuals, as indeed is its intensive examination of the classes in general. While, as I have already noted, it is dependent for much of the inspiration and some of the material of its interrogations on the *Summa aurea* of Hostiensis, there is ample indication that the author had a personal interest in the shortcomings of the legal cum administrative classes. His article, under the head of restitution, on

16 Oxford, Bodleian Library, MS Bodley 446, fols. 90v–3v.
17 *The Register of John Grandisson, Bishop of Exeter (A.D. 1327–1369)*, ed. F. C. Hingeston-Randolph, 3 vols. (London and Exeter, 1894–99), II, 809.

archdeacons and their ministers – on whom I will focus here as an illustration of his views on administration additional to the interrogatory for officials and deans edited below[18] – has no model in Hostiensis and, like his interrogatory for officials and deans, it is a consideration of a class much neglected in the *Summae confessorum*. In turn, his treatment – again under the head of restitution – of the assessors and counsellors of judges,[19] and of apparitors and other minor officers,[20] though suggested by Hostiensis, contains much apparently original comment.

As regards archdeacons, a principal preoccupation of the *Memoriale presbiterorum* is abuse in visitation and in particular the levying of procurations when there has not been personal visitation.[21] These were points referred to in William Doune's will, at a juncture where he made elaborate provision by proclamation within his archdeaconry for the restitution of any unjust receipts either by him or his servants.[22] Ironically, the provision regarding unjust receipts was interpreted by Hamilton Thompson as evidence of Doune's proclivity to abuses that were widespread rather than as evidence of peculiar sensitivity to abuses.[23] The benign reading is corroborated by the recurrence of a similar provision in the will of Doune's official in the archdeaconry and successor in the officiality, Mr John de Belvoir, who died in 1391. John de Belvoir's regard for Doune, by whom he appears to have been deeply impressed and to whom he certainly felt deeply indebted, is an explicit, pronounced and informative feature of his testamentary dispositions.[24]

The strictures of the *Memoriale presbiterorum* on the subject of archidiaconal and more generally of official corruption and the sensitivity evinced – on the above reading – by Doune and unmistakeably by John de Belvoir have their counterpart in the surviving administrative documentation. The concern is evidenced in a letter issued by Bishop Grandisson on behalf of the veteran Adam de Carletone, archdeacon of Cornwall, in 1342,[25] and in a general mandate issued by him in 1348, excommunicating those who levied procurations or other sums by colour of them without personal visitation and undertaking to address the question of past exactions.[26] Other abuses in visitation, notably the levying of pecuniary penances (another preoccupation of the *Memoriale presbiterorum*), had a history of legislation within the Exeter diocese,[27] and they evoked specific regulation from Grandisson, perhaps in

18 See below, pp. 126–31.
19 C, fols. 66r–v: Haren, 'A Study', II, 231–2.
20 C, fols. 67v–8r: Haren, 'A Study', II, 232–3.
21 C, fols. 65r–v: Haren, 'A Study', II, 223–6.
22 Thompson, 'The Will', p. 280.
23 A. H. Thompson, *The English Clergy and their Organization in the Later Middle Ages: the Ford Lectures for 1933* (Oxford, 1947), pp. 60–1.
24 See M. J. Haren, 'The Will of Master John de Belvoir, Official of Lincoln (d. 1391)', *MS* 58 (1996), 119–47 (135–7).
25 *Reg. Grandisson*, ed. Hingeston-Randolph, II, 956–7.
26 *Reg. Grandisson*, ed. Hingeston-Randolph, II, 1050.
27 See a statute of Peter Quinel of 1287: *Councils & Synods*, II, 1034–5.

1346 or somewhat earlier, as a prelude to his tackling the procurations issue.[28] Then, dramatically, from the period of John de Belvoir's officiality at Lincoln, comes a series of mandates over a period of twelve years (1377–89) that constitutes the most determined and ferocious onslaught evidenced in any medieval English diocese on illicit archidiaconal exactions.[29] In view of the evidence for the high regard in which John de Belvoir held his former principal and predecessor, William Doune, this campaign during the episcopate of John Buckingham may plausibly be regarded as the continuance at a remove of the reforming programme of Grandisson at Exeter and of preoccupations within his circle, as forcefully attested by the *Memoriale presbiterorum*.

I turn to my second selected aspect. If, as noted by Dr Pantin, 'a strong sympathy for the underdog, for the poor and the weak who are the victims of officials or powerful neighbours, and an outspoken criticism of clerical abuses' are thus a notable trait of the *Memoriale presbiterorum*, it is combined, as he also noted, 'with a strong sense of clerical *esprit de corps* and a championship of clerical rights against lay attacks'.[30] In this aspect, the treatise is peculiarly in keeping with a contemporary sensitivity, and, within the proposed context of its writing, the reason is not far to seek. While lay hostility to the church – as famously asserted by Boniface VIII's bull *Clericis laicos* – was a long-standing and recurring theme, there is evidence that friction between the two jurisdictions and perceived infringement of ecclesiastical liberties was of some particular topicality in England in the middle years of the fourteenth century. The published legislation of the Council of London of 1342 proclaims as much. It denounced a variety of lay transgressions, including matters of high principle, such as the impeding of actions in the church courts, the harassment of ecclesiastics over pecuniary penances and the seizure of the goods of intestates, as well as simple abuses, such as defective tithe-paying, particularly as regards ceduous wood, and harassment of collectors.[31] I do not suggest that there is anything novel about these complaints nor am I concerned to maintain that they were peculiarly justified. I am interested in them here primarily as evidence of sensitivity and of determination to address them. Though the history of the Council's deliberations is not known in detail, it seems that this aspect of its programme was given special prominence. The legislation on ecclesiastical liberties was probably the only series of the Council's constitutions to be published.[32] Bishop Grandisson, whose episcopate began in the shadow of the murder of Walter Stapledon, shows himself throughout

---

[28] *Reg. Grandisson*, ed. Hingeston-Randolph, II, 1008. I shall discuss these and other measures and the technical aspects of pecuniary penances and archidiaconal procurations in more detail in the monograph referred to above.

[29] See Haren, 'The Will of Master John de Belvoir', p. 137 and n. 96.

[30] Pantin, *English Church*, pp. 210–11.

[31] *Concilia Magnae Britanniae et Hiberniae*, ed. D. Wilkins, 4 vols. (London, 1737), II, 702–9.

[32] See C. R. Cheney, 'Legislation of the Medieval English Church', *EHR* 50 (1935), 415–17; C. R. Cheney, 'Textual Problems of the English Provincial Canons', in

his episcopate a hypersensitive defender of the sacrosanct character of the clerical estate and upholder of ecclesiastical rights against lay encroachment. 'To such audacity of madness do they now break forth that the more they inflict contumelies, damages and insults on churches and churchmen, the more they glory';[33] 'Does not the Lord say, "Touch not mine anointed?" ';[34] 'No power is attributed to laymen of judging the Lord's anointed';[35] 'To laymen and those exercising an office of secular power no licence or faculty pertains of judging priests and other ministers of the church, whom the word of Truth with prophetic mouth on occasion calls gods on occasion angels.'[36] This is an accurate reflection of the tone of Grandisson's register precisely in the years 1341–42. But it is equally a tone characteristic of the whole of his pontificate. 'The impiety of persecutors is the more strongly enflamed against churches and ecclesiastical persons the more half-hearted the opponents whom it encounters,' is his battle-cry a few years later.[37] While there was perhaps exceptional provocation on the last occasion (an attack on his manor of Tawton), it is also the case that in standing against infringements and transgressions that were the preoccupation of most medieval bishops Grandisson unfailingly finds the ground of elevated and unyielding principle. We know that, unable to attend personally a largely abortive session of a planned provincial council at London on 18 October 1341, he sent by his proctors, Hugh de Seton and Benedict de Paston, a dossier of proposed reforms.[38] From the circumstance that on 21 October 1342 he personally absolved in St Paul's, by authority of the bishop of London in whose cathedral he was and by that of the whole provincial council, John de Sodbury, priest, rector of Shepton-Mallet, we may deduce that he himself attended the council sessions held earlier that month. (In pursuance of a royal commission Sodbury had proclaimed outlawry against Master Paul Brey, professor of civil law, Richard Gifford (Grandisson's commissary), John Pilton and other clerks, in a dispute between the jurisdictions, and he had been excommunicated accordingly.)[39] If the argument is accepted for the context of the *Memoriale presbiterorum*, the hypothesis must be seriously entertained that Grandisson, whose zeal for ecclesiastical liberties is marked, may have been a principal

Cheney, *Medieval Texts and Studies* (Oxford, 1973), p. 122; B. Bolton, 'The Council of London of 1342', in SCH 7 (Cambridge, 1971), pp. 147–60.

33 *Reg. Grandisson*, ed Hingeston-Randolph, II, 946 (16 March 1341).

34 *Reg. Grandisson*, ed. Hingeston-Randolph, II, 946.

35 *Reg. Grandisson*, ed. Hingeston-Randolph, II, 947 (18 June 1341).

36 *Reg. Grandisson*, ed. Hingeston-Randolph, II, 962 (10 August 1342).

37 *Reg. Grandisson*, ed. Hingeston-Randolph, II, 1026–7 (1347).

38 *Reg. Grandisson*, ed. Hingeston-Randolph, II, 971: replying on 8 October 1341 to the citation, he excused himself on account of its late receipt, floodings, distance and ill-health and added, 'super reformandis, autem in dicto concilio cum religiosis et clero nostre diocesis deliberare curavimus, per nos et alios, in quantum temporis brevitas id permisit. Que in scriptis redacta, dicti excusatores nostri [sc. his proctors] vestre Dominacioni [sc. the archbishop], si placeat, exhibebunt.'

39 *Reg. Grandisson*, ed. Hingeston-Randolph, II, 968.

contributor to the deliberations on them and on some other points for which there is the same coincidence of evidence from his register and from the *Memoriale presbiterorum*, considered as a product of, so to speak, his think-tank. The suggestion will always be a hypothesis, in the absence of direct attestation, but medieval legislative programmes were not generated in a vacuum any more than are our own and we must attend to the promptings of the evidence, which in this case would point to Exeter as a centre of demonstrable, even strident, concern.

In a final brief exploration both of the rapport between the *Memoriale presbiterorum* and the administrative context to which it relates and of the theme of confession and social discipline, I turn to a topic of passing but recurrent comment in the treatise, the author's hostility to the confessional activity of the mendicant friars. His attitude on the point is conveyed in some dozen asides, where he interrupts his main theme to castigate the laxity or rapacity of mendicant confessors. This too was a feature that attracted the attention of Dr Pantin, who observed of the author that 'he takes much the same attitude as FitzRalph, with whom he may have had contact at the Curia *c.* 1337–44, and indeed he may have helped to inspire FitzRalph, whose attacks on the friars he anticipates by a few years'.[40] This shrewd perception – ignored by scholarship on FitzRalph in the interval since Pantin articulated it – is confirmed by the discovery of the circles in which the author moved. I have argued and shall argue elsewhere that his powerful and puritanical personality or the viewpoint at least that he so passionately advocates was an influence on the development of FitzRalph's central doctrines in relation to the pastoral cure and on that particular fusion of ideas which was so significant for FitzRalph the controversialist: the central importance of restitution in the penitential régime and the friars' alleged shortcomings in respect of it. Here, I confine myself to the implications for what I have been calling 'social discipline'. As FitzRalph came to see compellingly, perhaps disproportionately, one of the threats represented by the licensed intervention of the friars in the conduct of confessions and in the pastoral cure as a whole was that the voice of moral authority might consequently speak with diversity of tongues. The friars on this construction were perhaps the principal 'exit from the system', a principal point, in the eyes of their critics, at which that manipulation of the system adverted to by Alexander Murray elsewhere in this volume might occur.[41] The implication, as regards the perception of one critic (or set of critics), could hardly be clearer than from FitzRalph's fierce outburst in the full papal consistory in 1357: 'For I have in my diocese of Armagh, as I suppose, two thousand subjects who every year are involved in sentences of excommunication, on account of the sentences passed against wilful homicides, public robbers, incendiaries and the like; of whom scarcely forty in a year come to me or to my penitentiaries; and all such men receive the

---

[40] Pantin, *English Church*, p. 206.
[41] See above, pp. 71–2 and 77.

sacraments like other men, and are absolved or are said to be absolved; nor are they believed to be absolved by any others except by the friars, without doubt, for no others absolve them.'[42] The bond between the efficacy of moral authority and its unity and homogeneity is too perennial an issue ever quite to lose its topicality. Not for nothing were medieval prelates jealous on the point. The evidence of the *Memoriale presbiterorum* is that behind the lines of a campaign – FitzRalph's in the 1350s – which has been much noticed in its ecclesiological aspect lies a wider and older struggle, that for the right ordering of Christian society on a model of inflexible moral principle. This theme gives cohesion not only to the central preoccupations of the treatise itself in its approach to penitential discipline but to the outlook in so far as it can be separately constructed and inferred of the reforming circle in which the author began his career and from which he wrote. Though Grandisson's hostility to the friars is relatively late in emerging – it cannot be confidently documented from his register until the mid-1350s and earlier there are even some contrary indications[43] – he was a long-engaged, stalwart champion of a classically simple model of ecclesiastical organization founded on the parish unit.[44] Given the strength of view evinced by two members of the circle, by Doune (considered here – in respect of the strength of the view – as author of the *Memoriale presbiterorum*, though we are fortunate enough to be able independently to discern Doune's hostility to the mendicants)[45] and, rabidly, by FitzRalph, it is a fair surmise that Grandisson himself felt strongly on the central issue even in those years during which he is inscrutable. When his mask does drop he is quickly revealed as nothing short of apocalyptic in his fulminations and, as Fr Aubrey Gwynn long ago pointed out, he had studied in the Paris of Jean de Pouilli,[46] from where may ultimately derive the anti-mendicant strand within his circle. (I take licence to extend that term to include FitzRalph, who though not a member of the administration was a protégé of Grandisson from about 1328 or even earlier.) As regards 'social discipline' there can be little doubt that Grandisson, like the *Memoriale presbiterorum* and FitzRalph, from the time that he entered the lists, wanted an effective disciplinary framework by which all grave sinners, after initial

---

42   Richard FitzRalph, *Defensio curatorum*, in E. Brown, *Fasciculus rerum expetendarum et fugiendarum*, 2 vols. (London, 1690), II, 468. Cf. A. Gwynn, 'Richard FitzRalph, Archbishop of Armagh', *Studies* 25 (1936), 8–96 (pp. 94–5). The translation is Dr Pantin's; *English Church*, p. 156.

43   He had, for instance, acted as conservator of the Austins and he commissioned mendicant penitentiaries both in Cornwall – where their knowledge of the language recommended them – and, occasionally, elsewhere. For a comparative evaluation of this aspect of Grandisson's episcopate, see M. J. Haren, 'Bishop Gynwell of Lincoln, Two Avignonese Statutes and Archbishop FitzRalph of Armagh's Suit at the Roman Curia against the Friars', *Archivum Historiae Pontificiae* 31 (1993), 275–92 (p. 280).

44   The point will be developed and documented in my forthcoming monograph; cf. above, n. 4.

45   See Haren, 'The Will of Master John de Belvoir', pp. 135–6.

46   A. Gwynn, 'Archbishop FitzRalph and the Friars', *Studies* 26 (1937), 50–67 (p. 54).

screening by their parish confessor, would be answerable not less often than once a year to him or to his specially constituted penitentiaries. The category of grave sinners, in the interpretation of law advanced by the *Memoriale presbiterorum*, included everyone whose sin generated a problem of restitution. This régime for the control of endemic disease – eradication may be thought excluded by the Augustinian diagnostics – required constant and vigilant reference from general practitioner to surgeon.

The novelist's injunction to connect requires of the historian no great intellectual effort in the case of FitzRalph, once the identification of the author is accepted: one can even date precisely to the summer of 1343 the latest point at which they could have met.[47] There are other, more tenuous, connections to be pondered, fostered (if one may say so) only by engaging coincidences of outlook and context – no sooner generated than abandoned by the evidence. Abandoned, though: not disowned. In the first two instances, the prompting to adopt is a mere hint of family resemblance. To begin from the observations of Dr Pantin, who so accurately discerned the influence on FitzRalph, may deflect suspicion of partiality. 'He has something of the consciousness of social abuses which we have seen in the *Memoriale presbiterorum*', remarked Pantin of Henry of Lancaster, as known through his *Livre de seyntz medicines*. And, leaving aside completely the intensely self-critical character of the *Livre*, particularly marked as regards the confession of sins, one might add to the general impression of social conscience detected in it a particular hint of concern for faults committed by proxy, through one's agents,[48] that is one of the dominant features of the *Memoriale presbiterorum*, as it is a feature too of William Doune as testator.[49] It is a matter of judgement how far Henry of Lancaster's outlook requires the positing of specific influence but if an influence is looked for then the author of the *Memoriale presbiterorum* may be close to hand. John Gynwell had been Henry's chaplain and steward and undoubtedly owed episcopal promotion to his patronage.[50] As noted already, Doune was Gynwell's official from about 1352[51] (just two years before the date of the *Livre de seyntz medicines*). On 12

[47] William Doune accompanied Grandisson to Avignon then. Vatican City, Archivio Segreto Vaticano, *Registra supplicationum* 4 (formerly 5), fol. 89v.

[48] 'Et ainsi la ou jeo ne savoie par ma bouche gaigner altri biens ou terres, jeo louai bien altres bouches a parler pur moi, comme par plederies ou par trop legiers jugementz en ma courte ou en altrui, qui tout comme par ma bouche parloient, ou par ma promesse de bone louer avoir, ou par poour de grandes menaces': *Le Livre de seyntz medicines*, ed. E. J. Arnould (Oxford, 1940), p. 19.

[49] Doune made a specific bequest to the vicar of Melton Mowbray in recompense for receipts from him by Doune's servants 'as they have said': the impression is that they were quizzed on the point. Thompson, 'The Will', p. 280.

[50] See J. R. L. Highfield, 'The English Hierarchy in the Reign of Edward III', *TRHS* 5th series 6 (1956), 115–38 (p. 119); K. Fowler, *The King's Lieutenant: Henry of Grosmont, First Duke of Lancaster 1310–1361* (London, 1969), pp. 177, 179–80.

[51] He is first referred to as official on 12 October 1352, though he had been active in the diocese a year before. Lincolnshire Archives Office (subsequently LAO), Bishops' Registers 8, fols. 5r, 167v.

May 1354 he was appointed by the bishop as archdeacon of Leicester.[52] We are dealing here with a concrete context and, whatever about the genesis of the *Livre* and of the sensitive conscience that informed it, it is at least plausible to think that its introspective author and the punctiliously scrupulous author (as identified) of the *Memoriale presbiterorum* would have recognized one another as kindred spirits.

'As a critic of the social evils of the time, he invites comparison with Langland and Chaucer a generation later,' wrote Dr Pantin of the author of the *Memoriale presbiterorum*.[53] ('Generation' here refers, of course, to the time to writing of the treatise not to the span of activity of its author.) In critical tone, the kinship is more evident with Langland. Above all the kinship is evident on the subject of the overriding obligation of restitution. I need not labour the role of restitution in *Piers Plowman*. In the *Memoriale presbiterorum*, the subject occupies some thirty-five folios of C, more than one-third of the treatise, and both in bulk and in detail it is the most thorough-going treatment of the topic by any English moralist. If it were not for *Piers Plowman*, I might have said also the most fiercely committed treatment: in this they are equal first. Add to this the anti-mendicant theme common to both. If there is an influence here then its channel is beyond all but the most speculative surmise, except that its context would plausibly be Worcester diocese, within whose compass is set Langland's first vision and which was one of the two officialities held by Doune – from 1354 until his death in 1361. It must be acknowledged that Doune's activity in Lincoln diocese can be followed in more detail than his activity in Worcester. This however must in part be a trick of the sources: Bishop Brian's register as preserved is much less informative than Gynwell's. Even so, there is both explicit and implicit evidence for the closeness of Doune's connections with Worcester.[54]

My last speculation is a product of context only, so far as concerns any influence to be imputed to Doune. That is on the presence of so engaged and so puritanically critical a moralist in the archdeaconry of Leicester in the generation before the region became a centre of Lollardy. Although the records of the archdeaconry are lost, the presence can be documented both from Gynwell's register and from Doune's will. Nearby Stamford is something of a base for the exercise of the officiality. Again, the precise channel of any influence must be speculative. Contacts with the local gentry are one possibility. Preaching is another – as it is in Worcester. They are not mutually exclusive. We know from the will that Doune kept something perhaps resembling a sermon diary.[55] As to the implication, I cannot improve on the

---

52 LAO, Bishops' Registers 9, fol. 319v (roman numeration). Cf. Haren, 'The Will of Master John de Belvoir', p. 124.

53 Pantin, *English Church*, p. 210.

54 For some preliminary remarks on Doune as official of Worcester, see Haren, 'Bishop Gynwell', pp. 278, 279, 288 n. 64.

55 He bequeathed to the prior of Osney usufruct 'of all the books of my own sermons (*meorum propriorum sermonum*)'. Thompson, 'The Will', p. 284.

question posed by R. G. Davies in his suggestive study of Lollardy and locality: 'It has often been remarked that most of the long-term Lollard strongholds started life early. Was it the case perhaps that the celebrated missionary efforts only really impressed where the locals were under heavy influence to be impressed?'[56] Whatever the implication, I do not suggest that Doune was a Lollard fore-runner. His bent is in one cardinal respect too different: his Exeter context apart from the content of the treatise associates him indelibly with a jealous regard for the church's independence of lay encroachment, much less correction. I am thinking only of the effect on the threshold of moral sensitivity and particularly of the continuum that undoubtedly exists between orthodox religion and heterodoxy, particularly where the concern is with issues of 'conduct rather than belief', and the emphasis on 'personal morality'.[57] If Doune's own contribution on this count to the Leicestershire context is imponderable, there is a point of vicarious contact so close as to forbid its being ignored. Doune's official in the archdeaconry and successor in the officiality, John de Belvoir, Doune's influence on whom I have already noted, was official of the diocese precisely in that period when Lollardy enjoyed what K. B. McFarlane described as 'the obscurity of the tolerated and ignored'.[58] As part of the explanation, McFarlane proposed 'the temper of those educated and politic administrators who held the higher offices in the Church; this was too sceptical and too humane for them to become at once effective persecutors'.[59] As regards John de Belvoir's outlook, I have suggested that McFarlane's other perception, 'that the knights' views found more than an echo in many hearts, even those of some of the higher clergy',[60] may be at once the authentic psychological diagnosis and the convincing aetiology of the official paralysis.[61] The effect would be an important legacy from the earlier period of orthodox puritanism.

[56] R. G. Davies, 'Lollardy and Locality', *TRHS* 6th series 1 (1991), 191–212 (p. 194).
[57] See J. A. F. Thompson, 'Orthodox Religion and the Origins of Lollardy', *History* 74 (1989), 39–55 (p. 45).
[58] K. B. McFarlane, *Lancastrian Kings and Lollard Knights* (Oxford, 1972), p. 224.
[59] McFarlane, *Lancastrian Kings*, p. 224.
[60] McFarlane, *Lancastrian Kings*, p. 224.
[61] Haren, 'The Will of Master John de Belvoir', p. 129.

The Interrogatories for Officials, Lawyers and Secular Estates of the *Memoriale presbiterorum*

Michael Haren

The text edited and translated below constitutes the main part of the interrogatories prescribed for the different professions and conditions of penitents in the *Memoriale presbiterorum* and illustrates several of the author's characteristic preoccupations: concern with the vices of officialdom, equally in ecclesiastical as in secular context; the mutual responsibilities of the social orders; ecclesiastical rights; the demands of strict justice both as between the social orders and as touching personal relationships. In the treatise, the passages presented here follow the interrogatories for four types of clerical penitent, with which, 'beginning from the part of greater dignity',[1] the *ad status* section opens: 'Circa religiosos' ('Concerning religious' – that is, regular clergy), 'Circa claustrales et obedienciarios' ('Concerning the holders of cloistral office and obedientiaries' – whose distinction from religious at large itself reflects the author's keen interest in the conduct of administration), 'Circa clericos seculares' ('Concerning secular clerics') and 'Circa presbiteros' ('Concerning priests'). Apart from the interesting and significant distinction of regular office-holders, the treatment given to regulars is sketchy, as befitted a treatise addressed to parish clergy, who would not normally be concerned with their confessions unless serving also as episcopal penitentiaries. The interrogatories for secular clerics and priests are largely concerned with traditional disciplinary problems and breaches of canon law. The sequence that then commences, though not a unit in its own right, can be extracted without violence from its context. Both in concept and in content it represents the most original and systematic examination of vocational and social groups from a penitential perspective in the whole tradition of English manuals, and also one of the most original and systematic as measured against continental production. Surveyed in sequence are: officers of ecclesiastical administration; lawyers (these, in terms of the *Memoriale*'s original context, as it will be proposed elsewhere, are likely to have been proximately lawyers in the church courts, though some of the interrogation could be applied to any type of lawyer); seneschals and bailiffs of secular jurisdiction (who, as the interrogation shows, are thought likely to be themselves clerics); knights; merchants and burgesses; servants (the questions asked dictate this translation

---

[1] 'a parte digniori incipiendo': Cambridge, Corpus Christi College, MS 148 (*Memoriale presbiterorum*), fol. 13rb. Haren, 'A Study', II, 44.

of 'servientes' here, though at its recurrence later in the treatise, under the head of restitution,[2] the term may alternatively or in addition mean 'sergeants'); sailors (so far as I know, a unique occurrence in confessional literature); villeins; married women; and children (with whom the section on interrogation concludes).

As I have previously argued,[3] this whole programme of interrogation and the section on the obligation of restitution, which complements and extends it later in the treatise, takes its ultimate origin from that strand of practical morality identified by Grabmann among twelfth-century theologians, especially the members of the circle round Master Peter the Chanter at Paris.[4] Practical morality led directly to social morality. Both merged readily with and in substantial measure promoted the burgeoning interest in penance that is so pronounced a feature of the twelfth- and early thirteenth-century schools. The early method of this socially orientated moralising was highly casuistic. By manner of proceeding, therefore, as well as by content and focus, a body of thought that had received its most significant development from theologians was ripe for take-over by the masters equally of applied thought and of casuistry, the canonists. They, as Gratian's *Decretum* alone amply demonstrates, had already identified in penance a central topic requiring systematic elaboration. In the thirteenth century, as the access of Aristotelian texts claimed more and more of the attention of academic theologians, even within the pastorally directed mendicant orders, the theological contribution to the elaboration of social morality wanes as that of the canonists waxes. The precise prompting, mechanism and stages of this disciplinary shift require and would repay further investigation but by the mid-thirteenth century its fruits are abundantly evident in the important *Liber poenitentiarius* (completed in 1247) of the Bolognese canonist, Joannes de Deo, where the penitential and social dimensions fuse in a comprehensive and precisely conducted survey of the classes of society and their vices.[5] If Peter the Chanter and his circle stand as one, remote origin of the social focus of the *Memoriale presbiterorum*, Joannes de Deo can be taken as another and more proximate one. Within a few years of the emergence of Joannes de Deo's work, it was adapted and extended by the *Summa Aurea* of Henry of Susa (Hostiensis), written *c.* 1253, which is a principal source as well for the general shape of both the *Memoriale's* interrogatories and its chapters on restitution as for particular departures and technical doctrine within them. Although the most widely read of the fourteenth-century English pastoral manuals, the *Oculus sacerdotis*, was the

2 Cambridge, Corpus Christi College, MS 148, fol. 68rb. Haren, 'A Study', II, 234–5.
3 Haren, 'Social Ideas'.
4 See M. Grabmann, *Die Geschichte der scholastischen Methode nach den gedruckten und ungedruckten Quellen*, 2 vols. (Freiburg im Breisgau, 1909–11), I, 476–501; B. Smalley, *The Study of the Bible in the Middle Ages*, 3rd edn (Oxford, 1983), pp. 196–9; Baldwin, *Peter the Chanter*.
5 Cf. Haren, 'Social Ideas', p. 47; Michaud-Quantin, *Sommes*, pp. 26–7. Joannes de Deo's treatise is partially edited in *PL* 99, 1085–8. A full text is found in Oxford, Bodleian Library, MS Laud Misc. 112, fols. 325r–38v.

work of a canonist, William of Pagula,[6] the *Oculus* and the manuals that derive from or are related to it were comparatively little affected by the canonists' intensely detailed contribution to social morality. (These derived or related works include the *Regimen animarum*, the *Pupilla oculi* of John de Burgo, Mirk's *Instructions for Parish Priests* and the *Cilium oculi sacerdotis*.)[7] It is the *Memoriale presbiterorum*, rivalled only by the more arcanely organized *Septuplum* of John Acton,[8] that exhibits most within the English tradition of pastoral manuals the influence of this important and relatively neglected intellectual current. The present selection documents with what powerful effect it was received and channelled.

Method of the edition

Of the five known manuscripts by which the *Memoriale presbiterorum* is transmitted in whole or part,[9] three witness to the text of the interrogatories: Cambridge, Corpus Christi College, MS 148 (cited as C); London, Westminster Diocesan Archives, MS H. 38 (cited as W); and London, British Library, MS Harley 3120 (cited as H). The edition below follows the text of C, the earliest and generally the best of the manuscripts, except where departures from it are indicated in the critical notes. The text of H contains a high frequency of manifest errors and unintelligibilities, many of which are of interest only to the history of the version of H itself or of wider interest only in the unlikely event of the identification of further manuscripts of the treatise. Accordingly, not all the variants from H have been presented here, though all have been taken into account in reconstructing the stemma within the context of the complete edition.[10] On that stemma, C and H are related by descent from a common ancestor, while W, as noted above,[11] is dependent at a remove on C. Clearly, in these terms, variants from W are of no critical interest but since they are so few they have been presented comprehensively as a record and W occasionally serves as an alternative to editorial emendation of the text of C. In C (as in W), the chapters are numbered in two series, with 119 chapters included under the letter 'a' and ninety-eight under the letter 'b'. This reflects no distinction of subject-matter and is a mere convenience of numbering. C's enumeration is followed in the edition below. The chapter designated accordingly as a. xxxiii, with which the present selection commences, is located as follows in the several manuscripts: C, fol. 19v; W, 16v; H, fol. 25r.

In editing the text, spelling – as regards which some inconsistencies will be noted – has been left unemended except where it was felt that intelligibility was impaired.

6   See Boyle, '*Oculus*', and Boyle, 'Study'.
7   See Pantin, *English Church*, pp. 202–5, 213–14.
8   For a short survey of this treatise, see Haren, 'Social Ideas', pp. 48–9.
9   See above, p. 109.
10 See Haren, 'A Study', I, 12–21. The text is edited in the second volume of this dissertation.
11 See p. 109 above.

a. xxxiii. Circa officiales et decanos rurales iurisdiccionem
ecclesiasticam exercentes. Rubrica.

Tu confessor tibi caveas quod non indistincte admittas ad confessionem
officiales episcoporum vel archidiaconorum seu[a] eorum decanos nisi in
5   casibus tibi a iure permissis, sine licencia proprii episcopi. Quod[b] si te
contigerit forsan talem aliquem audire, diligenter inquiras ab eodem[c] infra
scripta, ita quod vultum[d] suum sibi racione officii sui[e] parcendo in nullo
pertimescas, nec aliqua adulando sibi dicas. Primo sic dicas: 'Audivisti iura
civilia et canonica, ita quod in singulis causis ecclesiasticis noveris iuste
10   iudicare, quia ignorans iura periculose agit et contra conscienciam facit, si
presumat sibi assumere[f] officium iudicandi[1] et sic agit ad Gehennam? /[fol.
20rC] Item, tulisti unquam iniustam vel iniquam sentenciam diffinitivam[g] in
aliqua causa ecclesiastica, matrimoniali vel alia,[h] forsan quia prius non
consuluisti[i] libros super hoc vel iuris peritos, ut debuisti, vel fecisti aliquid in
15   iudicio vel extra per graciam vel per sordes contra conscienciam tuam et contra
iusticiam in gravamen alicuius partis? Item, tulisti unquam aliquam[j]
sentenciam /[fol. 25vII] excommunicacionis maioris vel minoris in aliquem
sine scriptis, et causam excommunicacionis[k] propter quam eam protulisti[l] in
scriptis[m] non expressisti, vel alias[n] excommunicacionis sentenciam sine
20   maturitate debita fulminasti? Item, indixisti unquam alicui infamato
purgacionem nimis gravem,[o] et sic necessitate compulsus redemit vexacionem
suam solvendo tibi pecuniam hac de causa? Item citasti vel terminum
prefixisti[p] alicui subdito tuo causa ipsum gravandi et vexandi, in ultimis
finibus iurisdiccionis tue, vel in loco nimis remoto a loco[q] ubi subditus degebat
25   et sic laboribus et expensis superfluis fatigatus fuit, et forsan[r] pro redempcione
laboris tibi aliquid /[fol. 17rW] dedit? Item, observasti ordinem iudiciorum in
causis coram te sic ventilatis in quibus ordo iudiciarius necessario requiritur
observari? Item, recepisti[s] unquam aliqua munera vel dona ab aliqua parte
litigante[t] coram te, preter esculentum et poculentum quod in paucis diebus

---

[a] seu: sive *H*
[b] quod: et *H*
[c] eodem: eo *H*
[d] vultum: wultum *H*
[e] sui *om. H*
[f] sibi assumere *om. H*
[g] diffinitivam *per correctionem ex*
     diffinitam *C*
[h] alia: aliqua *H*
[i] consuluisti: consiluisti *W*; consulisti *H*
[j] aliquam *om. H*
[k] excommunicacionis *om. W*; maioris
     [. . .] excommunicacionis *om. H*

[l] eam protulisti: tulisti *H*
[m] in scriptis *om. H*
[n] alias: aliam *H*
[o] grande [*sic*] *H*
[p] prefixisti: posuisti *H*
[q] a loco *om. H*
[r] *add.* tibi *H*
[s] *add.* aliquando vel *H*
[t] vel dona [. . .] litigante: vel dona vel alia
     a partibus litigantibus *H*

[1] Cf. X. 2.13.13, Friedberg, II, 286–8.

a. xxxiii. Concerning officials and rural deans, exercising ecclesiastical jurisdiction

Take you care, confessor, that you do not without distinction admit to confession the officials of bishops and of archdeacons or their deans, except in the cases permitted to you, without licence of the proper bishop. But if it should fall to you, perhaps, to hear any such, inquire diligently from him on the points written below, in such a way that you tremble not the slightest at his countenance – sparing him by reason of his office – and that you do not say anything to him in flattering tone. Say first to him, as follows: 'Did you attend lectures in the laws, civil and canon, so that you might know to judge justly in individual ecclesiastical cases (because he who is ignorant of the laws deals perilously and acts against conscience, if he presumes to take upon himself the office of judging, and so makes straight for hell)? Item, did you ever pass unjust or unfair definitive sentence in any ecclesiastical case, matrimonial or other – perhaps because you did not first consult the books upon the matter or expert opinion, as you ought to have – or did you do anything in judgment or out of it through favour or through bribery, against your conscience and against justice, to the oppression of any party? Item, did you ever without written acts pass any sentence of major or minor excommunication against anyone and did you fail to specify in writing the cause of the excommunication – on account of which you promulgated it – or did you otherwise let fly sentence of excommunication without due deliberation? Item, did you ever prescribe for any accused person too burdensome a purgation and so, compelled by necessity, he redeemed his vexation by paying you money on this account? Item, did you cite or fix a term for any subject of yours, in order to oppress or harass him, in the farthermost bounds of your jurisdiction or in a place excessively removed from the place where the subject dwelled and thus he was worn out with labours and superfluous expenses, and perhaps gave something to you for redemption of his labour? Item, did you observe the order of judgments in cases aired before you, in which observance of judicial order is necessarily required? Item, did you ever receive any presents or gifts from any party litigating before you – beyond such food and drink as could be

poterat[u] consumi, et sic in preiudicium et /[fol. 20rbC] detrimentum partis[v]
adverse, sibi plus debito favebas? Item, commisisti unquam vices tuas alicui
fatuo, iura ignoranti vel capitoso, in aliquo negocio vel causa, ut sic
commissarius tuus magis posset gravare vel fatigare partes vel[w] earum
5 alteram, et[x] si hoc feceris odio,[y] prece vel munere corruptus? Item, imposuisti
unquam talleas[z][2] pauperibus presbiteris, forsan pro familia tua ditanda, et si
non contulerint hiis[a] quibus volebas, iuxta votum tuum, ipsos gravasti in bonis
suis vel laboribus fatigasti seu fatigari fecisti?[b] Item, opposuisti unquam
aliquos defectus vel crimina occulta vel pene[c] occulta, de quibus tuum non fuit
10 iudicare de iure, aliquibus subditis tuis, et sic ab eisdem[d] pecuniam
extorquebas hac de causa? Item, recepisti unquam pecuniam ab aliquo pro
delicto suo notorio,[3] pro quo puplicam debuit egisse penitenciam de iure?[4]
Item recepisti unquam[e] munera vel donaria[f] ab aliquo delinquente pro
fovendo vel tolerando ipsum in peccato suo vel forsan[g] aliquod annuum ab
15 eodem recepisti[h] ad opus domini tui,[i] liberas habenas peccandi locando et[j] in
peccatis suis diu stare sine correccione debita permittendo, quo casu particeps
es sui criminis vel delicti, ex quo suo errori ex officii tui debito desisti resistere,
et sic plus quam ipse de/[fol. 20vC]linquens merito ex hoc eris puniendus?[k]
/[fol. 26rH] Item, expedivisti unquam celeriter[l] negocia divitis coram te
20 agitata, forsan timore vel munere instigatus, et negocia consimilia pauperis
per te expedienda posuisti in respectu,[m] eo quod pauper nichil habuit quod
offeritur,[n] et sic dampnabilis[o] fuisti acceptor personarum? Item, procurasti vel
fecisti aliquem inhabilem racione persone sue, quia forsan notorie criminosus
fuit vel insufficiens[p] litterature vel quia nullum penitus aut falsum habuit
25 titulum vel de aliena diocesi forsitan[q] fuit oriundus, preter conscienciam

[u] poterat: poterit *H*
[v] partis: parti *H*
[w] vel: et *H*
[x] et *add. supra lineam C*
[y] *add.* vel *H*
[z] talleas: tallias *H*
[a] *add.* in *H*
[b] ipsos [. . .] fecisti: ipsos gravasti sive fatigasti *H*
[c] vel pene: et plene *H*
[d] eisdem: eis *H*
[e] unquam *om. H*
[f] donaria: dona *H*
[g] forsan: forte *H*
[h] *add.* ut *H*
[i] ad opus domini tui *om. H*
[j] locando et: permittendo *H*

[k] ex quo [. . .] puniendus: ex quo ab errore subditos ex officio suo tenetur emendare et sic fovens eos in peccatis plus quam illi delinquid [*sic*] et /[f. 26r] erit puniendus secundum quod patet in hiis versibus:
      Consensus negligit, suadens iuvat atque tenetur
      Hic minus, hicque minus, hic equaliter, hic plus *H*
[l] celeriter *om. H*
[m] *add.* tuo *H*
[n] offeritur: offerit tibi *H*
[o] dampnabilis: dampnabiliter *H*
[p] insufficiens: insufficientis *H*
[q] forsitan *per correctionem ex* forsati *C*: forsan *H*

[2] imposuisti unquam talleas: Cf. Hostiensis (Henricus de Susa), *Summa Aurea* (Basle, 1573), V, tit. 'De penitentiis et remissionibus', art. 24, col. 1416, 'primo'.
[3] Item . . . notorio: cf. ibid., 'tertio'.
[4] Cf. X. 5.37.3, Friedberg, II, 880–1.

consumed in a few days – and did you thus favour that party more than was due, to the detriment of the opposing party? Item, did you in any business or case ever commit your functions to any foolish person, ignorant of the laws or arbitrary, so that your commissary could the more oppress or fatigue the parties or one of them, and whether you may have done this being corrupted by hatred, entreaty or bribe? Item, did you ever impose tallages on poor priests, perhaps for the enrichment of your household, and if they should not have delivered to those whom you wished, in accordance with your will, you oppressed them in their goods or wore them out or caused them to be worn out with labours? Item, did you ever charge any of your subjects with any hidden or nearly hidden faults or crimes, concerning which it did not by law pertain to you to judge, and so you extorted money from them on this account? Item, did you ever receive money from anyone for notorious delict on his part, for which he ought by law to have done public penance? Item, did you ever receive gifts or bribes from any offender for cosseting or tolerating him in his sin or did you perhaps receive some annual payment from him for the upkeep of your lord, renting out the loose reins of sinning and permitting him to stand long in his sins without due correction, in which case you are partaker of his crime or delict, in that you neglected to resist his error as by duty of your office, and thus from this you stand worthily to be punished more than the offender himself? Item, did you ever process quickly the affairs of a rich man conducted before you, prompted perhaps by fear or reward, and did you put back the similar affairs of a poor man due to be processed by you, in that the poor man had nothing to offer, and so were you a damnable respecter of persons? Item, did you procure or cause anyone who was, in personal terms, incapable, because perhaps he was notoriously criminous or of insufficient learning or

ordinantis, ad minores vel ad sacros ordines[r] promoveri? Item, recepisti unquam ab aliquo[s] rectore vel vicario albam, vaccam vel aliquod[t] temporale equipollens[u] pro corporali induccione seu investitura sua[5] in ecclesiam suam vel vicariam per te facienda?'

Si igitur repperis[v] aliquem tibi premissa confitentem, dicas: 'Amice, vide in quantis mortaliter peccasti. Tu enim positus es ad corrigendum errores aliorum et tu ipse vilior omnium et deterior[w] esse conprobaris, quia, potestate tibi commissa[x] abutendo, primo contra Deum et secundario contra iura et eorum precepta et potissime[y] contra legem naturalem veniendo,[z] symoniam, dolum, fraudem et concussionem, hoc est crimen falsi, in lesionem tui proximi, vel ut domino tuo placeres vel tibi aliquod temporale[a] illicite adquireres, committere stu/[fol. 20vbC]duisti.' Et dicas sibi secure sic: 'In lege tua scriptum est, *Qui occasionem dampni dat (scilicet proximam[b]), dampnum dedisse intelligitur*,[c][6] nec dimittetur[d] tibi peccatum nisi[e] hiis quos contra Deum et iusticiam sic lesisti restitueris[f] omnia per te vel occasione tui ablata et deperdita. Preterea, Deum, iusticiam, officii tui debitum, /[fol. 17vW] conscienciam tuam propriam, naturam humanam et eciam proximum tuum per avariciam offendisti. Unde, quia in tot offendisti, pena multiplici, prout in iure tuo legitur,[g][7] merito debes puniri. Teipsum ergo in hiis recte iudica et caveas tibi, quia quilibet iudex qui talia facit suspensus est ab execucione officii sui /[fol. 26vH] per annum ipso iure,[8] et nichilominus irregularitatem incurrit, si durante suspensione huiusmodi dampnabiliter ingesserit se divinis.' Set certe, quicquid de peccatis iudicum[h] scribatur, hodie habet locum illud Danielis, *Quia egressa est iniquitas a senioribus iudicibus qui videbantur regere populum*.[i][9]

---

[r] minores vel ad sacros ordines: ad maiores sacros *H*
[s] aliquo: alieno *H*
[t] aliquod: aliquid *H*
[u] equipollens: permittit *H*
[v] repperis: reppereris *W*; recipias *H*
[w] vilior omnium et deterior: vilior et deterior omni *H*
[x] *add.* abiciendo sive *H*
[y] potissime: potentissime *H*
[z] veniendo: vivendo *H*
[a] aliquod temporale: aliquid spirituale *H*

[b] scilicet proximam: si proximo *H*
[c] intelligitur: videtur *H*
[d] dimittetur: dimittitur *H*
[e] *add.* in *H*
[f] restitueris: restitueres *H*
[g] legitur: inseritur *H*
[h] iudicum: iudicium *C*; iudicum scribatur *om. H*
[i] *add.* et species decepit eos non tam carnis quam pecunie *W*

[5] Item . . . investitura sua: cf. Hostiensis, *loc. cit.*, 'secundo'.
[6] See X. 5.36.9, Friedberg, II, 880.
[7] Cf. (?)D. 1 de pen. c.18, Friedberg, I, 1162.
[8] See Sext. 2.14.1, Friedberg, II, 1007.
[9] Daniel 13.5.

because he had no title at all or false title or was perhaps by origin of another diocese, to be promoted to minor or to sacred orders without the the ordainer's being apprised? Item did you ever receive from any rector or vicar (?)vestment <(?)or> cow or any temporal commodity of like value for his corporal induction or investiture to be performed by you to in respect of his church or vicarage?'

If, therefore, you have found anyone confessing to you as set out above, say: 'Friend, see in what great respects you have sinned mortally. For you were placed to correct the errors of others and you yourself are shown to be more base and abject than all, because, by abusing the power committed to you, offending first against God, secondly against the laws and their precepts and especially against natural law, you have made it your business to commit simony, deception, fraud and abuse of office – which comes under the crime of breach of faith – to the injury of your neighbour, either so that you might please your lord or so that you might unlawfully acquire some temporal gain for yourself.' And say to him as follows, without fear of error: 'In your law it is written "One who gives rise to the damage (that is to say, proximately) is held to have inflicted the damage" ', and the sin shall not be remitted you unless you restore to those whom you have thus injured, against God and justice, everything removed or wasted by you or by occasion of you. In addition, you have through avarice offended God, justice, the duty of your office, your own conscience, human nature and your neighbour too. In consequence, because you have offended in so many respects, you well ought to be punished by multiple penalty, as your law reads. Rightly judge yourself, therefore, on these points and take you care, because any judge who does such things is by law automatically suspended from execution of his office for a year and, beyond that, incurs irregularity if, while this suspension lasts, he should damnably presume to participate in divine offices.' But – it is a fact, whatever may be written of the sins of judges – today that text of Daniel holds good: 'Because there went out iniquity from the senior judges who seemed to rule the people'.

a. xxxiv. Circa advocatos et procuratores. Rubrica.[10]

Caveas tibi[j] tu confessor quod circa istos si eos audieris[k] diligenciam
5 adhibeas in quantum potes, quia licet scire dicantur iura in quibus versantur,
nonnulli tamen eorundem abutuntur[l] eisdem, et de abusu huiusmodi
necgligunt confiteri. Si igitur talis tibi confiteatur ad plenum, sufficere tibi
debet; alioquin si tibi visum fuerit[m] expediens inquirere poteris sic /[fol. 21rC]
ab eodem, primo sic:[n] dedisti unquam falsum consilium clientulo tuo pro
10 pecunia et sic partem adversam ledebas iniuste? Secundo fovebas unquam
subdole causam, prodeundo et decipiendo proprium clientulum? Talis enim
de iure prevaricator et infamis esse dicitur. Item fovebas unquam causam
desperatam, contra consciencia tuam, quia legitur quod nullus tenetur
improbum defendere de iure. Item instabas unquam erga iudicem ut
15 superfluas dilaciones optineres ad hoc tantum[o] ut causa in qua postulabas
plus debito protraheretur et eas optinuisti in lesionem partis adverse? Item
fecisti unquam pactum cum parte pro[p] qua litigabas super certa parte litis ad
grave dampnum ipsius litigatoris? Item certabas vel litigabas unquam verbis
probrosis quia forsan[q] ignorabas respondere iuribus contra te allegatis nec alio
20 modo sciebas te defendere, et sic clientulus[r] fuit indefensus et sic subdole
salarium tuum recepisti? Item fuisti unquam contentus minimo salario, puta
quattuor vel sex denariis advocando vel procurando in magna causa, unde
bonis advocatis seu procuratoribus te melioribus[s] sic in illa causa lucrum
subtraxisti? Item recepisti unquam nimis magnum salarium ultra quam,
25 inspecta facundia tua et quantitate[t] cause, considerato labore quem in ea
sustinuisti et fori consuetudine attenta, recepisse debuisti de iure, sic clien
/[fol. 21rbC] tulum tuum gravando fraudulenter? /[fol. 27rH] Item fecisti
unquam cavillosas posiciones ad decipiendum[u] partem adversam et sic[v] pars
illa incaute respondendo circumventa in causa succubuit iniuste? Item
30 induxisti unquam clientulum tuum ad degerandum,[w] vel ponendo vel
respondendo, et sic fuisti quasi auctor periurii? Item informasti vel instruxisti
falso testes in aliquibus causis et maxime matrimonialibus ad falsa[x]

[j] tibi *om. H*
[k] audieris: vis audire *H*
[l] abutantur *H*
[m] visum fuerit: videtur *W*
[n] primo sic *om. W H*
[o] ad hoc tantum *om. H*
[p] cum *H*
[q] forsitan *H*
[r] *add.* tuus *H*

[s] bonis [. . .] melioribus: bonus
   advocatus vel procurator te melior
   non tanti lucri esset contentus et *H*
[t] qualitate *H*
[u] decipiendum: decipiendam *H*
[v] sic *om. H*
[w] degerandum: deiurandum *H*
[x] falsum *H*

[10] From 'Secundo fovebas . . .' (line 10), the interrogation under this head is based on
Hostiensis, *op. cit.*, art. 32, col. 1418, except as regards the advocate's fee (lines 21–2)
and the emphasis on matrimonial causes (line 31).

a. xxxiv. Concerning advocates and proctors

Take you care, confessor, that you apply what diligence you can as regards such men, if you hear them [sc. in confession], because although they may be said to know the laws in which they practise, some of them nevertheless abuse the same and concerning this abuse they neglect to confess. If therefore such a one should confess fully to you, that ought to suffice for you. Otherwise, if it shall have seemed to you expedient you can inquire of him in the following fashion, and first in this way: 'Did you ever give false counsel to your client for money and did you thus injure the opposing side unjustly? Secondly, did you ever foster a cause duplicitously, betraying and deceiving your own client? Such a one, by the way, is said in law to be a prevaricator and to suffer infamy.[1] Item, did you ever foster a desperate cause, against your conscience, because it is read that no one is required by law to defend the reprobate. Item, did you ever pressurise a judge in order to obtain unnecessary postponements, for the purpose only that the cause in which you were pleading should be protracted more than was right, and did you obtain them to the detriment of the opposing side? Item, did you ever make a pact with the party on whose behalf you were litigating over [sc. your receiving] a certain part of the matter at issue, to the grave damage of the litigant in question? Item, did you ever in contending or litigating employ abusive language, because perhaps you did not know how to reply to the laws pleaded against you and knew in no other manner how to defend yourself, and thus the client was undefended and thus you received your salary deceitfully? Item, were you ever content with a paltry salary, say four or six pence, while acting as advocate or proctor in a large case, with the result that you deprived good advocates or proctors, better than yourself, of profit in that case? Item, did you ever receive too great a salary, beyond what you ought by right to have received, having regard to your eloquence and the size of the case, taking into account the labour that you expended in it and allowing for the custom of the court, thus fraudulently oppressing your client? Item did you ever enter cavilling points, for the purpose of deceiving the opposing party, and thus the party, tricked by responding incautiously, unjustly went under in the case? Item, did you ever induce your client to commit perjury, either in deposing or in responding, and thus you were as one might say the author of the perjury? Item did you ever brief or instruct witnesses falsely as to deposing falsehoods in any cases, and especially matrimonial cases, or did you knowingly make use of their [sc. false]

---

1   That is, to labour under legal disabilities.

deponendum vel eorum deposicionibus scienter usus fuisti, quia omnes tales
advocati et procuratores falsi et^y homicide dicuntur esse et perpetua notantur
infamia? Item proposuisti unquam vel proponi fecisti in causis
matrimonialibus aliquas excepciones frivolas vel quascunque alias maliciose
5   ne ipsa matrimonia debitum possent sortiri effectum, vel ut processus
causarum huiusmodi / [fol. 18rW] contra iusticiam diucius suspenderentur^z
et sic excommunicacionis^a maioris sentenciam incurristi ipso facto?[11] Item
studuisti diligenter pro causa clientuli tui, et circa eam vigilasti,^{b} quia multi
sunt advocati et procuratores qui postquam receperint^c salarium suum non
10 curant de causis suis et sic propter eorum necgligenciam clientuli sui bonas
causas nonnunquam amittunt? Preterea multi sunt advocati et procuratores
ydiote et insufficientes, propter quorum insufficienciam clientuli frequenter
suas^d / causas amittunt, et tamen magnum salarium recipiunt ab eisdem, et sic
graviter peccant, dolum et fraudem committendo. Talibus autem tu confessor
15 debes dicere sic:^{e} 'Ecce quod oportebit te illos quos predictis modis lesisti
competenter satisfacere, si volueris perpetuum inferni cruciatum effugere,^{f}
nec credas quod in die iudicii habere poteris de allegacionis tue eloquencia
subsidium.' Item de periurio quod frequenter procuratores incurrunt debes
inquirere, et de aliis peccatis et^g eorum circumstanciis ut^h supra notatur.
20

a. xxxv. Circa senescallos et balivos. Rubrica.

Tu confessor si contingat te aliquando audire aliquem talem, debes insistere
25 viriliter ad eruendam^i veritatem, quia tales cavillosi sunt valde,^{j} et omnino
avaricie et falsitati dediti, et ceca cupiditate ducti, que radix est omnium
malorum; nec curant de Deo, vel de sancta ecclesia, vel eius ministris, set
tantummodo de lucris et muneribus consequendis. Et primo debes
considerare utrum talis senescallus vel ballivus fuerit clericus vel laicus,^{k} et si
30 clericus, tunc utrum fuit^l beneficiatus vel non. Si vero^m fuerit clericus^n
beneficiatus cum cura, et per consequens sacerdos, debes sibi^o dicere quod
canon prohibet sibi^p sub interminacione anathematis, ne senescallus vel

y	et *om.* H	h	ut: prout H
z	suspenderentur: suspenderetur H	i	eruendam: erudiendam H
a	sic excommunicacionis *per*	j	*add.* et omnia mala vere perpetrant H
	emendationem ordinis verborum C	k	vel laicus *om.* H
b	vigilasti: evigilasti H	l	fuit: fuerit H
c	receperint: ceperunt H	m	vero *om.* H
d	frequenter suas *om.* H	n	clericus *om.* H
e	sic *om.* W	o	sibi: ei W
f	effugere: evadere W	p	canon prohibet sibi: canone prohibetur
g	*add.* de W		H

[11] See canon 4 of the Council of Oxford: *Councils & Synods*, II, 107.

depositions (because all such advocates and proctors are said to be false and assassinous and are branded with perpetual infamy)? Item, did you ever propound in matrimonial cases any frivolous points of order or any other such maliciously with a view that the same marriages should be unable to take due effect or so that the proceedings of the cases in question should be drawn out contrary to justice (and thus you automatically incurred sentence of major excommunication)? Item, did you apply yourself diligently as regards your client's case and keep watch over it, because many are the advocates and proctors who, after they have received their salary, do not care for their cases and thus, on account of their negligence, their clients sometimes lose good cases? In addition, there are many advocates and proctors unlearned and inadequate, on account of whose inadequacy clients often lose their cases, and yet they receive great salary from them, and they sin gravely, committing deceit and fraud. But to such, confessor, you ought to say the following: 'Look how it behoves you to satisfy competently those whom you have damaged in the fashions mentioned, if you wish to escape the eternal torment of hell. And do not believe that in the day of Judgment you will be able to have support of the eloquence of your pleading.' Item, you ought to inquire concerning perjury, which proctors often incur, and concerning other sins and their circumstances, as is noted above.

a. xxxv. Concerning seneschals and bailiffs

Confessor if it chances that you hear from time to time such a one in confession, you must strive manfully to extract the truth, because such people are exceedingly cavilling and altogether given to avarice and falsity and led by blind greed which is the root of all evils; nor do they care for God or for holy church or its ministers, but only for securing profits and rewards. And first you ought to consider whether such a seneschal or bailiff was a clerk or layman, and if a clerk, then whether he was beneficed or not. If, indeed, he was a beneficed clerk with cure, and consequently a priest, you ought to say to him that the canon forbids him under the threat of anathema from being seneschal or bailiff of secular jurisdiction. Accordingly, it will be necessary for him speedily to resign office, never to resume it, because it is certain that in this he

balivus iurisdiccionis secularis fiat.[12] Unde oporte / [fol. 21vbC] bit ipsum^q celeriter illud dimittere officium, nunquam illud resumpturus,^r quia constat quod ipse^s peccat in hoc mortaliter, propter quod est ipso facto excommunicatus a canone, secundum quosdam doctores, et secundum alios
5   est excommunicandus tamquam pro mortali. Unde non poterit agere veram penitenciam, ipso durante in illo officio. Inquiras igitur primo sic,^t tam a clerico quam a laico : dedisti unquam alicui mediatori, vel domino temporali vel alicui de ministris suis aliquam pecuniam vel aliquod^u donum, pro adipiscenda et^v habenda balliva vel potestate seculari,^w vel constituisti te
10 soluturum domino tuo aliquod annuum pro baliva tua tenenda. Et si sic fecit,^x constat quod in hoc^y graviter peccavit, contra iuris prohibicionem, quia ius presumit quod talis senescallus et^z balivus balivam suam^a emens, levabit a pauperibus hominibus balive sue quicquid dedit ipse^b vel solvit pro baliva sua habenda, ipsos iniuste opprimendo et^c gravando. Item si unquam recepit
15 munera ab aliqua parte, ut adversarium ipsius gravaret vel attachiaret iniuste. Item si subditus suus non fecit semper^d voluntatem suam, et^e ob hoc attachiaverit^f eum et perdere fecit^g bona sua, hac de causa. Item si pro^h extorquenda pecunia posuit aliquos debiles et impotentesⁱ aut pauperes vel ali/[fol. 22rC]os^j ignaros in assisis vel inquisicionibus, et sic redimebant suam
20 vexacionem aliquid sibi dando. Item si aliquid recepit^k ab aliquo pro differenda^l execucione sentencie vel iusti precepti iudicis, in gravamen et lesionem partis alterius, que promte non potest^m consequi iusticiam suam, propter impedimentum cavillosum et fraudulentum /[fol. 18vW] ballivi. Item si unquam concupivit terras, domos vel possessiones seu alia bona immobilia
25 seu mobilia vicini sui, et quia illa sibi vendere, locare, vel donare noluit, gravavit ipsum vel gravari /[fol. 28rH] procuravit in rebus suis vel persona, vel bona forsan huiusmodi per oppressionem amisit hac de causa. Item si incarceraverit vel incarcerari mandaverit seuⁿ procuraverit aliquem iniuste, et sic taliter incarceratus amisit bona sua conferendo ea sibi vel eciam aliis
30 quibuscunque pro liberacione sua habenda et sua vexacione iniuriosa

^q ipsum: eum *H*

^r resumpturus: recepturus *W H*

^s ipse: ille *W*

^t sic *om. H*

^u aliquod: aliud *W*

^v et: vel *W H*

^w vel potestate seculari *om. W*

^x si sic fecit: sic *H*

^y in hoc *om. H*

^z et: vel *W H*

^a balivam suam: de baliva sua *H*

^b ipse *om. H*

^c et: vel *H*

^d semper *om. H*

^e et *om. H*

^f attachiaverit: attachiavit *H*

^g fecit: fecerit *H*

^h pro *add. supra lineam C*

ⁱ et impotentes *om. H*

^j vel alios *om. H*

^k recepit: reciperit *[sic] H*

^l differenda: 'da' *post emendationem C*; deferenda *H*

^m que prompte non potest: quo pars non potest *H*

ⁿ seu: *add. supra lineam C;* vel *H*

¹² Cf. X. 1.37.1, Friedberg, II, 210.

sins mortally, on account of which he is by the canon automatically excommunicate, according to some doctors, and according to others he stands to be excommunicated, as for a mortal [sc. sin]. Accordingly, it would not be possible for him to do true penance, while remaining in that office. You should inquire, therefore, first as follows, both from a clerk and from a layman: 'Did you ever give to any middle man or temporal lord or any of his servants any money or any gift for acquiring and having bailiwick or secular power, or did you contract to pay to your lord any annual sum for holding your bailiwick?' And if he did so it is certain that in this he sinned gravely, against the prohibition of the law, because the law presumes that such a seneschal or bailiff, buying his bailiwick, will raise from the poor men of his bailiwick whatever he himself gave or paid (or pays) for having his bailiwick, oppressing and harassing them unjustly. Item, if he ever received gifts from any party that he might harass or attach an adversary of the same unjustly. Item, if a subject of his did not always do his will and on this account he attached him and caused him to lose his goods for this reason. Item, if in order to extort money he placed any feeble and incapable or poor or other ignorant men on assises or inquisitions, and they thus redeemed their harassment by giving something to him. Item, if he received anything from anyone for deferring execution of a sentence or other just direction of a judge, to the oppression and damage of the other party, which could not promptly pursue the justice belonging to it, on account of the cavilling and fraudulent delaying tactic of the bailiff. Item, if he ever lusted after the lands, houses or possessions or other immovable or movable goods of his neighbour, and because the latter was unwilling to sell, rent or give them to him, he harassed him or procured his harassment in his goods or person or he lost the goods in question, perhaps, by oppression, for this reason. Item if he shall have imprisoned or ordered or procured the imprisonment of anyone unjustly and so the person thus imprisoned lost his goods by conferring them on him or even on others in order to have his release and redeem his injurious vexation. Item, if he shall have beaten or consented to the act of those beating or have arrested or have

redimenda. Item si verberaverit vel verberantibus consenserit vel ceperit[o] seu
capi procuraverit vel mandaverit seu in vinculis tenuerit invitum[p] aliquem
clericum, sic excommunicacionis sentenciam incurrendo[q] ipso facto. Item si
ingrediebatur unquam aliquam possessionem ecclesie et bona ibidem inventa
5   attachiavit vel asportavit seu capi et asportari fecit contra volun/[fol.
22rbC]tatem custodum eorum,[r] contra libertatem ecclesie. Item si extraxerit
unquam ab ecclesia vel ipsius cimiterio vel extrahi mandavit seu extrahentibus
consensit aliquem fugientem ad illam pro ipsius immunitate et tuicione
habenda seu vite necessaria sibi[s] dum erat in ecclesia ministrari prohibuit vel
10 ne ministrarentur impedivit. Item si senescallus unquam recepit munera ab
aliqua parte litigante coram se, ad differendum celerem facere iusticiam in
gravamen partis alterius. Item si unquam recepit munera ab utraque parte
litigancium et sic ei qui plus dedit plus debito fovebat, vel illam contra partem
adversam favebat[t] in iniuria sua. Item si compellebat aliquos subditos suos ad
15 falso[u] iurandum et dicendum contra veritatem, in preiudicium alicuius, sive in
iudicio sive extra. Item si unquam fecit[v] pactum cum aliqua parte coram se
litigante quod haberet quicquid posset[w] consequi in iudicio si haberet pro se
sentenciam, vel eciam composuit secum de habenda certa parte rei iudicate, et
sic fuit pars et iudex in una et eadem causa. Item si in iudicio probris et rixis
20 contendebat aliquem subditum suum vituperando plus debito, vel minis seu
terroribus comminando, ita quod pauper subditus non audebat ius suum
coram se prosequi vel forsan ali/[fol. 22vC]as[x] bona sua hoc[y] pretextu amisit
iniuste. Item si unquam contra aliquem falsam vel iniquam tulit sentenciam
contra / [fol. 28vH] conscienciam suam et in hoc peccant hodie multi in tali
25 potestate constituti, prece vel precio seducti, fabricantes sibi consciencias
largas causa lucri temporalis consequendi nec hodie tales se credunt in hoc
peccare[z]; set certe male decipiuntur. Item si unquam spoliavit[a] ecclesias vel
viros ecclesiasticos[b] bonis suis ecclesiasticis[c] de quibus nec de iure debuit nec
potuit sana consciencia se intromittere vel iudicare.[d] Item si[e] unquam precepit
30 vel statuit aliqua fieri vel observari[f] subditis ballive sue in preiudicium ecclesie
vel lesionem virorum ecclesiasticorum. Item si unquam amerciavit in curia sua
aliquam personam ecclesiasticam racione delicti personalis, de quo delicto non
potuit nec debuit de iure iudicare, et amerciamentum levari fecit per
capcionem bonorum ipsius.[g] Item si bona alicuius monasterii vel[h] ecclesie

o   ceperit: cepit *H*
p   invitum: vinctum *H*
q   incurrendo *bis canc. C*
r   custodum eorum: custodiencium *H*
s   sibi *om. H*
t   favebat: fovebat *W H*
u   falso: falsa *H*
v   fecit: fecerit *H*
w   posset: poterit *H*
x   alias: alia *H*
y   hoc: huiusmodi *H*

z   peccare: peccasse *H*
a   spoliavit: expoliavit *H*
b   ecclesiasticos: religiosos *H*
c   ecclesiasticis *om. H*
d   se intromittere vel iudicare:
    intromittere *H*
e   si *add. supra lineam C*
f   *add.* a *H*
g   ipsius: illius *H*
h   alicuius monasterii vel *om. H*

procured or ordered the arrest or have detained in bonds against his will any clerk, thus automatically incurring sentence of excommunication. Item, if he ever entered on any possession of the church and attached or removed the goods found thereupon or caused them to be taken and removed against the will of their custodians, in breach of the liberty of the church. Item, if he ever extracted from a church or its cemetery or ordered the extraction or consented to the act of those extracting anyone fleeing to it to have its immunity and protection or if he forbade the necessities of life to be ministered to him while he was in the church or impeded their being ministered. Item, if a seneschal ever received gifts from any party litigating before him, for postponing to do rapid justice, to the oppression of the opposing party. Item, if he ever received gifts from both the parties of litigants and thus he fostered more than due that one which gave the more or favoured it in its lack of right, against the opposing party. Item if he compelled any subjects of his to swear falsely and to speak against truth, to the prejudice of anyone, whether in or outside of judgment [sc. court proceedings]. Item, if he ever made a pact with any party litigating before him that he should have whatever it might win in judgment, if it had sentence for it, or even arranged with it about having a certain part of the matter adjudged, and thus he was party and judge in one and the same case. Item, if in judgment he disputed in opprobrious and quarrelsome fashion, disparaging beyond propriety any subject of his or intimidating him with threats or terrors, so that a poor subject did not dare to pursue his right before him or perhaps otherwise unjustly lost his goods by this circumstance. Item, whether he ever delivered false or wicked sentence against anyone, contrary to his conscience, and in this sin many today, constituted in power of the kind, being seduced by entreaty or bribe, constructing for themselves extended consciences for the sake of winning temporal gain; nor do such men today believe that in this they sin; but certainly they are badly deceived. Item, if he ever despoiled churches or churchmen of their ecclesiastical goods, concerning which he neither ought nor could by law with a sound conscience intrude himself or judge. Item, if he ever ordered or enacted any acts to be done or observed by the subjects of his bailiwick to the prejudice of the church or the damage of churchmen. Item, if he ever amerced in his court any ecclesiastical person by reason of personal delict (concerning which delict, by law, he could not and ought not to judge) and caused amercement to be levied by seizure of the goods of the same. Item, if he occupied the goods of any monastery or

parochialis cuius dominus suus patronus est[i] tempore vacacionis /[fol. 19rW]
eiusdem ecclesie occupavit vel per alios capi et[j] occupari mandavit ipsa bona
in utilitatem domini sui vel eciam in utilitatem suam propriam convertendo.
Item si unquam aliquas possessiones vel aliqua bona[k] alia de aliquo per
5   oppressionem vel metum sue potestatis adquisivit iniuste, quia talia bona
/[fol. 22vbC] omnia et singula[l] ut pretangitur contra iusticiam adquisita habet
taliter adquirens necesse restituere hiis quibus de iure fuerint restituenda si
salvari voluerit. Si vero talis senescallus vel ballivus fuerit clericus non
beneficiatus, inquiras si aspiret ascendere ad honorem[m] clericalem ordines
10 sacros recipiendo, et si sic, dicas quod ordinari non potest nec debet de iure
quamdiu fuerit astrictus tali officio seculari et potissime si fuerit obligatus ad
reddendum compotum de administracione sua, quia tales ad raciocinia
obligati prohibentur de iure promoveri. Multa alia peccata committunt falsi[n]
senescalli et ballivi de quibus quilibet[o] iuxta suam conscienciam seipsum
15 debet[p] accusare.

a. xxxvi. Circa milites. Rubrica.[13]

20 Inquirere debes a[q] milite si fuerit superbus, vel adulter, vel alias luxuriosus,
secundum quod sunt quasi[r] omnes moderni, vel si uxorem suam a se
abiecerit.[s] Item si spoliaverit vel privaverit ecclesias, vel viros ecclesiasticos,
iuribus, possessionibus vel bonis suis ecclesiasticis. Item si extorserit ab
eisdem pensiones, vel procuraciones.[14] Item si traxerit clericos ad curiam
25 suam[15] contra eorum /[fol. 29rH] voluntatem,[t] compellendo eos ibidem
litigare vel respondere in spiritualibus accionibus vel causis ad forum
ecclesiasticum spectantibus, et eosdem amerciando sive multando, per se vel
per senescallum suum ipso sci/[fol. 23rC]ente et hoc ratificante, gravavit. Item
si fecerit vel permiserit per balivos suos clericos distringi vel attachiari per
30 bonorum suorum capcionem contra libertatem ecclesiasticam, maxime si
clericus non tenet ab eo temporalia. Item si unquam per se vel per alium ipso
iubente aliquod manerium episcoporum seu clericorum aliorum
quorumcunque seu grangias vel alia loca eorum[u] hostiliter ingressus fuerit, et

[i]	fuit *add. in marg. altera manu C post*	[o]	quilibet *om. H*
	corr. ex est *in textu:* est *H*	[p]	suam conscienciam seipsum debet:
[j]	capi et *om. H*		suas consciencias seipsos debent *H*
[k]	aliqua bona: alia *H*	[q]	a: de *H*
[l]	omnia et singula: de aliquo per	[r]	quasi: communiter *H*
	oppressionem et metum *H*	[s]	a se abiecerit: subiecerit *H*
[m]	honorem: ordinem *H*	[t]	voluntatem: voluntates *H*
[n]	falsi *om. H*	[u]	eorum: illorum *H*

[13] Several of the sins included in Hostiensis, *op. cit.*, art. 35–40, as appropriate to various
secular rulers are applied under this heading to knights.
[14] Item si extorserit . . . procuraciones: ibid., art. 36, col. 1421.
[15] Item . . . ad curiam suam: ibid.

parish church of which his lord is patron, in time of vacancy of the said church, or ordered their being taken or occupied by others, converting the said goods to the utility of his lord or even to his own utility. Item, if he ever acquired unjustly any possessions or any other goods from anyone by oppression or fear of his power, because all and single such goods, acquired, as indicated above, contrary to justice, the person acquiring in that manner is held necessarily to restore to those to whom by law they must be restored, if he wishes to be saved. If, indeed, such a seneschal or bailiff be a non-beneficed clerk, inquire whether he aspires to ascend to [sc. further] clerical dignity, by receiving sacred orders, and if so, say that by law he cannot nor ought not to be ordained so long as he may be constricted by such secular office, and especially if he be obliged to render account for his administration, because such persons, bound to account, are by law forbidden to be promoted [sc. to sacred orders]. False seneschals and bailiffs commit many other sins, of which each ought to accuse himself in accordance with his conscience.

a. xxxvi. Concerning knights

You ought to inquire of a knight if he was proud or an adulterer or otherwise lecherous, as they almost all are nowadays, or if he has put away his wife. Item, if he has despoiled or deprived churches or churchmen of their ecclesiastical rights, possessions or goods. Item, if he has extorted from them pensions or procurations. Item, if he has drawn clerks to his court against their will, compelling them to litigate or make answer there in spiritual actions or cases belonging to the ecclesiastical forum, and if he oppressed them by amercing or mulcting them, himself or, knowing and ratifying this, through his seneschal. Item, if he has caused or permitted through his bailiffs that clerks be distrained or attached by seizure of their goods against ecclesiastical liberty, especially if the clerk [sc. in question] does not hold temporalities from him. Item, if, acting personally or through another, on his orders, he ever entered in hostile fashion any manor of bishops or of any other clerks, or granges or other places of the same and invaded and removed goods found there, against the

bona ibidem inventa invaserit et abstulerit contra voluntatem domini[v] vel balivi sui, vel alterius qui ad bonorum ipsorum custodiam fuerat[w] deputatus. Item si unquam sacrilegium commiserit, res sacras vel non sacras a loco sacro auferendo. Item si clericum incarceraverit vel[x] in vinculis detinuerit vel teneri
5   mandaverit invitum, seu manus in ipsum iniecerit temere violentas. Item si terras vel possessiones alienas occupaverit violenter, et eas celeriter non restituerit vero domino, quia nunquam salvari poterit, nisi omnia bona per ipsum occupata qualitercunque iniuste ac eciam possessiones sic occupatas, cum omnibus fructibus et proventibus[y] inde per eum vel per alium suo
10   nomine perceptis et quos verus dominus percepisse potuisset, integre restituerit. Item si conspiraverit in mortem principis vel domini sui, cui iuramento fidelitatis est astrictus. Item si unquam commiserit crimen usure. Item si unquam presentavit[z] ad ecclesiam /[fol. 23rbC] cuius est patronus vel eciam procuravit presentari ad ecclesiam cuius non est patronus aliquem
15   clericum[a] vel aliquem procuravit[b] ordinari mediante pecunia, vel quacunque alia re temporali, symoniam aliquo modo committendo. Item si integre solverit[c] et per[d] suos ministros solvi preceperit[e], decimas Deo et ecclesie ab eo debitas.[16] Item si ediderit, statuerit, /[fol. 19vW] edi[f] vel statui fecerit in curia sua aliquas constituciones vel statuta contra ecclesiasticam libertatem,[17]
20   utputa, milites quandoque rectores, vicarios et capellanos parochiales ecclesiarum in quarum parochiis habent maneria sua odio persequuntur, nonnunquam ex levi et frequencius ex nulla causa, cuius pretextu, in preiudicium et gravamen ecclesiarum, sibi subtrahunt vel subtrahi faciunt iura sibi debita, et consuetudines laudabiles tollunt, et suis rusticis et
25   tenentibus precipiunt et precipi faciunt per balivos suos, ut subtrahant ecclesiis laudabiles /[fol. 29vH] consuetudines, in quarum possessione ecclesie ipse fuerant ab antiquo, quo casu milites precipientes et eorum balivi precepta huiusmodi exequentes et rustici ea observantes sunt excommunicati ipso[g] facto.[18] Item si talliis et exaccionibus indebitis suos tenentes et maxime
30   pauperes rusticos gravaverit,[19] quia scire debet quod non potest[h] nec debet[i] de iure divino a suo tenente quicquam exigere vel violenter /[fol. 23vC] extorquere, ultra id quod sibi debetur racione terrarum quas ab eo tenet vel

[v]   contra voluntatem domini: contra   [b] aliquem procuravit *om. H*
      voluntatem vel domini permissionem   [c] solverit: solvit *H*
      H   [d] et per *C W*: et *add. supra lineam C*: vel *H*
[w] fuerat: fuerit *W H*   [e] preceperit: precepit *H*
[x] incarceraverit vel *om. H*   [f] edi *om. H*
[y] proventibus: provenientibus *W*   [g] ipso: eo *W*
[z] presentavit: presentaverit *H*   [h] non potest *om. W*
[a] cuius non est patronus aliquem   [i] nec debet *om. H*
      clericum *om. H*

[16] Item si integre . . . debitas: cf. ibid., art. 38, col. 1423, 'octavo'.
[17] Cf. ibid., art. 37, col. 1422, 'secundo'.
[18] X. 5.39.49, Friedberg, II, 910.
[19] Item si talliis . . . gravaverit: cf. Hostiensis, *op. cit.*, col. 1423, 'peccant autem duces'.

will of the lord or the latter's bailiff or of anyone else who had been deputed to the custody of the said goods. Item, if he has ever committed sacrilege, by carrying off from a sacred place sacred or non-sacred things. Item, if he has imprisoned a clerk or detained him in bonds or ordered him to be held against his will or has temerariously laid violent hands upon him. Item, if he has violently occupied lands or possessions of another and has not speedily restored them to the true lord, because he can never be saved unless he restore in full all goods occupied by him, in whatever manner, unjustly, and also [sc. in case of] possessions thus occupied, with all fruits and proceeds taken thence by him or by another in his name and which the true lord could have taken. Item, if he has conspired to the death of his prince or lord, to whom he was bound by oath of fealty. Item, if he ever committed the crime of usury. Item, if, in consideration of money or of any other temporal thing, he ever presented to a church of which he is patron, or even procured to be presented to a church of which he is not patron, any clerk, or procured anyone to be ordained, committing simony in any manner. Item, if he has fully paid and ordered payment by his servants of tithes due from him to God and the church. Item, if he has issued, enacted [or] caused to be issued or enacted any constitutions or statutes against ecclesiastical liberty: as, for instance, knights sometimes from hatred persecute rectors, vicars and parish chaplains of churches in whose parishes they have their manors, on occasion for light cause, more frequently for none, on pretext of which, to the prejudice and oppression of churches, they withdraw or cause to be withdrawn rights due to the same, and do away with laudable customs, and they order their villeins and tenants – and cause orders to be issued them by their bailiffs – to withdraw from churches laudable customs, in possession of which the churches in question had been from of old, in which case the knights giving the orders and the bailiffs executing them and the villeins observing them are automatically excommunicate. Item, if he has oppressed his tenants and especially his poor villeins with undue tallages and exactions, because he ought to know that by divine law he cannot and ought not to exact or violently extort from his tenant anything beyond what is owed him by reason of the lands held from him or what by reason of personal delict

quod[j] racione delicti personalis vel alia legitima de[k] causa sibi de consuetudine prestare debet. Quod si fecerit, rapinam committit. Item si habuerit capellam in manerio suo et in ea celebrari fecerit sine licencia et auctoritate pape vel proprii episcopi, et[l] oblaciones forsan in ea[m] factas fecerit
5   imbursari et asportari in preiudicium matris ecclesie,[20] ipsam ecclesiam temere privando suo iure. Item si in curia sua iusticiam servari et fieri fecerit equaliter pauperi sicut et[n] diviti.[21] Item si domino suo, regi forsan, comiti vel baroni aliquando favebat, vel[o] fovebat eum[p] in peccatis carnalibus vel aliis illicitis, vel si eum ad bellum iniustum stimulabat, vel eum in eo iuvabat
10   pugnando scienter[q] iniuste. Item si frequentaverit torneamenta,[22] que de iure canonico sunt interdicta. Multa alia peccata committunt milites[r] frequenter, furta videlicet, rapinas, blasphemias, homicidia, decepciones, detracciones, symoniam, et irreverenter se habent et gerunt in ecclesia dum audiunt missam, garulando cum astantibus de frivolis, et indevoti sunt, vix aut nunquam unam
15   oracionem dominicam dicendo, set[s] ut plurimum immiscendo periuria, mendacia et similia, de quibus te confessorem cavere oportebit diligenter.

a. xxxvii. Circa mercatores et burgenses. Rubrica. /[fol. 23vbC]
20

Primo inquirere debes tu confessor a mercatore et eciam a[t] burgense si solverit fideliter decimas suas personales ecclesie[23] in qua audit divina et ecclesiastica percipit sacramenta, de iusto suo lucro, quia illi[u] ecclesie et non[v] illi infra cuius parochiam emit et vendit, decime huiusmodi de iure debentur.
25   Item si unquam fecerit compensacionem lucri ad dampnum,[w] hoc modo, videlicet: hodie emet merces, et vendendo lucratur viginti;[x] cras vendet[y] /[fol. 30rH] merces[z] alias et perdet viginti, et sic non vult solvere decimas de viginti primo lucratis, quia[a] perdit[b] alia[c] viginti de aliis mercibus venditis, set certe in hoc peccat mortaliter, defraudando ecclesiam iure suo, quia de iure talis
30   compensacio est penitus reprobata. Item si sub specie liberalitatis vel pietatis crimen usure commiserit,[24] quia forsan pauperi vel diviti carius vendit, pro

j	quod *om. H*		t	eciam a *om. H*
k	de *om. H*		u	illi: ille *H*
l	et: ut *H*		v	non: eciam *H*
m	forsan in ea: in ea *W*; sibi *H*		w	ad dampnum: cum dampno *H*
n	et *om. H*		x	*add.* et *H*
o	favebat vel *om. H*		y	vendet: vendens *H*
p	eum *om. H*		z	merces *om. H*
q	*add.* et *H*		a	quia *add. supra lineam C*
r	milites *om. H*		b	perdit: perdidit *H*
s	set *om. H*		c	alia *om. H*

[20] Item si habuerit . . . ecclesie: cf. ibid., 'tertio'.
[21] Item . . . diviti: cf. ibid., 'quinto'.
[22] Item si frequentaverit torneamenta: cf. ibid., art. 40, col. 1424, 'quarto'.
[23] Cf. ibid., art. 41, col. 1424.
[24] Item si sub specie . . . commiserit: cf. ibid., 'secundo'.

or other lawful cause he ought by custom to render him. If he does so, he commits rapine. Item, if he has had a chapel on his manor and has caused celebration in it, without licence and authority of the pope or the appropriate bishop, and has perhaps caused offerings made in it to be pocketed and taken off, to the prejudice of the mother church, temerariously depriving that church of its right. Item, if in his court he has caused justice to be observed and done equally to poor as to rich. Item, if he at any time encouraged his lord, the king, perhaps, [or] earl or baron, or nurtured him in carnal sins or other unlawful things or spurred him on to unjust war or knowingly aided him unjustly by fighting in the same. Item, if he has frequented tournaments, which are banned by canon law. Knights often commit many other sins – namely, thefts, rapines, blasphemies, homicides, deceptions, detractions, simony – and they hold and conduct themselves irreverently in church while they are hearing mass, chattering with bystanders about trifles, and they are undevout, hardly ever or never saying a single Lord's Prayer but generally intermingling perjuries, falsehoods and such-like, concerning which, confessor, you will need diligently to be on your guard.

a. xxxvii. Concerning merchants and burgesses[2]

You ought first to inquire, confessor, from a merchant and also from a burgess if he has faithfully paid his personal tithes, from his just gain, to the church in which he hears divine offices and takes the ecclesiastical sacraments, because by law such tithes are owed to that church and not to the church within whose parish he buys and sells. Item, if he has ever made compensation of gain as regards loss, in this manner namely: today he will buy goods and in selling gains twenty; tomorrow he will sell other goods and will lose twenty; and so he does not wish to pay tithes of the first twenty gained, because he loses another twenty on the other goods sold. But certainly in this he sins mortally, defrauding the church of its right, because by law such compensation is utterly discountenanced. Item, if under pretence of liberality or piety he has committed the crime of usury, because perhaps he sells to a

---

2 Most of the questions, though translated here in the masculine, are not gender-specific.

longi termini dilacione,[d] alias non sic venditurus, set pro longe minore precio, /[fol. 20rW] si precium incontinenti recepisset. Ecce quod sola cupiditas lucrandi inducit talem usurarium ad sic vendendum. Item si in aliis speciebus usure unquam deliquerit, verbi gracia, aliquis mutuavit tibi decem usque ad
5 annum, pro quibus obligasti sibi[e] fundum tuum, et creditor[f] percipit[g] fructus illius fundi; in fine anni, tu solvis sibi[h] illa decem; set creditor non computat in illis decem fructus quos percepit.[i] Certe usuram committit.[j] /[fol. 24rC] Et sic de aliis.[k] Item si unquam decepit proximum suum, vendendo sibi merces falsas pro veris, asserendo merces venditas certa pondera vel mensuram[l]
10 continere[25] vel sanas et integras esse, set[m] postea totum contrarium reperitur, et emptor decipitur. Vel si vendiderit, scienter decipiendo emptorem ultra dimidium[n] iusti precii,[o] quibus casibus, si quid[p] ultra iustum precium recepit,[q] turpe lucrum recipere de iure reputatur. Item si carius vendiderit peregrinis et aliis transeuntibus, quam vicinis suis propriis.[26] Item si per falsa
15 pondera vel[r] falsas mensuras quibus dolose utitur alicui quicquam vendiderit.[27] Item si periurium vel mendacium in vendendo commiserit, verbi gracia, mercator dicit sic : 'Ecce res ista, tantum costavit[s] mihi, et nulla melior invenietur, et pro tanto precio habebis, et non pro minori', et hoc affirmat iurando per omnia membra Christi, et mentitur expresse. Ecce ergo quod in
20 hoc facto quatuor mortalia peccata committit, videlicet, mendacium, periurium, blasphemiam, et decepcionem proximi.[28] Item si unquam choierit[t] societatem cum aliquibus vel[u] cum aliquo et fidem prestiterit vel iuraverit super librum quod fideliter se haberet in societate huiusmodi, set postea fraudem faciendo fidem non servavit. Item si unquam iuravit[v] solvere ad
25 certum terminum precium conventum vel rem promissam, et in termino non solvit /[fol. 30vH] et tamen solvisse potuisset, si /[fol. 24rbC] voluisset. Item si unquam transtulerit[w] se, habens uxorem in uno regno vel provincia, ad[x] aliud regnum vel provinciam, et ibi, fingens[y] se solutum, contraxerit matrimonium

---

[d] pro longi termini dilacione: pro longe [*sic*] tempore scilicet pro dilacione habenda *H*
[e] sibi *om. W*
[f] creditor: credit *W; add.* interim *H*
[g] percipit: percepit *H*
[h] sibi: illi *W*
[i] *add.* medio tempore *H*
[j] usuram committit: usura esse constat *H*
[k] Et sic de aliis *om. H*
[l] mensuram: mensuras *H*
[m] set *om. W*

[n] dimidium: medietatem *H*
[o] *add.* de *H*
[p] quid: quis *H*
[q] recepit: receperit *H*
[r] vel *om. C W*
[s] costavit: constat *H*
[t] choierit: statuerit *W*; iniecerit *H*
[u] cum aliquibus vel *om. H*
[v] iuravit: iuraverit *H*
[w] transtulerit: abstulerit *H*
[x] ad: et in *H*
[y] et ibi fingens: fingit *H*

[25] Item si unquam decepit . . . continere: cf. ibid., 'quinto'.
[26] Item si carius . . . propriis: cf. ibid., 'quarto'.
[27] Item si per falsa pondera . . . vendiderit: cf. ibid., 'quinto'.
[28] Item si periurium . . . proximi [excepting: per omnia membra Christi]: cf. ibid., 'sexto'.

poor man – or a rich – at a higher price, on long credit, not being disposed otherwise to sell on those terms, but for a much lower price, if he had received the price there and then. It is quite plain that only greed for profit induces such a usurer to sell in that way. Item, if he ever offended in the other types of usury, for example, someone lent you ten for a year, in respect of which you pledged your estate to him, and the creditor takes the fruits of the estate; at the end of the year, you pay him those ten but the creditor does not calculate in the ten the fruits which he has taken. Certainly, he commits usury: and so on concerning the other types. Item, if he ever deceived his neighbour, selling him false goods for true, alleging that the goods sold contained specified weights or measure or were sound and whole, but afterwards quite the contrary is found and the buyer is deceived. Alternatively, if he has sold knowingly deceiving the buyer beyond one half of the just price. In which cases, if he received anything beyond the just price, he is deemed by law to receive dishonest gain. Item, if he has sold at higher price to pilgrims and other travellers than to his own neighbours. Item, if he has sold anything to anyone by false weights [or] false measures which he deceitfully uses. Item, if he has committed perjury or falsehood in selling: for example, the merchant says, 'Look, that item cost me such an amount and no better example will be found and you shall have it for such a price and not for less', and this he affirms by swearing on all the limbs of Christ and he is telling an outright lie. Just look how in this act he commits four mortal sins, namely, falsehood, perjury, blasphemy and deception of his neighbour. Item, if he has ever formed a partnership with any persons or person and has pledged his faith or sworn upon the book that he would conduct himself faithfully in the partnership but afterwards, committing fraud, he did not keep faith. Item, if he has ever sworn to render at a specified term an agreed price or item promised and at the term has not done so, though he could have, had he wished. Item, if, having a wife in one realm or province, he has ever transferred to another realm or province and there, pretending that he was single, has contracted marriage de facto with another woman or, even

cum aliqua de facto vel eciam non contrahendo adulterium commiserit.[29] Item
si burgensis locaverit scienter domos suas meretricibus pupplicis ad
inhabitandum, vel si postquam novit ipsas esse meretrices, non expulit eas, set
inhabitare permisit, et sic earum turpem vitam approbando lenocinium
5   commisit. Alia autem sunt[z] peccata quasi infinita quibus mercatores et
burgenses involvuntur,[30] de quibus oportebit te confessorem diligenter
meditando precavere.

10   a. xxxviii. Circa servientes. Rubrica.

Licet peccata serviencium et potissime garcionum omnibus per facti
experienciam sint nota, pauca tamen hic de eis[a] perstringam. Inquiras igitur tu
confessor a talibus servientibus,[b] primo sic : 'Iurasti vel fidem dedisti ad
15   serviendum fideliter domino tuo?', et si dicat quod sic, inquiras sic:[c] 'Fecisti
unquam fraudem in servicio tuo?', quod sit[d] multis modis, prout quilibet
discretus per se novit de facto explicare. Item: 'Furatus fuisti quascunque res
domini tui? Item consumpsisti vel male expendidisti bona domini tui quorum
habebas custodiam, in dampnum domini tui? Vel dedisti ea alicui persone
20   suspecte /[fol. 24vC] puta, mulieri levis opinionis, vel alii persone cuicunque?
Item mentitus fuisti domino tuo dicens te aliquid fecisse, vel non fecisse, et sic
falsum dicendo, /[fol. 20vW] dominum tuum decepisti? Item denudasti vel
eciam retulisti unquam alicui, et maxime inimico domini tui, secreta domini
tui, et sic per hoc status domini tui fuit decoloratus,[e] vel dominus tuus aliquo
25   modo gravari potuit? Item permisisti unquam scienter et prudenter quod
aliquis fecit dampnum in bonis[f] domini tui vel audivisti quod aliquis
predicavit sinistra de domino tuo et factorem dampni non impedivisti, vel
super hiis dominum tuum non premunivisti?[g] Item necglexisti unquam facere
servicium tuum fideliter et diligenter, ita quod, racione necgligencie tue, bona
30   domini tui perierunt vel necgligenter fuerunt[h] deperdita? De blasphemia,
iurando incaute et de consuetudine, de lenocinio, de adulacione, fornicacione
et aliis peccatis /[fol. 31rH] inquiras prout videris expedire.

---

z   sunt *add. supra lineam* C
a   hic de eis: de hiis H
b   servientibus *om.* W
c   sic: secundo H *add.* si H
d   quod sit: quod fit W; que fit H
e   decoloratus: deterioratus H

f   quod aliquis fecit dampnum in bonis:
    quod aliquod dampnum datum fuit in
    rebus H
g   premunivisti: premonuisti W
h   fuerunt: fuerint W

---

29   Item si unquam choierit . . . commiserit: cf. ibid., 'septimo' *et seq.*
30   Alia autem . . . involvuntur: cf. ibid.

without contracting, has committed adultery. Item, if a burgess has leased his houses knowingly to public harlots for habitation or if, after he knew them to be harlots, he did not expel them but allowed them to live there, and thus by approving their shameful life-style he was guilty of pandering. There are almost infinite other sins in which merchants and burgesses are involved, concerning which, confessor, you will need to be on your guard by diligent pondering.

a. xxxviii. Concerning servants

Although the sins of servants and especially of menials are well known to everyone by actual experience, I will nevertheless set down a few points about them. Inquire therefore, confessor, from such servants, first as follows: 'Did you ever swear or give faith to your lord to serve faithfully?' and if the answer be yes, inquire as follows: 'Did you ever commit fraud in your service?' – which occurs in many ways, as any man of discretion himself knows to explain from experience. Item, 'Did you ever steal any of your lord's things? Item, did you consume or badly spend the goods of your lord, of which you had custody, to the damage of your lord? Or did you give them to any suspect person, for instance to a woman of light reputation, or to any other person? Item, did you lie to your lord, saying that you had done something or not done something and thus, by speaking false, deceived your lord? Item, did you ever reveal or even report to anyone, and especially an enemy of your lord, the secrets of your lord, and thus by this act your lord's state was tarnished or your lord could be damaged in any way? Item, did you ever knowingly and deliberately permit that anyone caused damage in the goods of your lord or did you hear that anyone spread evil reports of your lord and you did not impede the perpetrator or did not alert your lord upon these points? Item, did you ever neglect to perform your service faithfully and diligently, so that by reason of your negligence your lord's goods perished or were negligently lost?' Inquire as you may see fit concerning blasphemy, incautious and habitual swearing, pandering, flattery, fornication and other sins.

a. xxxix. Circa nautas.

Tu confessor, si contingat te audire aliquem nautam in confessione, necesse
5   habebis caute et studiose te habere in[i] inquirendo, quia scire debes quod vix
sufficit calamus scribere peccata quibus involvuntur. Tanta est enim illorum
malicia, quod omnium[j] hominum aliorum peccata[k] excedit. Scire igitur debes
quod naute peccant: primo[l] sunt male creden/[fol. 24vbC]tes et male fidei.
Item dum sunt in terra necgligunt confiteri, et licet fuerint confessi, nunquam
10   peragunt penitenciam sibi iniunctam. Item blasphemant Christum et sanctos
eius, iurando per singula[m] membra Christi[n] de consuetudine et deierando[o] et
Deum negando. Item non reverenter se habent erga[p] ecclesiam Dei nec
sacerdotes vel alios[q] ecclesie ministros. Item verberant presbiteros et clericos,
et aliquos interficiunt, in casibus sibi a iure non permissis, unde sunt
15   excommunicati ipso facto. Item non solum occidunt clericos et laicos dum sunt
in terra, set eciam, quando sunt in mari, piraticam exercent pravitatem,
rapiendo bona aliorum et potissime mercatorum mare transeuncium, et eos
crudeliter interficiunt.[r] Quo casu omnes naute et eciam quicunque alii alios
Christianos quoscunque bonis suis spoliantes in mari vel eciam naufragium
20   pacientes hodie sunt excommunicati ipso facto,[31] nec a tali sentencia poterit
taliter spolians aliqualiter absolvi, nisi prius restituerit taliter spoliatis omnia[s]
spoliata, et occupata, si habuerit in bonis unde satisfacere poterit.[t] Set si non
habuerit unde, tunc tene quod scribitur infra de restitucione male
adquisitorum. Item ita sunt superbi et elati, quod omnes homines cuiuscunque
25   condicionis fuerint, exceptis personis maioribus, quibus resistere vel pares
esse non possunt, contempnunt et absque misericordia crudeliter tractant,
dum eos in suis navibus[u] /[fol. 25rC] ducunt, et maxime pauperes peregrinos,
eorum bona violenter auferendo. Item quasi omnes sunt usurarii, fenus
nauticum exercentes. Item omnes sunt adulteri et fornicatores, quia in singulis
30   terris et regionibus quas ingrediuntur vel contrahunt matrimonia de facto cum
diversis mulieribus, credendo hoc sibi licere, vel fornicantur passim et
indistincte cum meretricibus. Item sunt gulosi quia vix aut nunquam
ieiunant:[v] eciam in die Parasceves[w] bis comedunt aliqui, absque causa
necessaria. Item dum sunt super terram, totum tempus suum, in quo[x] bonum
35   operari debeant, expendunt circa comessaciones, ebrietates, luxurias, luctas,

---

[i]	in *om.* H	[q]	*add.* clericos H
[j]	*add.* malorum H	[r]	interficiunt: tractant H
[k]	aliorum peccata *om.* H	[s]	*add.* bona H
[l]	*add.* quia W	[t]	poterit: potest H
[m]	singula: sanguinem W	[u]	navibus: manibus H
[n]	Christi: eius H	[v]	*add.* ac H
[o]	et deierando: iurando H	[w]	s *add. supra lineam* C: Parasceve H
[p]	se habent erga: honorant H	[x]	in quo: dum H

[31] See X. 5.17.2, Friedberg, II, 808.

a. xxxix. Concerning sailors

Confessor, if it befalls you to hear any sailor in confession, you will have of necessity to conduct yourself cautiously and zealously in making inquiry, because you ought to know that the pen scarcely suffices to write the sins in which they are involved. For so great is their malice that it exceeds the sins of all other men. You ought to know, therefore, that sailors sin [sc. as follows]: first, they are ill believers and of weak faith. Item, while they are on land they neglect to confess and, even though they may have confessed, they never perform the penance enjoined on them. Item, they blaspheme Christ and his saints, swearing habitually by each and every limb of Christ and committing perjury and denying God. Item, they do not conduct themselves reverently towards the church of God nor priests nor other ministers of church. Item, they strike priests and clerks and kill some, in cases not permitted them by law, on account of which they are automatically excommunicate. Item, not only do they kill clerks and laymen while they are on land but also, when they are at sea, they practise the depravity of piracy, plundering the goods of others and especially of merchants crossing the sea and cruelly do they slay them. In which case, all sailors and also others, whoever they be, despoiling any other Christians of their goods on the sea or, also, [sc. despoiling] those suffering shipwreck, are today automatically excommunicate, nor could such a despoiler be in any respect absolved from such sentence unless he were first to restore all the goods taken or occupied to those who suffered the spoliation, if he should have in his resources the capacity to make satisfaction. But if he should not have the resources, then observe what is written below concerning the restitution of what has been wickedly acquired. Item, they are so proud and elated that they despise all men, of whatever condition they may be – excepting the really great, to whom they can neither offer resistance nor be equal – and they treat them cruelly, without mercy, while they conduct them in their ships, and especially poor pilgrims, violently carrying off their goods. Item, almost all are usurers, practising the sea-loan. Item, they are all adulterers and fornicators, because in the single lands and regions which they enter, they either contract marriages de facto with several women, believing that this is permitted to them, or fornicate generally and promiscuously with harlots. Item, they are gluttonous, because they seldom or never fast; even on Good Friday some of them eat twice, without necessary reason. Item, while they are on land, the whole time in which they ought to be doing good they waste on feasting, drunken orgies, lecheries, brawls, contentions and quarrels,

contenciones et rixas, de quibus vel de huiusmodi temporis amissione,
nunquam volunt[y] ali/[fol. 21rW]qualiter confiteri. Item fraudem faciunt in
contractibus suis; vix alicui fidem prestitam vel promissam observant. Item
falsas et corruptas merces pro veris et integris fallaciter vendunt. Et ut breviter
5   me expediam,[z] plura sunt eorum peccata, quam tu[a] sensu humano poteris
cogitare.[b] Et certe nonnumquam peccant contra mentem legis Rodie[32] de iactu.
Hoc est in periculo maris constituti proiciunt[c] merces de navi, causa navis
alleviande, parcendo[d] bonis unius mercatoris, precio corrupti, et dampnum
dando alii[e] mercatori in bonis suis; de quibus omnibus necesse habent confiteri
10   et penitere, satisfaciendo dampnum pas/[fol. 25rbC]sis de omnibus dampnis
per eos sibi datis si penas Gehennales voluerint evitare.[f]

a. xl. Circa rusticos. Rubrica.

15

Scire debes tu confessor quod isti rustici tamquam homines bestiales sua
bursali[g] racione utentes,[h] vix aut nunquam possunt induci, ut Deo et eius
preceptis pareant, in hiis <quibus>[i] sibi et sue[j] ecclesie sunt astricti. Et quia
difficile est mancipia trita et veterana[k] ad bonos mores reformare, magis erit in
20   suis confessionibus audiendis[l] laborandum, ut a suis erroribus valeant
salubriter revocari. Inquiras ergo[m] tu confessor si rusticus solverit decimas
suas prediales integre,[n][33] quia aliqui deducunt expensas suas circa
colleccionem fructuum factas, solvendo stipendia mercenariorum suorum
antequam decimas suas solvant. Et alii partem quintamdecimam, alii
25   vicesimam vel tricesimam solvunt de fructibus, loco decime, furtum
committendo. Alii decimam solvunt numero,[o] tamen illud[p] quod est vilius et
deterius in fructibus et animalibus, exemplo Chayni, pro decima solvenda
plerumque solvunt. Item[q] furantur decimas, postquam fuerint separate ab
acervo. Item alii erga[r] suum rectorem vel vicarium moti, causa se vindicandi
30   vel ipsum gravandi longe a se proiciunt garbas decimatas, /[fol. 32rH]

[y]	volunt: velint *H*	[i]	quibus: que *mss.*
[z]	expediam: expedam *H*: expendiam *C*	[j]	sue: sancte *H*
[a]	tu: in *H*	[k]	mancipia trita et veterana: eos *H*
[b]	cogitare: excogitare *W*	[l]	audiendis *om. W*
[c]	proiciunt: percuciunt *H*	[m]	ergo: igitur *H*
[d]	parcendo: partem de *H*	[n]	integre: integras *H*
[e]	alii: altero *W*; alio *H*	[o]	numero: omnino *H*
[f]	evitare: evadere *W*	[p]	tamen illud: cum id *H*
[g]	bursali: bestiali *H*	[q]	*add.* alii *H*
[h]	utentes: exercentes *H*	[r]	erga: ergo *W*

32 Digest, 14.2: *Digesta Iustiniani Augusti*, ed. Th. Mommsen and P. Krueger, 2 vols.
(Berlin, 1870), I, 419–22.
33 Inquiras . . . integre: cf. Hostiensis, *op. cit.*, art. 42, col. 1424.

concerning which or concerning the waste of time involved they never wish in the least to confess. Item, they commit fraud in their contracts; hardly ever do they keep their pledged faith or promise to anyone. Item, they fraudulently sell defective and deteriorated goods as being true and whole. And, to make a long story short, their sins are more than from a decent perspective you could imagine. And, for sure, they frequently sin against the purpose of the Rhodian Law on jettison. That is to say, when put in peril of the sea they throw merchandise overboard in order to lighten the ship, sparing – corrupted by a bribe – the goods of one merchant and inflicting damage on another merchant in his goods. Concerning all of which they have of necessity to confess and repent, making satisfaction to the victims in respect of all the damages inflicted by them, if they wish to avoid the pains of hell.

a. xl. Concerning villeins

You should know, confessor, that those villeins, like brutish men, possessing a purse-orientated mentality, can scarcely or never be induced to obey God and his commandments in those things in which they are bound to him and his church. And, because it is difficult to convert old worn-out servitors to best practice, more work will have to be expended in hearing their confessions, in order that they may be wholesomely recalled from their errors. Inquire, therefore, confessor, if a villein has paid his predial tithes in full, for some deduct their expenses, incurred in the collection of the fruits, paying the wages of their hired hands before they pay their tithes. And others pay the fifteenth part of the fruits, others the twentieth or thirtieth, in place of the tenth, committing theft. Others pay an actual tenth, but they pay as tithe, of fruit and animals, that which is worth least and is in worst condition, on the model of Cain. Item, they steal the tithes, after they have been separated from the main part. Item, others moved against their rector or vicar, to vindicate themselves or injure him, fling the tithed sheaves far from them, shaking off the ears from

excusciendo[s] grana de spicis et eas exponunt animalibus devo/[fol. 25vC]randas; nec curant quid mali in hiis agant, dummodo rector vel vicarius gravari possit. Item in[t] decimis personalibus solvendis varie peccant, prout quilibet curatus singulis diebus de facto poterit experiri. Item inquiras si
5   iuramentum suum fidelitatis domino suo prestitum inviolabiliter observaverit, quia vix aut nunquam reperietur rusticus qui iuramentum suum huiusmodi voluerit observare. Ecce enim quam[u] irreverenter se habent aliquando[v] erga dominum suum, ipsum non reverendo, set contra ipsum insurgendo et sibi totis viribus resistendo. Item si[w] subtrahere sibi nititur et
10 eciam[x] subtrahit[y] iura[34] debita et servicia consueta. Item si[z] furatur bona domini sui, et eciam res ab aliis furata, furibus consenciendo, receptat. Item si[a] facientibus dampna in bonis domini sui clausis oculis consentit, nec eis vult resistere licet possit, nec dampna data seu auctores dampni detegendo domino[b] vult nunciare, vel alii per quem in hoc domino poterit provideri.[c]
15 Peccat eciam talis[d] quia non observat[e] festa sanctorum prout in ecclesia precipitur et a iure statuitur,[35] plus laborando in illis diebus, in casibus[f] a iure non concessis, quam in aliis diebus profestis.[g] Preterea rustici, lege fusiacanina,[36] licet ab[h] olim abrogata, more canino utentes, aliis nocere satagunt in quantum possunt; set sibi ipsis in nullo /[fol. 25vbC] prosunt. In
20 primis ineunt inter se et faciunt conventicula et pacciones illicitas, coniurando et /[fol. 21vW] conspirando contra proximos et maxime contra pauperes, qui non habent quid eis offerant, et ipsos exheredant, et multis aliis modis opprimi procurant in curiis dominorum suorum, contra Deum et iusticiam, et tamen sibi ipsis ex hoc nichil accrescit. Item fidem vix alicui observant, ubi credunt
25 per aliquam cautelam ad sui com<m>odum evadere posse. Item contra ecclesias et viros ecclesiasticos ac libertatem ecclesiasticam coniurando et conspirando,[i] frequenter statuunt inter se laudabiles consuetudines ecclesiarum, que pia fidelium devocione sunt inducte et inconcusse[j] observate ab antiquo, non debere ulterius inter se observari, et sic sentenciam

[s] excusciendo: excuciendo *W H*
[t] Item in: Unde de *H*
[u] quam: quod *W; om. H*
[v] aliquando *om. H*
[w] si *add. supra lineam C: om. H*
[x] *add.* sibi *H*
[y] subtrahit: subtraherit *H*
[z] si *om. H*
[a] si *add. supra lineam C: om. H*
[b] domino: suo *W*
[c] provideri: previderi *H*

[d] peccat eciam talis: peccant enim tales *H*
[e] observat: observunt *[sic] H*
[f] in casibus *om. H*
[g] quam in aliis diebus profestis: et tam in diebus festis quam in profestis *H*
[h] ab *om. H*
[i] contra proximos [. . .] conspirando *om. H*
[j] inducte et inconcusse: introducte et concesse *H*

[34] Item si subtrahere . . . iura: cf. ibid., col. 1425, 'tertio'.
[35] Peccat . . . statuitur: cf. ibid., 'quarto'.
[36] *recte* Fufia Caninia. Institutionum, 1.7; *Imperatoris Iustiniani Institutionum Libri Quattuor*, ed. J. B. Moyle, 5th edn (Oxford, 1912), p. 121.

the blades, and set them before their animals to be devoured; and they care not what evil they do in this respect, provided that the rector or vicar can be injured. Item, they sin variously in paying personal tithes, as anyone with cure of souls could verify every day as a matter of fact. Item, inquire if he has kept inviolably his oath of fealty sworn to his lord, because scarcely or never will be found a villein who has willed to keep such oath of his. Look, too, how disrespectfully they sometimes conduct themselves towards their lord, not revering him, but revolting against him and resisting him with might and main. Item, if he strives to withdraw and does withdraw from him due rights and customary services. Item, if he steals the goods of his lord and also if he is a receiver of things stolen by others, thus consenting to the thieves. Item, if he consents, by shutting his eyes, to those causing damage to the goods of his lord, and wills not to resist them, though he could, and will not apprise his lord – or someone else through whose agency the lord's interest in this matter might be consulted – by revealing the damages done nor the authors of the damage. Such a person [sc. a villein] sins too in that he does not observe the feasts of the saints, as is enjoined in church and enacted by law, labouring more on those days, in cases not conceded by law, than on other days leading up to them. Moreover, villeins, availing themselves in canine fashion of the *Lex Fufia Caninia*, though abolished long ago, busy themselves to harm others so far as lies in their power, even while they are conferring no advantage on themselves. In the first place, they combine and make conventicles and unlawful pacts, jointly swearing and conspiring against their neighbours and especially against the poor, who have nothing to offer them, and they disinherit them, and in many other ways procure their being oppressed in the courts of their lords, against God and justice, and yet no profit accrues to them thereby. Item, they keep faith with scarcely anyone, when they believe they can escape to their benefit by some circumvention. Item, jointly swearing and conspiring against churches, churchmen and ecclesiastical liberty, they often enact among themselves that laudable church customs which were established by pious devotion of the faithful and were firmly observed from of old ought no longer to be observed among them, and so they incur sentence of

excommunicacionis incurrunt *ipso* facto. Preterea rusticus dives in maioribus peccare nititur, et minus peccare formidat quam nobilis sensu regulato ductus. De tali enim divite dicitur: *Reus dives nullam culpam pertimescit, quam nummis se redimere existimat.*[37] Unde tales divites dicuntur infelices iuxta illud[k] versus:

> Diviciis uti (scilicet[l] male) res est adversa saluti.
> Paucos crede bonos, quos beat eris honor.[38]

Item rustici frequenter accusant vicinos suos fraudulenter erga dominos suos et eorum balivos, super criminibus /[fol. 26rC] et defectibus fictis, et sic fatigantur /[fol. 32vH] iniuste, et bona sua amittunt. Item quilibet rusticus invidet alii; vix unum bonum verbum vult dicere de eo, nisi precio conductus, et quilibet alii detrahit,[m] falsa de eo[n] mendaciter predicando. Item quilibet rusticus, furando terram vicini sui terre sue contiguam, terminos ad discernendum huiusmodi terras positos avellere nititur, et de facto, obscurandorum huiusmodi finium causa, terminos positos[o] tollit ex toto.[p] Unde talis si hoc dolo[q] male fecerit per legem agrariam[39] debet puniri pena capitis. Quanto magis de iure canonico debet excommunicari, et certe multo magis, quia in hoc peccat mortaliter.[r] Item rustici confidunt in auguriis et garritu avium, et ea sequ<u>ntur.[s] Item confidunt in quibusdam malis[t] sortibus[u] et supersticionibus quas vetule plurime tenent et faciunt, et sic deviant a recta et vera fide, et male sunt credentes.

a. xli. Circa mulieres coniugatas, et eciam viduas necnon alias corruptas.

Expedias te sic circa istas[v] tu confessor[w] inquirendo. Primo[x] si use fuerint superfluo, pomposo, monstruoso et inordinato apparatu capitum suorum, quia cornute et monstruose incedunt, quod est species superbie. Item si non obedierint maritis suis tanquam dominis, debitam reverenciam et subieccionem in domo, in mensa et in lecto exhibendo, quia multe

k　illud: illos *H*
l　scilicet *om. H*
m　alii detrahit: aliis detrahunt *H*
n　falsa de eo: fallendo eos *H*
o　terras [. . .] positos *om. H*
p　tollit ex toto: et ex toto tollit *H*
q　unde talis si hoc: unde si talis *H*
r　*add.* et tenetur accione finium regundorum que ipsum infamant [*sic*] *H*

s　item [. . .] sequ<u>ntur *om. H*
t　*notatur altera manu in margine C ad v.* malis: alias aliis
u　Item [. . .] sortibus: item confundunt in aliis sordibus *H*
v　circa istas *om. H*
w　*add.* contra istos [*sic*] *H*
x　*add.* sic *H*

37　C. 11 q. 3 c. 72, Friedberg, I, 663.
38　See Hostiensis, *loc. cit.*, col. 1425.
39　Digest 47.21.3. *ed. cit.*, II, 792.

excommunication automatically. Moreover, a rich villein strives to sin in larger matters and is less afraid to sin than a noble, led by a regulated instinct as the latter is. Of such a rich man it is said: 'A rich culprit fears [sc. to commit] no fault which he thinks he can redeem with money.' Accordingly, such rich people are said to be unfortunate, in keeping with that sentiment of the verse:

> To dispose of wealth (that is, badly) is a thing at odds with health
> Believe few blest who have a treasure chest.

Item, villeins often deceitfully accuse their neighbours to their lords and their bailiffs of fictitious crimes and defaults and so they are harassed unjustly and lose their goods. Item, each villein envies the other; scarcely one good word will he say of him, unless bribed to do so, and each detracts the other, mendaciously telling falsehoods of him. Item, each villein strives to tear up the boundary marks placed to distinguish lands, stealing the land of his neighbour next to his own land, and, in order de facto to obscure the boundaries in question, wholly removes the boundary marks placed. Accordingly, such a one, if he has done this wicked deed with malice aforethought, ought by the Agrarian Law to be punished with death. How much more ought he to be excommunicated by canon law, and certainly much more, because in this he sins mortally? Item, villeins trust in certain wicked casting of lots and superstitions which very many old women hold and practise, and so they stray from right and true faith and are ill believing.

a. xli. Concerning married women and also widows and other sexually-experienced women

Proceed briskly as regards these, confessor, inquiring in the following fashion: first, if they have worn extravagant, vainglorious, outlandish and inordinate apparel on their heads, because they go about wearing horns[3] and looking outlandish, which is a category of pride. Item, if they have not obeyed their husbands, as being their lords, manifesting due reverence and subjection in home, at board and in bed, because many women despise their husbands

---

3 The reference is to the pointed hats of medieval fashion.

contempnunt maritos suos, et ab eis recedunt, seorsum commorando. Et multe
volunt dominari que tamen debent subesse, et sic reddunt se inobedientes.
Item si fucaverint[y] facies suas ipsas unguendo collinirio vel unguento, ita
quod rubicundiores vel candidiores hominibus appareant. Talis enim unccio
5   dicitur adulterina fallacia,[z] qua[a] frequenter tam mariti quam alii[b] decipiuntur,
et ad deserviendum[c] demonibus adhibetur, et sic falsi crimen committunt et
de hiis sic scribitur versus:

Si vicium frontis alienus fucus inauret,
10   Gloria frontis obit, cum color hospes abit.

Item si induxerint[d] maritos suos seu amasios vel amatores suos inhonestos[e]
ad vendendum bona sua pro apparatu huiusmodi pomposo sibi inveniendo,
et sic ad paupertatem nimiam eos deduxerunt et bona eorum non absque dolo
15   consumunt, et sic dolum et quasi /[fol. 22rW] rapinam committunt. Item si
unquam /[fol. 33rH] dederit amasio suo inhonesto[f] aliqua bona mariti sui,
occasione peccati secum commissi vel committendi, prout plereque[g] magne
domine et maxime burgenses[h] consueverunt, quia sic dando, furtum
committunt. Item econtra si ipsa receperit unquam ab aliquo inhonesto
20   amatore suo aliquod donum pro peccato secum commisso, vel committendo,
quia in utroque casu tenetur /[fol. 26vC] mulier furtive donans vel inhoneste
recipiens ad restitucionem faciendam tam donatorum quam receptorum,
prout hoc infra dicetur suo loco.[i] Et hoc quod hic dicitur de muliere adultera
seu alia meretrice ex turpi causa donante[j] seu dona recipiente debet[k] intelligi et
25   dici de quocunque adultero[l] et fornicatore, ex huiusmodi causa turpi donante
seu recipiente, quia isti non iudicantur ad imparia in casu isto. Item inquiras de
adulterio, de incestu, de fornicacione et eorum circumstanciis, ut supra
scribitur. Item inquiras si unquam fuerit pronuba vel si permiserit aliquos[m]
scienter simul commiscere in aliquo loco ubi potuit eos impedivisse, si
30   voluisset. Item inquiras si coniugata unquam concepit[n] filium vel filiam in
adulterio et si filius[o] sic susceptus successit in hereditate vel succedere
deberet[p] patris sui putativi, et sic verus heres exheredatur; quo casu vix salvari
poterit, nisi hereditatem vero heredi restitui fecerit, vel eciam vere penituerit,
prout infra scribitur suo loco. Item an unquam[q] oppresserit proprium filium

[y] fucaverint: sulcaverint *H*
[z] adulterina fallacia *per emendationem ordinis verborum C*
[a] qua: quia *H*
[b] tam mariti quam alii: illi *H*
[c] deserviendum: serviendum *H*
[d] induxerint: induxerunt *W*
[e] inhonestos *om. W*
[f] inhonesto: inhoneste *H*
[g] plereque: plerumque *H*
[h] *add.* facere *H*
[i] dicetur suo loco: scribitur in loco suo *H*
[j] donante: donatura *H*
[k] debent *C W*
[l] adultero: adulterio *W*
[m] aliquos: alios *H*
[n] concepit: conciperit *[sic] H*
[o] filius *om. H*
[p] deberet *om. W*
[q] unquam: nunquam *C*

and withdraw from them, dwelling apart. And many women want to dominate, though they ought to be subject, and so they render themselves disobedient. Item, if they have painted their faces, greasing them with cosmetic or unguent, so that they may appear ruddier or paler to men. That sort of greasing is called adulterous trickery, and by it often both husbands and other men are taken in, and it is applied to the service of demons, and so they commit the crime of fraud and of them this verse is written:

> If the face's flaw is gilt with paint on loan
> The face's brightness dies when the visiting colour's gone.

Item, if they have induced their husbands or sweethearts or disreputable lovers to sell their goods in order to find the means for them of this vainglorious apparel and thus they brought them to an extreme of poverty; and they consume their goods, not without guile; and so they commit guile and as one might say rapine. Item, if she has ever given her disreputable sweetheart any goods of her husband, by occasion of sin committed or to be committed with her, as a good many great ladies and especially burgesses are accustomed to do, because by so giving she commits theft. Item, conversely, if she herself has ever received any gift from her disreputable lover for sin committed or to be committed with him – because in either case, the woman furtively gifting or dishonourably receiving is obliged to make restitution both of gifts and of receipts, as this matter will be declared below in due course.[4] And this statement here concerning the adulterous woman or other harlot gifting or receiving from shameful cause ought to be understood and made concerning any male adulterer and fornicator, gifting or receiving from a similar shameful cause, because they are not judged by different standards in this case. Item, inquire concerning adultery, incest, fornication and their circumstances, as is written above.[5] Item, inquire if she has ever been a bawd or if she has knowingly permitted any to commingle in any place where she could have stopped them, had she wished. Item, inquire if a married woman ever conceived a son or daughter in adultery and if the son, thus acknowledged, succeeded or stood to succeed in the inheritance of his putative father, and thus a true heir was disinherited; in which case she could scarcely be saved, unless she were to cause the inheritance to be restored to the true heir or at least[6] truly repent, as is written below in due course. Item, if she has ever

---

4   The author refers to treatment of the topic in the section on restitution, later in the treatise.
5   The reference is to earlier treatment of the circumstances of action.
6   literally 'also': but this is imperfect sense.

suum vel eciam[r] aliquem de die vel de nocte, et an hoc fecerit[s] ignoranter vel
scienter. Item an unquam exposuit filium suum – hoc est, quando fatue
mulieres ponunt filios suos in ecclesia vel extra et eos relinqu<u>nt sine
custodia, et /[fol. 26vbC] tales expositi in anglico[t] vocantur 'fundlinges'.[u] Item
si unquam potabat vel aliis dederit ad potandum aliquas potaciones vel[v]
succum[w] herbarum ne possit concipere ab aliquo, vel dedit aut potabat ad
faciendum aborsum, hoc est ad interficiendum[x] fetum vel conceptum in utero,
quia forsan latenter concepit, de dampnato[y] coitu, et in isto casu caute debes
inquirere an partus fuerit vivificatus in ventre an non, quia secundum hoc
moderanda /[fol. 33vH] erit[z] penitencia infligenda.[a] Item inquiras de
sortilegiis et de incantacionibus quibus mulieres male credentes[b] uti varie
consueverunt.[c] Item inquiras de ypocrisi quia plereque mulieres simulant[d] se
esse sanctas, simplices et[e] Deo et sanctis suis devotas, plurimum[f] ecclesias
frequentando et orando et ieiunando, et tamen interius demonio sunt plene,
odia, invidias et iracundias sectantes, aliis maledicentes et detrahentes, et alia
peccata infinita committentes. Item si aliquando contraxerit clandestine
matrimonium cum aliquo per verba de presenti, eciam carnali copula non
subsecuta, vel eciam contraxerit per verba de futuro,[g] carnali copula
subsecuta, et postea de facto clam vel palam contraxerit cum alio. Item si
permiserit se post huiusmodi contractum cognosci carnaliter ab aliquo, sic
adulterando. Item si contraxerit sponsalia cum aliquo et postea contraxit
matrimonium cum aliquo,[h] fidem /[fol. 27rC] suam primo sponso datam
absque causa legitima violando. De periuriis, de blasphemia, rixis, /[fol.
22vW] contencionibus, diffamacionibus et aliis peccatis poteris et debebis
inquirere, prout condicio persone tibi confitentis exigerit inquirendum.

---

[r]　vel eciam: an *H*
[s]　hoc fecerit: fecit *H*
[t]　anglico: anglice *H*
[u]　fundlinges: foundlynges *W*; fundelyng
　　H
[v]　vel: sive *W*
[w]　succum: succos *H*
[x]　aborsum [. . .] interficiendum *om. H*
[y]　dampnato: dampnatu *W H*
[z]　erit: est *H*

[a]　infligenda: iniungenda *H*
[b]　credentes: credunt *H*
[c]　uti varie consueverunt: et varie hiis
　　diebus *H*
[d]　simulant: similant *W*
[e]　et *om. W*
[f]　plurimum: plurimas *H*
[g]　eciam [. . .] futuro *om. H*
[h]　et postea [. . .] cum aliquo: et postea
　　[. . .] cum alio *W*; *om. H*

overlain her own child or anyone, for that matter, by day or night, and whether she did this unknowingly or knowingly. Item, whether she ever exposed her own child – that is when foolish women place their children in a church or outside it and leave them without anyone to look after them, and children exposed in that way are in English called 'foundlings'. Item, if she ever drank or gave others to drink any draughts or juice of herbs so that they should be unable to conceive by anyone, or gave or drank to induce abortion – this is to kill the foetus or that conceived in the womb – because perhaps she conceived surreptitiously, of prohibited union, and in that case you ought circumspectly to inquire whether the foetus was quickened in the womb or not, because in accordance with this will be adjusted the penance to be inflicted. Item, inquire about sorceries and charms which ill-believing women are variously wont to employ. Item, inquire about hypocrisy, because a good many women pretend that they are holy, simple and devoted to God and his saints, greatly frequenting churches and praying and fasting, and yet inwardly they are full of the demon, the eager attendants of hatreds, envies and wraths, reviling and detracting others and committing infinite other sins. Item, if she has ever contracted marriage with anyone by words of present consent, even if carnal union did not ensue, or has contracted by words of future consent, with subsequent carnal union, and afterwards, de facto, has contracted secretly or openly with another. Item, if she has allowed herself, after such contract, to be carnally known by anyone, thus committing adultery. Item, if she has contracted espousals with anyone and afterwards contracted marriage with anyone [sc. else], violating without lawful cause her faith given to the first partner. You could and should inquire concerning perjuries, blasphemy, brawls, contentions, defamations and other sins, according as the condition of the person confessing to you may dictate inquiry.

a. xlii. Circa pueros. Rubrica.[40]

Scire debes tu confessor quod si puer fuerit doli capax,[i] proximus pubertati,
5   tenetur omnia peccata sua confiteri saltem semel in anno. Inquiras ergo[j] ab
eodem si unquam commiserit sacrilegium, res sacras vel non sacras ab[k]
ecclesia auferendo, vel si furtum fecerit in rebus parentum suorum vel
extraneorum, secundum quod faciunt plures, tam garbas decimatas quam
alias furando in autumpno. Item si fuerit ingratus erga suos parentes, ipsos
10 probris afficiendo seu contumeliis ipsis improperando seu maledicendo, seu
ipsis debitam reverenciam non exhibendo. Item si blasphemus fuerit, iurando
incaute de consuetudine per singula membra Christi. Item si adulterium,
fornicacionem vel incestum commiserit.[l] Intelligas tamen[m] tu confessor quod
micius erit agendum in penitenciis infligendis[n] cum tali puero delinquente,
15 propter etatis sue fragilitatem, quam cum sene, et maxime quando delinquitur
circa carnis[o] lapsum, quia in sene calores naturales tamquam frigidi et quasi
consumpti extingu<u>ntur, set in iuvene exardescunt. Unde de hiis /[fol.
27rbC] scribitur sic:[P]

20   Militat in teneris amor velud hospes amenus,
              Et in canicie ridiculosa Venus.

---

[i] puer fuerit doli capax *om. H*
[j] ergo: igitur *H*
[k] ab: de *W*
[l] *add.* item *H*

[m] tamen *om. H*
[n] infligendis: affligendis *H*
[o] circa carnis: contra carnalem *H*
[P] *add.* versus *W*

[40] The section is based on Hostiensis, *op. cit.*, art. 43, col. 1425, to whose outline
interrogatory the author of the *Memoriale presbiterorum* adds the introductory
comment and the following elaborations: lines 6–7: 'res sacras . . . auferendo'; lines
7–9: 'in rebus . . . autumpno'; lines 9–12: 'erga . . . Christi'; line 13: 'vel incestum'; lines
15–21: 'propter etatis . . . Venus'.

a. xlii. Concerning children

You ought to know, confessor, that if a child be capable of wrongdoing, near to puberty, he[7] is obliged to confess all his sins at least once a year. Inquire therefore from the same if he has ever committed sacrilege, abstracting from a church things sacred or non-sacred, or if he has committed theft as regards the property of his parents or of outsiders, in the way that many do, in autumn stealing sheaves, as well tithed as others. Item, if he has been ungrateful towards his parents, behaving insolently towards them or heaping contumelies on or reviling them, or not showing them due reverence. Item, if he has been blasphemous, rashly and habitually swearing by all the limbs of Christ. Item, if he has committed adultery, fornication or incest. Understand, however, confessor, that one should act more leniently, in the infliction of penances, with such a delinquent child, on account of the vulnerability of his age, than with an old person, and especially when the sin is sexual, because in an old person the natural heats are dying out as it were of cold and exhaustion but in a young person they are aflame. Accordingly, of these is written as follows:

> Cupid in the tender ranks a pleasant guest
> While Venus in the grey-haired is the butt of jest.

---

7   The remarks under this head are not, in Latin, gender specific.

Confessors' Manuals and the Avoiding of Offspring[1]

Peter Biller

In 1962 Pierre Michaud-Quantin published a useful general survey of *summae* of cases and confessors' manuals written between the twelfth and the sixteenth centuries.[2] Among the shorter manuals, two to which he gave special attention were written around 1300, the *Confessionale* of John of Freiburg and a work of less certain authorship which is usually known by its opening words, *In primis debet sacerdos*. Before looking at avoidance of conception in these two manuals, let me outline my aim in this investigation and comment on the most important modern account of medieval avoidance of offspring.

I am (a) asking questions about people in the past trying to avoid offspring, and looking at pastoral literature as possible evidence for this theme. I argue (b) that pastoral concern with particular sins varied. This variation came in part from their pastoral expertise about trends in people sinning – from their observation that a particular sin was being committtted more than it had been. I am, therefore, (c) examining the texts written by pastoral experts, looking for traces in these texts of people sinning in their efforts to avoid offspring. More specifically, the ups and downs of pastoral concern in these texts – less or more concern at different times, or in different regions of Europe – may have had some rough correlation with the degree to which people *in fact* tried to avoid offspring: more at some periods or in some places, less at other times or in other regions. If indeed their behaviour has left such a *varying* deposit in these pastoral texts, the latter become valuable evidence for the demographic historian.

The most useful guide to these themes is a book we have now had for over thirty years, the fundamental history of the Catholic Church's theological and canon-legal teaching on contraception which was written by John Noonan.[3]

---

[1] When describing the thoughts and actions of medieval people in this chapter, I am using 'avoiding of offspring', which translates the medieval Latin phrase *vitatio prolis*, to avoid the anachronism of words and concepts which may accompany the use of such words as 'contraception' and 'birth-control'.

[2] Michaud-Quantin, *Sommes*.

[3] J. T. Noonan Jr., *Contraception. A History of Its Treatment by the Catholic Theologians and Canonists* (Cambridge, Mass., 1966). Among modern work, see J. W. Baldwin, *The Language of Sex. Five Voices from Northern France around 1200* (Chicago, 1994), pp.

There are three problems about Noonan's account of avoiding offspring in the Middle Ages – and if these have to be recapitulated here, I hope that the reader does not forget my praise of Noonan. The first flaw is that Noonan's Middle Ages were dominated by a challenge-and-response theory, manifested in heretical (Cathar) hostility to procreation and their practice of contraception, and Church response to this. Antecedent to this lay the preoccupation of the period during and after the second Vatican Council, when the past historical variability of the Church's teaching on birth-control was important for anyone trying to scrutinise the validity of the modern Catholic Church's ban.

Now, however colourful the Cathars, they were never a majority in any region, not even in Languedoc. Occupying centre-stage in Noonan's account, they drove off it the people who should have been there. These were the vast majority of people, ordinary Catholic Christians. Of course Noonan did not entirely ignore them. What is at issue, however, is the primacy of his focus on a small heretical minority. Clearly more important were the marriages of ordinary Christians and the extraordinary development in the eleventh to thirteenth centuries of the Church's ceremonial, legal and penitential framework for these marriages. This development is the principal intelligible context for the Church's teaching on 'contraception', and it is the sins of these millions of ordinary Christians which were principally in the eyes of the Church's pastoral experts.

A second problem is not Noonan's fault – his theme was contraception, not contraception and abortion. Abortion crops up in his book, of course, and so the inattentive reader may be misled into thinking that the proportion of attention Noonan paid to the two topics (viz. much less to abortion) parallels the proportion of attention which medieval texts paid to them. Most of the time, in fact, the opposite prevailed – usually medieval texts paid more attention to abortion.

A third problem lay in the Church texts which Noonan used. With massive erudition Noonan presented many of the relevant theological and canon-legal sources from the central and later Middle Ages. They are numerous, varied and overlapping. The topics which *may* bear upon avoidance of conception – such as the Augustinian marriage-good (offspring), the purpose of the sexual act, and so-called unnatural forms of sex – are to be found variously and ubiquitously in most of these sources. Faced with all this, how are we to set the texts into some sort of relation with the sins of past, ordinary Christians? And how are we to pick out significant threads? The strength or weakness, presence or absence of a particular topic may be mainly to do with the complex inter-relations of these texts: mainly a textual matter. How are we to discern

214–16, and J. M. Riddle, *Contraception and Abortion from the Ancient World to the Renaissance* (Cambridge, Mass., 1992), an uncritical account which has nevertheless performed an important job in drawing attention to the problem of the effectiveness of herbal methods. J. M. Riddle's *Eve's Herbs. A History of Contraception and Abortion in the West* (Cambridge, Mass., 1997) was not available to me at the time of writing. For the earlier Middle Ages, see n. 77 below.

developments in these texts which may represent shifts in pastoral observation of sins – and patterns of sinning – among ordinary Catholic Christians?

What can we do? Well, we can see the evidence – records of marriage courts, canon law, quodlibets on marriage-cases from later thirteenth century Paris, marriage sections of commentaries on the *Sentences*, and so on – as the archaeological-textual remains of a system which involved the Church and the marriages and sins of these ordinary Catholic Christians, and we can sort out these remains into various strata. Having done this, we can mount an enquiry in which we exercise control by carefully selecting and sticking to one narrowly defined seam of texts, and within that seam, one topic only.

We begin with people's efforts to avoid offspring. *Then* these actions may have been as much hidden and in the dark as they have been in most periods of history because they were regarded as illicit or felt to be shameful. Given such secrecy at the time and the general scarcity of evidence about many ordinary matters of daily life in the Middle Ages, we might despair. What hope have we got? Surely this – of all areas of human activity – is the furthest from the historian's grasp? Perhaps. But a woman or man told a parish priest or mendicant secrets when confessing – their sins – and some of these were sexual, some specifically to do with avoiding offspring. Behind the priest hearing confession were the bishops' penitentiaries who received and dealt with complicated sins, and others who talked about sin: discussion of trends in sin was presumably obsessive for the professionals, pastoral experts gathered at a synod of the diocese, or in a convent among those mendicants who specialised in preaching and hearing confessions. Behind the priest were the experts who occasionally got down to writing a guide, a confessors' manual, advising priests how to deal with the penitents who came to them to confess. Further off in the background lay treatment of these themes in theology and canon law faculties in universities, and reading and commenting upon those sections in the *Sentences* or compilations of canon law which dealt with these sins.

We can see the general interrelations of these areas of activity, thought and writing, and also survey the patchy survival of texts which preserve some sort of deposit from any one of them. Thus, on the one hand I know no texts that preserve the conversations I conjectured in the previous paragraph, while on the other the textual remains of reading and commenting upon the *Sentences* are enormous. What of the meeting-point of individual confessing penitent and priest? Well, Alexander Murray has demonstrated wonderfully how priests' experiences of individual confessions supplied material for tales in thirteenth-century *exempla* collections, and how these tales can be used – in reverse, as it were – to get back into these past secrets.[4] *Exempla* can bear upon our theme quite closely – well-known is Caesar of Heisterbach's story about two Rhineland peasants, questioned by their parish-priest about making love

---

4   Murray, 'Confession'.

to their wives during Lent[5] – but unfortunately they do not do so often enough for our purposes. The evidence which both survives well and bears most closely upon our theme is that found in confessors' instruction manuals.

The instructional material which could be surveyed is vast, and here I propose to control it, and to try to discern significant developments, by restricting it in two ways. First, I intend to look only at avoidance of offspring. 'Only': that is to say, I am only looking at those confessional interrogations or descriptions where it is explicitly spelled out that avoiding offspring is the intention of specific medical or physical actions. This means the exclusion of confessional material which does r ɔt talk directly about avoidance and only analyses the purpose of contracting marriage, or the purpose of the sexual act in marriage, or the naturalness or unnaturalness of certain acts. Such discussions may all have some sort of relevance or connection, insofar as they hint at or suggest avoidance of offspring or mention acts which inevitably preclude generation. However, there are advantages in excluding them. In one topic which crops up, 'unnatural acts', avoidance of generation may be no more than an inadvertent consequence, not in sinners' minds at all. Talk about positive 'purposes' of sex in marriage may well *hint* at the opposite, but it is nevertheless self-evidently weaker evidence than explicit statements about avoidance. But, beyond these considerations, there is the desirability of having contours on a map. The nearly universal presence of the *indirectly* relevant topics leaves any modern map of pastoral literature grey and undifferentiated: but if we trace on it only the presence and absence of direct treatment of avoidance of offspring we may be able to see a contour.

Secondly, I only look at those works of instruction which are common or garden texts, 'confessors' manuals'. These are those very short and simple works which were intended for the common-run of mendicant friars and parish priests, the how-to-do-it guides whose small physical size also meant that they were cheap, and could fit into their users' hands and pockets. This means excluding large and expensive penitential works like Raymond of Peñafort's *Summa de poenitentia* (1234), John of Freiburg's *Summa confessorum* (1298), and the enormous Italian *summae* of cases of the fourteenth century and later. The contents of these were for the learned, and their size and expense meant that their place and role was to be chained up in libraries to be consulted for the rarer and more canon-legally complex matters.[6] The idea behind this is simple. It is that that the presence or absence of instruction to question on some theme, when observed in common booklets which were intended for the ordinary priest, may be significant guides to general pastoral facts: pastors' concern with Christians' common-or-garden sins, and perhaps the greater or

---

5   Caesar, *Dialogus*, III.xl, I, pp. 160–1; discussed in P. Biller, 'The Common Woman in the Western Church in the Thirteenth and Early Fourteenth Centuries', in *Women in the Church*, ed. W. J. Sheils and D. Wood, SCH 27 (1990), 127–57 (p. 134).

6   The contrast between the short manuals and the long *summae* is discussed in Michaud-Quantin, *Sommes*, pp. 9–10; on the academic character of the long *summae*, see Boyle, '*Summa confessorum*', especially pp. 235–6.

lesser prevalence of these sins at different periods or in different areas of Christendom.

I begin, then, with two texts from around 1300 – one very, and the other fairly, little and common. First I look at what these texts contain explicitly about avoidance of offspring. Then I ask what contemporary sectors of thought about avoidance of offspring hover in the background – independently of the pastoral material, or possibly converging with it. Finally I ask what is shown when such little books are looked at regionally, and over long periods of time.

1. The Two Manuals

John of Freiburg's *Confessionale* has an interrogatory directed 'to those who are married', *Ad coniugatos*, and its last question is this:

> Item, if the woman has brought about some impediment to avoid conceiving; and the same question concerning the man; and if she has procured an abortion. (Item, si mulier aliquod impedimentum fecit ne conciperet; et idem de viro; vel si aborsum procuravit.)[7]

The *In primis debet sacerdos* begins with a short manual for confession, and whereas estate interrogatories dominate John's manual, here it is the ten commandments and the seven deadly sins which are to the fore. The questions come under the sixth commandment, 'Thou shalt not kill', and abortion leads the way.

> The confessor should ask therefore . . . whether she/or he has brought about the loss of the foetus, or taught how it should be killed, or acted in some other way in order not to conceive. Because women who have many children, more than they want, do not pay the debt and guard themselves from their husbands. Item, they do worse than this, because after their husbands have made use of them, they rise up or move around in another way in order not to conceive. Therefore there should be careful questioning of them, whether they do anything to avoid conceiving, either before or after carnal intercourse, or whether they have taken some potion of herbs or of some other thing for the same reason. (Querat igitur . . . si conceptum mulieris perdidit, vel occidi docuit vel aliquo modo quod non conciperet. Et quia mulieres habentes [sic] multos filios, plures quam vellent, non reddant debitum et deffendunt se a maritis. Item, faciunt peius, quia postquam cum eis viri usi fuerint, surgunt vel aliter se movent ne concipiant. Unde caute queratur ab eis, si faciunt aliquid ne concipiant, sive ante carnalem

---

7 Oxford, Bodleian Library, MS Laud. Misc. 278, fol. 361va; checked against Paris, Bibliothèque Nationale, MS Lat. 3532, fol. 393a.

copulam sive postea, vel si sumpserint aliquam potionem herbarum, vel alicuius alterius rei, propter illam causam.)[8]

A few words first about the author of the *Confessionale*, John.[9] He was born in Freiburg-im-Breisgau around the mid-thirteenth century, joined the Dominicans in Freiburg, and studied in Strasbourg before 1272 and perhaps in Paris. He spent most of the rest of his life, as far as we know, in the Dominican convent in Freiburg, dying perhaps in 1314. At the convent he had become lector in 1280, giving lectures to Dominicans in the convent and local clergy if they wanted to attend. His writings are almost entirely on confession, and they fall into two groups. One group is essentially an extension to the very large canon-legal text on penance and marriage which had been composed by Raymond of Peñafort (second recension 1234)[10] and then glossed in the mid-thirteenth century by William of Rennes.[11] John composed an index and an addition to these,[12] and then, finally, in 1297–98, a *Summa confessorum*[13] which broadly incorporates Raymond and William as well as commenting upon them and adding to them. This is a work familiar to many readers not only through its easy availability in printed form but also through its use by modern historians of confession, such as Thomas Tentler,[14] and the magnificent analysis of its sources by Leonard Boyle.[15] The second group consists of a *Manuale confessorum*[16] (which is not discussed in this paper) and the *Confessionale*, which was quoted above; its cross-references to the *Summa confessorum* of 1298 presumably indicate a slightly later date of composition.

In the *Summa confessorum* John embraced the expansion of learned theology and canon law of the mid-thirteenth century, and in so doing produced a work of about 120,000 words, which is still extant wholly or in part in 176 manuscripts.[17] It is likely that many of these and the other now-lost earlier manuscripts, in which the *Summa confessorum* was copied and diffused, did not differ greatly in their essential characteristics from the early printed editions which modern scholars usually consult: large in size, very expensive, and

---

8   Paris, Bibliothèque Nationale, MS Lat. 3265, fol. 36v.
9   Michaud-Quantin, *Sommes*, pp. 43–4; L. E. Boyle, 'The *Summa confessorum* of John of Freiburg and the popularisation of the moral teaching of St Thomas and some of his contemporaries', Boyle, *Pastoral Care*, III, 246–7; *SOPMA* II, 428, and IV, 151.
10 Michaud-Quantin (*Sommes*, p. 34) gives 1220–21 for the first recension, while *SOPMA* (III, 285) gives 1224–26.
11 Around 1240–45, according to Michaud-Quantin, *Sommes*, pp. 40–1; around 1241 according to *SOPMA*, II, 156.
12 Boyle, *Pastoral Care*, III, pp. 247–8; *SOPMA* II, 428–9.
13 Michaud-Quantin, *Sommes*, pp. 44–8; Boyle, *Pastoral Care*, III; and '*Summae confessorum*', pp. 236–7; *SOPMA* II, 430–3.
14 Tentler, *Sin*.
15 Principally in Boyle, *Pastoral Care*, II–III.
16 Michaud-Quantin, *Sommes*, p. 44; Boyle, '*Summa confessorum*', p. 237 and note 13.
17 *SOPMA* II, 430–3, and IV, 151–2.

located in a library. The *Confessionale*,[18] by contrast, takes up less than 20,000 words. One hundred and sixty-four manuscripts[19] of it are still extant – and we may conjecture that its lesser size and cost than the *Summa confessorum* have led to greater losses, that is, that its 164 manuscripts are a much smaller proportion of the medieval copies that once circulated than are the 176 manuscripts of the *Summa confessorum*. An idea of the characteristics of these extant and lost copies of the *Confessionale* may be given by Munich, Bayerische Staatsbibliothek, MS CLM 28427.[20] This is 21 by 15 centimetres in size, and contains the *Confessionale* in the first thirty leaves, and a few confessional formulae and two letters of penance from the diocese of Augsburg in the final four leaves: a small, easily portable and relatively inexpensive book intended for use in the administration of confession and penance. Even more portable would have been a copy now in Trier, which measures 9.5 by 13.3 centimetres.[21]

In writing such contrasting texts John puts himself forward as a writer making deliberate choices, for two different audiences. John opens the *Confessionale* with words which introduce himself as an author with one audience in mind, 'Desiring to instruct the simpler and less expert confessors about the way to hear confessions' (Simpliciores et minus expertos confessores de modo audiendi confessiones informare cupiens).[22] As we shall see, the author of *In primis debet* wrote, as he said, for 'priests who have no knowledge [about confession]'.[23] Formulaic though these phrases may be, there is a useful appproximation between what they suggest and our modern phrase 'idiot guides'.

Where there is a pair of opposites in John's picture of two sets of readers – the *periti*, the learned, who read the *Summa confessorum*, and the *inperiti*, the simple, who read the idiot-guide called the *Confessionale* – there is also a pair of opposites in the selection or non-selection of contents. On the one hand, material in the large *Summae* of Raymond and John was unselective: it reflected the comprehensiveness of law which tried to cover all possible eventualities, regardless of rarity. When 'rare and difficult problems come up', writes John, the confessor who has the *Confessionale* needs to go off to the comprehensive texts: 'read [about them]', writes John, 'in the *Summa* of the

---

18 Michaud-Quantin, *Sommes*, pp. 49–50; Boyle, '*Summae confessorum*', p. 237.
19 *SOPMA* II, 433–6, and IV, 152.
20 G. Glaucke, *Cod. Lat. 28255–28460*, in C. Halm *et al.*, *Catalogus codicum manuscriptorum Bibliothecae Regiae Monacensis*, I– (Munich, Wiesbaden, 1868–), IV, part 8, pp. 258–60.
21 M. Keuffer, G. Kentenich *et al.*, *Beschreibendes Verzeichnis der Handschriften der Stadtbibliothek zu Trier*, 10 parts (Trier, 188–1931), V, 27–8, number 564. Another manuscript, Stuttgart, Württembergische Landesbibliothek, MS HB I 60, from Weingarten, contains the *Confessionale* in 66 leaves of a manuscript measuring 21.5 by 15 centimetres, J. Autenrieth *et al.*, *Die Handscriften der ehemaligen Hofbibliothek Stuttgart* (Stuttgart, Wiesbaden, 1963–), I, part 1, 95–6.
22 MS Laud Misc. 278, fol. 354ra.
23 The text is quoted more fully below.

blessed Raymond, in the *Book of Case-questions* and specially and more fully in the *Summa of Confessors'*[24] – the second and third references here being to two of John's own works. On the other hand when writing the *Confessionale* John was like someone writing an exam essay and with a word-limit: he had to select severely and stick to his theme. And the theme is the *more common* sins. This is spelled out straightforwardly and simply in his preamble:

> I have divided this treatise into two parts . . . In the second part, on the questioning which should be done with certain people, [people] of various dignities, estates and occupations, I have given special instruction according to the sins which are more frequently committed by such people. (Hunc autem tractatum in duas partes distinxi . . . Secundo autem de interrogacionibus faciendis circa quasdam personas diversarum dignitatum, statuum et officiorum instructionem specialem tradidi secundum peccata que a talibus frequencius committuntur.)[25]

John opens the second part by repeating this formula, while underlining it by spelling out the contrast with the questions which have just been paraded, in the first part, under the heading of the seven deadly sins:

> After intruction on questioning about those sins which for the most part can be found commonly among men [people][26] of any estate, I have judged it useful to provide some things on the enquiries which should be made about some particular sins which are more frequently committed by people of various dignities, estates and occupations. (Post instructionem de interrogationibus eorum peccatorum que ut plurimum inveniri possunt in hominibus cuiuscunque status communiter, utiliter iudicavi aliqua tradere de inquisitionibus faciendis de aliquibus peccatis specialibus que a quibusdam personis diversarum dignitatum, statuum et officiorum frequencius committuntur.)[27]

As we then read John listing clergy and religious, judges, lawyers, doctors, teachers, nobles and so on and ascribing typical sins to them, we can see someone who is looking in several directions. He is looking at an existing tradition of such estates lists.[28] He is looking backwards to the large, learned and unselective *summae*, to which he provides handy cross-references. Finally, he is looking towards his contemporary world in and near Freiburg, the other friars and clergy whom he taught and for whom he wrote, and beyond them to

---

[24] '. . . erga rara et dubia, cum occurrerint, lege in summa fratris Raymundi et in libello questionum casualium, specialiter autem et plenius in summa confessorum'; MS Laud Misc. 278, fol. 354ra.

[25] MS Laud Misc. 278, fol. 354ra.

[26] 'Men' (*homines*) is intended here to cover both sexes.

[27] MS Laud Misc. 278, fol. 358va.

[28] See Haren, 'Social Ideas' on estates lists, and p. 55, on the *Confessionale*; see also in this volume, chapter 6 above, pp. 110–11.

the German-speaking men and women of whose more frequent sins he was trying to provide a brief 'sociography'. Thus, John writes, under the questions to be put to 'peasants and farmers', such a person should be asked, 'whether he has moved [*or* altered] field-boundaries, which in German are called "Markstein" '.[29] A pub-landlord (*tabernarius*) is to be asked about misleading customers about wine, selling wine purporting to come from one country or estate when in fact it came from another.[30]

Writing for Latin-reading priests who are going to interrogate ordinary people in German, John occasionally intrudes a vernacular word into his Latin text. Notably, when John came to formulating a question under 'Lechery' about 'inordinate' forms of sex with women ('Did you have any inordinate gestures [*or* motions] with women?') he decided to provide it both in Latin and the vernacular. 'Habuisti aliquos gestus inordinatos cum mulieribus? Teutonice, hetest du iede heme geberde mit vrowen die niht zimelich waren?'[31] It is the only time in the *Confessionale* that John writes the whole question in both tongues: very clear are the simple practicality and directness both of John's pastoral observation and his prescriptions for confessors who talked to couples about sex.

Less can firmly be said about the origin of *In primis debet sacerdos.*[32] Michaud-Quantin dates it at the end of the thirteenth century.[33] The majority of the extant manuscripts do not attribute it to an author, while there are also a few with clearly wrong attributions, and some with a quite plausible attribution – to Bérenger Frédol the Older. Bérenger, who originated in the Montpellier region, studied in Paris and Bologna, where he became a noted canon lawyer; he was bishop of Béziers (1294–1305) and from 1305 cardinal and grand penitentiary in Avignon, dying in 1323.[34] While seeing no conclusive argument for Bérenger's authorship, Michaud-Quantin regards it as very probable.[35]

---

29 'Ad rusticos et agricolas . . . si mutavit terminos agrorum, qui dicuntur teutonice Markstein'; MS Laud Misc. 278, fol. 362va. In the photographic reproduction of this manuscript which I am using, *mutavit* appears to have been written *mutitavit*, with *it* partly erased.

30 MS Laud Misc. 278, fol. 362rb.

31 MS Laud Misc. 278, fol. 355ra. *Geberde* is preceded in the manuscript by *geb* whjich appears, in the photographic reproduction I am using, to be partly erased. Cf. Paris, Bibliothèque Nationale, MS Lat. 3532, fol. 367ra: 'Teuthonice, hattest du iede heme geberde mit vrowen die niht zimelich wearen'. *Inordinatos gestus* is a hold-all question, which could embrace positions and the question of 'unnaturalness' per se, but, given John's preoccupation with avoidance of offspring, withdrawal to avoid conception was probably the principal concern.

32 Michaud-Quantin, *Sommes*, pp. 50–1, and 'La "Summula in foro poenitentiali" ', *Studia Gratiana* 11 (1967), 145–67.

33 Michaud-Quantin, 'Summula in foro poenitentiali', p. 162.

34 P. Viollet, 'Bérenger Frédol, canoniste', *Histoire littéraire de la France* 34 (1914), 62–178. He appears often in B. Guillemain's *La cour pontificale d'Avignon, 1309–1376. Étude d'une société* (Paris, 1966).

35 Michaud-Quantin, 'Summula', p. 164.

The author of *In primis debet sacerdos* was writing a fairly short *summula*, and, as already mentioned, like John he was intending an idiot guide. This is made abundantly clear in the (paradoxically long) title: 'Short and useful little summa for the forum of penance, and very useful to priests, especially those who have no knowledge in this area' (Summula in foro poenitentiali brevis et utilis valdeque necessaria sacerdotibus, maxime super hoc notitiam non habentibus).[36] The work acquired wide diffusion, though not as wide as John's,[37] and Michaud-Quantin's comments on the appearance of the manuscripts (often produced with care, by professional scribes) may indicate a little distance between this work and the commonest and roughest little confessors' manuals.[38] Unlike John the author of *In primis debet sacerdos* did not use an estates list. This means that there is not such a sharp sense in his work of a 'sociography' of sin, although he does show some sign of a pastoral expert's and canonist's interest in such generalisation, in his introduction to summaries of canon law on matrimonial cases and questions in matrimonial matters, where he writes that these are things which occur frequently.[39]

Here then, around 1300, are two idiot-guides for confessors based more or less explicitly on a 'sociography' of sin, that which most commonly occurs: and they are direct and emphatic on avoidance of offspring. In John's case avoidance is not treated as something outside marriage or the married – as a concern of careful fornicators, for example. It is located *among* the married: something which is done by a married woman or a married man to avoid conception, and put alongside (but also distinguished from) abortion. Saturating earlier theological and canon-legal discussions of avoiding conception is a phrase, 'to procure poisons of sterility', *venena sterilitatis procurare*. The popularity of this phrase had rested in part on its use in a key-text by St Augustine, and probably in part on the reality of people's use of herbal potions. Marked, then, in John's text is his avoidance of 'poisons of sterility' and his preference for a phrase using the word 'impediment' (*impedimentum*), 'impediment in order not to conceive'. This is a phrase which seems to be acquiring currency in the late thirteenth century,[40] and it is tempting to speculate that its intrusion and occasional success in toppling St Augustine's phrases came from the pressure of the words and phrases used by ordinary women and men at that time.

What of the author of the *In primis debet sacerdos*? As we saw, his questioning came under a commandment rather than the estate of the married, and this meant that his questions do not necessarily exclude the unmarried or underplay avoidance of conception outside marriage. Now, his material is not specifically shaped by an estates category; that is to say, he is not being

---

36 Michaud-Quantin, 'Summula', p. 149.
37 Michaud-Quantin, 'Summula', pp. 166–7, provides a provisional list of fifty-eight manuscripts.
38 Michaud-Quantin, 'Summula', p. 165.
39 Michaud-Quantin, 'Summula', p. 150.
40 Biller, 'Pastoral geography', pp. 72–3.

encouraged to address a particular estate by what may be, partly, a literary-topical reason rather than by his pastoral experience and – assuming he is Bérenger of Frédol – by his learning and experience specifically as canonist, bishop, and papal penitentiary. The absence of this pressure, then, lends more significance to what we learn through his passing reference to husbands: namely that he is thinking, and perhaps thinking mainly, about avoidance of conception by the married. Like John, the author of the *In primis debet sacerdos* avoids 'poisons of sterility'. Unlike John he provides both a catch-all phrase, 'do something not to conceive', and also a variety of methods. These range from wives repelling their husbands to post-coital movements and the drinking before or after sex of herbal drugs directed against conceiving. He differs from John in placing more emphasis on a wife's actions, and he more than makes up for what his treatise lacks in not having an estates-interrogatory by briefly establishing a distinct group of wives: these are the mothers with many children who do not want any more.

2. Bordering Areas of Contemporary Thought: Generalisation, and Medicine

I would like here to relate avoidance of offspring to two broader and bordering areas of thought around 1300, (i) generalisation and (ii) medicine.

The first concerns the moral generalisation which is presented to us more or less explicitly in these texts. Generalisations of two sorts are going on. There is the mapping of sin according to groups, and the slow emergence of general descriptive statements about groups. If we broaden the theme, briefly, to include abortion, infanticide and fertility, we can see a brief history of different estates and ascribed typical sins in these areas which would include the following milestones. In late twelfth century Paris Peter the Chanter, a member of the minor French nobility of the Beauvaisis, commented on noble girls stifling their offspring.[41] From the twelfth century on many authors, usually living in Paris, commented on low fertility among prostitutes.[42] In the 1280s a

---

[41] Chanter, *Summa*, III(2a), p. 280 (earlier cited in Biller, 'Pastoral Geography', p. 79): 'Some noble girls who stifle their offspring (upon which crime the bishop's advice is required) are so ashamed that in no way are they willing to confess except to some private priest: what should happen?' (Quedam nobiles puelle que suffocant partus suos de quo facinore consilium requiritur episcopi, ita uerecunde sunt quod nullo modo uolunt confiteri nisi alicui priuato sacerdoti, quid fiet?)

[42] The observation and the question – 'Why do prostitutes infrequently conceive?' – seem to go back in western learned literature to William of Conches (ob. after 1154). See D. Jacquart and C. Thomasset, *Sexuality and Medicine in the Middle Ages*, transl. M. Adamson (Oxford, 1988), pp. 25 (on the theme in William of Conches), 64 (Vincent of Beauvais), 81 (Albert the Great); J. Cadden, *Meanings of Sex Difference in the Middle Ages. Medicine, Science and Culture* (Cambridge, 1993), pp. 93–4 (on the theme in a group of twelfth-century anonymous questions, influenced by Wiliam of Conches); Baldwin, *Language of Sex*, pp. 216–17 (on the theme in William of Conches, *The Prose*

bishop of Exeter commented on the sin of pride in glorying in one's offspring, beginning with their large number, and he ascribed this sin to the estate of nobles.[43] John of Freiburg around 1300 is making avoiding conception an ascribed typical sin of the married – using his terms, a sin more frequently committed by members of the estate of the married. By 1330–32, when we get to Alvarus Pelagius, there is the first hint of ascribing one method to members of one particular estate: peasants, *rustici*, avoid conception simply by abstaining.[44]

Alongside this thin but developing strand of generalisation about sin in relation to one particular estate is another strand of a different sort of generalisation. This is the mental leap of placing side by side on the one hand individuals committing sexual sin and on the other hand the human race or 'multitude' (*multitudo*, the preferred term for 'population'), and ultimately the size of this 'multitude'. The sin of sodomy and the related increase or decrease of the human race is a theme in Peter the Chanter,[45] marriage-regime (Christian or Muslim) and the related size of population is a theme in an earlier thirteenth-century treatise on the sacrament of marriage written by William of Auvergne,[46] and Peter was reaching many readers in the later thirteenth and early fourteenth centuries through the adoption and adaptation of his material in the Dominican William Peyraut's *Summa of Vices and Virtues*.[47]

Salernitan Questions, and the fabliau *Richeut*); P. Biller, 'Birth-control in the West in the Thirteenth and Early Fourteenth Centuries', *Past and Present* 94 (1982), 3–26, at p. 18 and n. 64 (on the theme in Vincent of Beauvais and Giles of Rome).

[43] Peter Quinel, *Summula*, 13, *Councils & Synods*, II, 1066: [On Pride and taking pride in natural goods]. Item [taking pride] in nobility, if one is from a great family, [taking pride] in one's offspring, for example, if one has many or beautiful or good boys or girls' ('Item ex nobilitate, si est ex magno genere, ex prole ut si habet multos vel pulchros vel bonos filios vel filias').

[44] Alvarus Pelagius, *De planctu ecclesie* ii.43 (Venice, 1560), fols. 146vb–7rb: [Now] we are to describe the vices of rustics or labourers or farmers . . . thirteenth: they often abstain from sex with their wives in order to avoid generating children, fearing that they cannot feed so many, on the grounds of poverty, [and] in this they sin most gravely' (Rusticorum vel laboratorum vel agricultorum vitia designemus . . . 13o abstinent sepe a coitu uxorum: ne filios generent timentes non tot posse alere paupertatis praetextum [r. praetextu] in quo gravissime peccant).

[45] The text in the long version of Peter's *Verbum abbreviatum* is edited in Baldwin, *Language of Sex*, p. 248.

[46] The passage is quoted and discussed in P. Biller, 'Applying Number to Men and Women in the Thirteenth and Early Fourteenth Centuries: An Enquiry into the Origins of the Idea of Sex-Ratio', in *The Work of Jacques Le Goff and the Challenges of Medieval History*, ed. M. Rubin (Woodbridge, 1997), pp. 27–52 (at p. 40). On William of Auvergne see Lesley Smith's chapter in this volume. The treatise on marriage is part of the *Tractatus de sacramentis* which Lesley Smith discusses; see her list of its manuscripts, pp. 98–9, n. 8.

[47] William Peraldus, *Summa de vitiis et virtutibus*, II, iii, 3, 3 (2 vols., Antwerp, 1571, II, fol. 14r) repeats the passage referred to in n. 38 above from Peter the Chanter, and Biller, 'Pastoral Geography', p. 74 notes and translates William of Pagula's use of the text.

Then, in the years after 1270, dramatic new pressure was being provided by the presence in Latin in Paris and in the libraries of more academic mendicant convents of Aristotle's *Politics*, which drew together the two themes in book 7. On the one hand there was the ideal size, the ideal 'multitude' or population of a political community, and on the other hand those actions which achieved this by moderating the numbers of children who would be generated and brought up.[48]

Running parallel, then, were estates generalisations about sin and Aristotelean as well as moral-theological strands, all juxtaposing and beginning to hint at links between avoiding conception and the size of the population. In England in the first half of the fourteenth century we begin to get 'sociographic' generalisations in this area. One is implied by William of Pagula in the 1320s, who juxtaposes married couples (and others) avoiding conception and the 'sin against nature' in a way which suggests that he is principally thinking of *coitus interruptus*, and then says that 'many these days' (multi . . . hiis diebus) do not regard this as a sin. Another is offered by the Dominican John Bromyard, in a work written between the 1320s and 1340s. Referring more obliquely to technique, talking of 'abusum operis' (abuse of the sexual act), in marriage, he writes of 'many' (multi) – many being worried, he says, about the resulting lack of offspring in marriages.[49] He continues elsewhere make various 'demographic' comments, including this: 'However in [this] modern time, just the limits of lands and holdings are contracting, because [their] owners and inhabitants are increasing in number, [and] the land scarcely suffices for them . . . (Moderno vero tempore . . . sicut terrarum termini et possessiones arctantur, quia possessores et habitatores multiplicantur, quibus terra vix sufficit . . .)'.[50] John and the author of the *In primis debet sacerdos* are slightly earlier, and neither would have dreamed of including such material in their idiot guides. But they themselves were learned men, living and working in the milieux in which such generalising thought was developing and men were commenting (in modern language) on contemporary trends in population and birth-control. Working in this world, they decided to lay such emphasis on avoidance of offspring by the married.

Around 1300 a second, bordering, area of thought is medicine. For one region of Europe, the kingdom of Aragon, there has been a brilliant recent demonstration of 'medicalisation' in the years around 1300.[51] With a wealth of detail Michael McVaugh has shown the dense and increasing presence, especially in towns and much thinner in the countryside, of a learned medical

---

[48] This is discussed in my forthcoming *Medieval Demographic Thought*.
[49] Earlier quoted and discussed in Biller, 'Birth-control', pp. 15 and 22–5, and Biller, 'Pastoral Geography', p. 73.
[50] John Bromyard, *Summa praedicantium*, Mors, 14 (Venice, 1586), fol. 71rb.
[51] M. R. McVaugh, *Medicine before the Plague. Practitioners and their Patients in the Crown of Aragon, 1285–1345* (Cambridge, 1993).

profession and its learned texts,[52] led by public demand; this 'medicalisation' was further shown in learned medicine's increasing intrusion into such areas as criminal investigation, treating the insane, providing sex advice and so on.

Notable for us are the learned medical texts and the material they contained on avoidance of conception. Chronology: though translated into Latin in the twelfth century, Avicenna's *Canon of Medicine* never utterly displaced a simpler set of texts from the university curriculum, and it was only coming on stream slowly, acquiring wider currency in the later thirteenth century,[53] when some other important but rather late translations were beginning to come through, especially Averroes' *Colliget*, translated into Latin perhaps in the third quarter of the thirteenth century.[54] Important accessions of material about sex and conception were among the roots of one of the western medical developments of around 1300, a proliferation of sex treatises at Montpellier, especially concerning sterility and fertility:[55] a textual accompaniment to the 'medicalisation' of sexual matters and behaviour which McVaugh has documented in the kingdom of Aragon.[56]

Three themes are relevant here, the first being this expansion in the medical material about conception in general. The second is to do with a well-known theme, the two-seed theory, whereby, in traditional Galenic medicine, conception needed the emission of both male and female seed.[57] The problem of women who had *apparently* not experienced pleasure but nevertheless conceived had already been aired in the twelfth century.[58] But, with the introduction of Averroes, the necessity of emission of female seed was being demolished with a comprehensiveness which needs to be read to be appreciated, and this by an author who appealed to the knowledge of many women, whom he claimed to have questioned on the theme:

> It [lack of need of woman's emission of seed] is manifested to sense [observation] and known by argument; by sense, because a man sees that a woman is impregnated without her emitting seed. And after I read

---

[52] See McVaugh, *Medicine*, pp. 87–95, on the diffusion of learned texts, and the telling example on p. 87 of the presence (pre-1297–1324) of a physician who owned Avicenna (part or all of the *Canon*) in Vic, a high and isolated town of about 4,000 inhabitants.

[53] N. Siraisi, *Taddeo Alderotti and His Pupils. Two Generations of Italian Medical Learning* (Princeton, N.J., 1981), pp. 97, 103, 105–9, 153 (noting slow reception).

[54] D. Jacquart and F. Micheau, *La médecine arabe et l'occident médiéval* (Paris, 1990), p. 182 and n. 30; see also n. 56 below, for the work being used by *c.* 1276.

[55] L. E. Demaitre, *Doctor Bernard de Gordon: Professor and Practitioner*, Studies and Texts 51 (Toronto, 1980), pp. 85–6; E. M. Cartelle, ed., *Tractatus de sterilitate. Anónimo de Montpellier (s. XIV) (Atribuido a A. De Vilanova, R. De Moleriis y J. De Turre)*, Lingüística y Filología 16 (Valladolid, 1993), pp. 18–19.

[56] McVaugh, *Medicine*, pp. 200–7.

[57] Often discussed, the theme is notably clear in Siraisi, *Alderotti*, pp. 195–201.

[58] For this and early to mid thirteenth century discussion, see, for example, Jacquart and Thomasset, *Sexuality and Medicine*, pp. 63–4, 68, and Cadden, *Meanings of Sex Difference*, pp. 126–7, 142–3.

Aristotle's books, I asked many women about this, and they replied that many women have been impregnated without emitting seed, and even if coitus displeased them. And I also saw very many of these, impregnated women who had been raped by males . . . (manifestatur sensu et cognoscitur per argumentum; per sensum quia homo vidit quod mulier impregnatur absque eo quod spermatizet. Et postquam legi libros Aristotelis ego quesivi a multis mulieribus de hoc et responderunt quod plures impregnate fuerunt absque spermatizatione: et etiam si displicuisset coitus. Et etiam vidi quamplures ex istis impregnatas que fuerant a masculis violate.)

Such material is usually used nowadays in the study of construction of gender in the Middle Ages. The old-fashioned theme of the nature and development of people's medical ideas – complementary to rather than incompatible with the study of gender – should not be forgotten, nor should the currently unfashionable theme of progress in ideas be entirely abandoned. It is arguable that learned medicine's advice on how to conceive may often have served to provide the less licit advice on how to avoid conceiving, with the tacit message 'do the opposite'. If so and insofar as learned medicine had diffusion and influence, it is difficult to see anything but muddle and failure in the long part of the central Middle Ages during which learned medicine insisted on woman's emission of seed as necessary for conception. What was now being introduced at a learned level was a greater realism about how conception takes place, a realism which could both act as a model in itself and bear upon the opposite theme, avoiding conception. Learned medicine now hinted more sharply at *coitus interruptus*. Slightly further on in the same section of the *Colliget* Averroes mentioned that 'there are some women who cannot be impregnated while they lactate (sunt alique mulieres que non possunt impregnari dum lactant)'.[59] Again, there is a large step *towards* realism, and an addition to the west's stock of ideas on the conditions in which conception does or does not occur.

Much less well-known is another theme whose history has not been written for this period – thought both among the learned and among ordinary people about the *time* in a woman's cycle which was likely to favour conception. In earlier material it is easier to find the notion that conception occurred during or just after menstruation, while by the early fourteenth century we can find in learned medical literature recommendations which implied the opposite. Further research may show both change in this theme, and also persistent intertwining of the old and the new. On the one hand, a *consilium* on remedying sterility by Taddeo Alderotti (ob. by 1295)[60] was still advising sex

---

[59] Averroes, *Colliget*, II.x (Venice, 1497, unfoliated). Giles of Rome's use of the *Colliget* on women conceiving without emission of seed in a work he wrote around 1276 is discussed by M. A. Hewson, *Giles of Rome and the Medieval Theory of Conception* (London, 1975), p. 87.

[60] On Taddeo, see Siraisi, *Taddeo Alderotti*.

during menstruation,[61] while on the other hand an early fourteenth century Montpellier treatise on sterility recommended abstinence to couples who wanted to conceive, saying the following:

> Moreover, it helps with conception if the man and woman abstain from coitus, and embraces, for five days or more before menstruation and throughout the whole time of the flow of menstruation and after this menstruation for three or four days and these nights. (Confert autem ad conceptum si vir et mulier abstineant a coytu et amplexibus per V dies vel amplius ante menstrua et toto tempore fluxus menstrorum et post ipsa menstrua III vel IIIIor diebus et illis noctibus.)[62]

Let me set against this background the Dominican convent in Paris, St Jacques, around 1310. One person present there is John of Naples,[63] who held a quodlibetic discussion here or in Naples on several moral problems arising from medical practice, including therapeutic abortion, parallelling a medical question about the morality of therapeutic abortion by another Italian, but a doctor rather than a mendicant, Gentile da Foligno.[64] Present at the same time as John in the Paris mendicant convent, and sometimes working with him, was Peter of La Palud,[65] who was about to 'read' the *Sentences*. Palud's commentary on the marriage distinctions of the fourth book of the *Sentences* is dense with discussion of avoidance of conception. Convergence with medicine is possibly detectable in the physical precision of Peter's descriptions of *coitus interruptus*. With this in mind, let us look at Peter commenting on distinction 32, and the question of sex during menstruation. Peter's discussion is characteristically laborious and compendious – his is one of the longest commentaries on book 4 written in the early fourteenth century – but darting through it are sharp, sceptical and informed comments. 'Also', writes Peter, 'a woman cannot conceive then, according to some [authorities]. . . . It is not certain that she conceives then (mulier concipere non potest secundum quosdam . . . Non est certum utrum tunc concipiat)'. Peter provides a long list of various motives and conditions of married couples having sex during the wife's period and their sinlessness or degree of sin, and this list includes the following:

> Fourthly, [having sex at this time] knowing or believing probably that [a child] is not generated: for example, if she is sterile; or because she is not

---

61 Taddeo Alderotti, *I "Consilia"*, 13, ed. G. M. Nardi (Turin, 1937), p. 33, in the course of advice on how to achieve conception: 'And also that there should be coitus when the menses have not been got rid of' (Et etiam quod coytus fiat menstruis non evacuatis).

62 *Tractatus de sterilitate*, 9, ed. Cartelle, p. 150.

63 On John, see P. Biller, 'John of Naples, Quodlibets and Medieval Theological Concern with the Body', in *Medieval Theology and the Natural Body*, ed. P. Biller and A. J. Minnis (York, 1997), pp. 3–12.

64 Biller, 'John of Naples', pp. 8–9, and notes 28, 30, and 31.

65 On Peter, see J. Dunbabin, *A Hound of God. Pierre de la Palud and the Fourteenth-Century Church* (Oxford, 1991).

wont to conceive then. For husbands know the conditions of their wives better, through experience, and vice-versa [viz. wives know the conditions of their husbands]. Similarly he does not sin, [or] at least [does not sin] mortally. (Quarto, sciens non generari vel probabiliter credens: quia sterilis vel quia non consuevit tunc concipere – quia viri cognoscunt melius conditiones uxorum et e converso per experientiam – similiter non peccat, saltem mortaliter.)[66]

According to Dunbabin, Peter had not finalised the text we have of this commentary on book 4 until 1315.[67] At some stage before this Peter seems to have been noticing contemporary medical opinion: and both the specific notion that women could not conceive at this time and also the fact that learned opinion on this was not universal. He had also been noticing a pastoral fact, couples having sex during menstruation while knowing or holding as probable that because of this timing conception would not occur, and basing this knowledge or probability on 'experience', which meant knowledge of the 'conditions' of the wife. Learned medicine, pastoral observation, and the practical experience and actions of married couples and pastoral experience all seem to be present.

At this period, then, medicine and moral theology seem to be converging: moral theologians are well aware both of learned medicine and practice. This is what is at issue in one of the remarkable elements of the author of the *In primis debet sacerdos*, his specification of method. Alongside such long-attested actions as the drinking of contraceptive herbal drugs, and the catch-all phrase of 'do something to avoid conception', which probably mainly meant *coitus interruptus*, he also specifies in detail post-coital movements by a wife, in a passage which I repeat – 'after their husbands have made use of them, they rise up or move around in another way in order not to conceive'. This parallels passages in the Montpellier sex treatises, one which, the anonymous *De sterilitate*, is quoted here.

. . . or sterility happens because immediately after coitus the woman jumps or moves too quickly or dashes up and down the stairs, which are all grounds for the seed not being retained in the womb. (. . . aut accidit sterilitas quia mulier statim post coytum saltat aut nimis cito movetur aut subito scalas ascendit et descendit, que omnia sunt cause quare semen non retinetur in matrice.)[68]

---

[66] Peter of la Palud, *In quartum sententiarum*, 32 (Venice, 1493), fols. 162vb–3ra.
[67] Dunbabin, *Pierre de la Palud*, p. 42.
[68] *Tractatus de sterilitate*, I, ed. Cartelle, p. 72. For other examples from this period, see Bernard de Gordon, *Lilium medicinae*, VII.xiv (Lyons, 1574), p. 618: '[Sterility] occurs when she jumps after coitus, or moves too quickly' ([Sterilitas] accidit quando post coitum saltat, aut nimis velociter movetur); and the *Compilatio de conceptione*, in Arnald of Villanova, *Opera omnia* (Lyons, 1532), fol. 214ra, which puts reasons for failure to conceive in brief, tabular, form, including 'Sudden rising up of the woman. Big jump (Subita erectio mulieris. Saltus magnus)'. The suggestion being made here is of wider diffusion of the idea, not its novelty. For the idea of jumping to dislodge

Two things are certainly converging here, medical vocabulary and confessors' manuals (and behind them such pastoral experts as the Dominicans John of Naples and Peter of la Palud), and a third with high probability, the thought-world of the couples whose typical sins were being mapped by contemporary experts in the 'sociography' of sin. These comments apply to two manuals of one period, around 1300, and perhaps one region. 'Perhaps' because, while the pastoral and regional setting of John's *Confessionale* is clear, there is uncertainty about *In primis debet sacerdos*. If it is southern, and by Bérenger, a legal-academic author originating in the Montpellier region, we should be thinking of the possibility of some influence of Montpellier medicine, and perhaps less input from pastoral experience.

3. Long-Distance Regional and Chronological Patterns

Let us stand back and raise questions about possible long-distance regional and chronological patterns. First, regional. In an earlier study of pastoral literature I suggested investigating manuals from different regions of Latin Christendom, seeing if some elements in them constituted reactions to local conditions. The difficulty and delicacy of such an investigation is clear, given the universal theology and canon law of the church and the influence of Paris and Bologna, all overlaying reactions to local conditions and – in England – the continuation of a local tradition in its pastoral literature. Comparing early fourteenth-century common denominator priests' manuals, I pointed to the heavier attention paid to avoidance of offspring in northwestern European texts.[69] Can we discern a northern/southern pattern of contrasts in the idiot confessors' guides we have been examining? If we do, the pattern has two elements, one of contrasting emphasis on avoidance itself, the other of contrasting medical milieux. We could select a southern text to compare with the northern text, John's *Confessionale*. One candidate is a work written by the Italian Franciscan Marchesino of Reggio Emilia a few years before 1315.[70] Its title (*Confessionale*) is identical, its length comparable (about 18,000 words), and the intention of the author is similar, though it is expressed with a verbal frivolity which would have been alien to John. The author presented himself as 'simplex simplicibus simplicia scribens simpliciter (a simple man writing

---

seed had been present for some time in learned medicine (see for example, Noonan, *Contraception*, p. 204, on jumping in Avicenna's *Canon*), and abortifacient jumping had been also present in one confessor's treatise of *c.* 1216 (Chobham, *Summa*, pp. 464–5, quoted in translation in Biller, 'Pastoral Geography', p. 81).

[69] Biller, 'Pastoral geography', p. 74.

[70] On the work, see Michaud-Quantin, *Sommes*, pp. 55–6, 118; on manuscripts see also M. W. Bloomfield *et al.*, *Incipits of Latin Works on the Virtues and Vices, 1100–1500 A.D.* (Cambridge, Mass., 1979a), pp. 223, no. 257, and 500, no. 5782. It is found printed among St Bonaventure's works, and the edition used here is St Bonaventure, *Opera omnia*, ed. A. C. Peltier, 15 vols. (Paris, 1864–71), VIII, 359–92.

simple things simply for simple men)'.[71] What we find is a contrast. Where in John there is stark emphasis, practicality, and clarity, in Marchesino there is less attention to the theme of avoidance. There is only a question about abortion, none about avoiding conceiving: 'if he [*or* she] killed, hampering the foetus or procuring an abortion, [even] though perhaps the effect of this sort of thing did not follow (si occidit, conceptum praepediendo, vel abortum procurando, licet fortassis effectus in hujusmodi non fuerit subsecutus)'.[72] At one point Marchesino chooses a word – *praepediendo* (shackling, fettering, hampering) – which does not help clarity.

We could also set the lack of hint of connections with learned medicine in the *Confessionale*, with the strong hint of such connections or infuence in *In primis debet sacerdos*. This last would fit what is being suggested by modern research into the history of 'medicalisation'. The picture put forward by McVaugh is of 'medicalisation' taking place in the kingdom of Aragon around and after 1300; in advanced Italian cities earlier (in the mid-thirteenth century); and in northern Europe, by implication, much later. The *Confessionale* and *In primis debet sacerdos* may carry traces, therefore, of such a northern/southern contrast in the (observed) impact of learned medicine on people trying to avoid offspring. This observation is presented here as a conjecture, a hypothesis useful for further research.

Secondly, what of chronology in the north? If we go back earlier in the thirteenth century, looking at common-denominator texts, we can look at the confession tracts which were copied into the brief booklets of statutes of a diocese, which each parish priest was required to have,[73] and also at earlier mendicants' manuals, going back to the 1220s.[74] Now, these texts contain a great deal on forms of sex which would in themselves have precluded conception, even if avoidance is not spelled out as the motive, and, as the thirteenth century wears on, much about the various degrees of licitness of sex in marriage which included reference to procreative purpose. However, what is usually absent in these booklets is what we find so easily around 1300, namely the explicit and direct treatment of 'avoidance of conception' as a subject in itself. If we confine our attention to little booklets, what we see emerging around 1300 is new.

This development in confessional literature parallels a development in preaching which we can see in England. Through English synodal statutes we see gradually developing and expanding the themes which any priest should preach on each Sunday – and, suddenly and sharply with William of Pagula in

---

71 Marchesino, *Confessionale*, Preface, ed. Peltier, p. 359b.
72 Marchesino, *Confessionale*, II.xiii, ed. Peltier, p. 364b.
73 An example is Bishop Alexander Stavensby's tract on confession, copied into his statutes for the diocese of Coventry and Lichfield, *Councils & Synods*, I, 220–6.
74 The examples used here are the *Summula Magistri Conradi* and the tract *Quia non pigris*, edited in *Trois sommes*, II. Note, however, the discussions of authorship in *Trois sommes*, I, 77–9 and 125–6, which make mendicant authorship plausible but not certain.

the 1320s, these are expanded to include the instruction that a parish priest 'frequenter publicare debet quod vir cognoscendo uxorem suam vel aliam mulierem carnaliter nihil faciat neque uxor eius propter quod impediatur concepcio partus (ought frequently to make public [the warning] that a man when carnally knowing his wife or another woman ought to do nothing – nor should his wife do anything – on account of which conception of a foetus is impeded)'.[75] So, what we have seen in this paper is that short tracts on confession confirm a pattern, while adding a chronological nuance. The change of emphasis in pulpit warnings, discernible in a northern treatise written in the 1320s, is present also when northern tracts advising on confession are laid out in a row, but in the latter it can be seen by around 1300.

In earlier discussion[76] this development in preaching was juxtaposed with demographic and economic situation of the time. Economic and demographic historians have seen increasing pressure in the conditions of the thirteenth and very early fourteenth centuries. Population had been growing for a long time and the available land was decreasingly able to support it. By around 1300, or a little earlier, there was a crisis of overpopulation. Now, we have seen the comments of the northern pastoral experts of around 1300. John Bromyard related growing numbers of inhabitants to the amount of land available, and he also talked about the worries of many about marriages not producing offspring through abuse of the marriage act. William of Pagula made a remarkable innovation in instructions to parish priests to make frequent pulpit warnings against couples avoiding offspring, and the special emphasis on this sin in the *Confessionale* of John of Freiburg implies his expert pastoral experience that this was in fact a common sin among the married. Brought together, then, around 1300 are the following: overpopulation; writers who are well equipped by the tradition in which they are writing to make generalising observations about human behaviour; generalisations by them about couples avoiding offspring; and, glimpsed through their texts, something of the reality of the women and men who were living then, who were in part reacting to overpopulation by trying harder and more often (and perhaps with better knowledge) to avoid conceiving. If we are to believe Bromyard, many were successful.

This cluster from 1300 has been resumed here schematically in order to underline the parallels with a ninth-century cluster, which supply our third and even more conjectural question about chronological and regional patterns. The little booklets of the *earlier* Middle Ages were the little penitentials, whose practical and actual use is argued persuasively by Rob Meens elsewhere in this volume.[77] Can we see a trend in the absence or presence of 'avoidance of offspring' as a topic in these 'little booklets' (*codicelli*)? Careful analysis of them

---

[75] Oxford, Bodleian Library, MS Rawlinson A 361, fol. 50r.
[76] Biller, 'Birth-control', p. 20, and 'Pastoral geography', p. 73.
[77] See chapter 2 above.

by Noonan and others[78] has not sufficiently highlighted one aspect of them, which is that the theme of deliberate avoidance of conception has a definite chronology, and may also be regional.

In the earlier penitentials there is the sin of abortion but not of avoidance of offspring. It is not difficult to find sexual sins which by their nature could not have resulted in generation. But 'not resulting in generation' is incidental to these sins, and it is something pointed out by a modern historian like Noonan, not by the authors of the penitentials. What is difficult to find is description of the sin of performing this or that sexual act *in order* not to conceive.

Then earlier absence is then followed by remarkable intrusion of the sin into penitential literature, in the period between the early (or mid) ninth century and just after 900 and in one northern region. There are two manuscripts which contain the most extensive treatment of avoidance of conception to be found anywhere in a penitential. Headed *De potionibus mulierum* (*On the potions of women*), the text goes like this:

> If anyone has taken potions, so that woman does not conceive, or has killed [aborted] the conceived, or if the man has spilled his seed from sex with the woman, in order not to conceive, as the sons of Judah did in Thamar. (Si quis potiones acceperit, ut mulier non concipiat, aut conceptos occiderit, aut vir semen effuderit a coitu mulieris, ut non concipiat, sicut filii Judae fecerunt in Thamar . . .)[79]

The earlier of the two manuscripts comes from St Hubert in the Ardennes, and was written some time in the early to mid-ninth century. To be put alongside this is the text *Si aliquis*:

> If someone to satisfy his lust or in deliberate hatred does something to a man or woman so that no children be born of him or her, or gives them to drink, so that he *or* she cannot generate or conceive, let this person be held to be a murderer. (Si aliquis causa explendae libidinis vel odii meditatione, ut non ex eo soboles nascatur, homini aut mulieri aliquid

---

[78] Noonan, *Contraception*, pp. 152–70, provides the basic survey; see also R. S. Callewaert, 'Les pénitentiels du moyen âge et les pratiques anticonceptionelles', *La vie spirituelle, Supplément* 18 (1965), 339–66; P. J. Payer, 'Early Medieval Regulations concerning Marital Sexual Relations', *Journal of Medieval History* 6 (1980), 353–76 (at pp. 359–60), and *Sex and the Penitentials: The Development of a Sexual Code, 550–1150* (Toronto, 1984), especially p. 117 on the general lack of censure of contraceptive sex in the penitentials.

[79] *Poenitentiale Hubertense* 56, ed. F. W. H. Wasserschleben, *Die Bussordnungen der abendländischen Kirche* (Halle, 1851), p. 385. For details of editions, studies and conjectured date of the St Hubert penitential, see C. Vogel, *Les 'Libri paenitentiales'*, Typologie des sources du moyen âge occidental 27 (Turnholt, 1978), pp. 75–6; the same work, revised by A. J. Frantzen (Turnholt, 1985), p. 30; Meens, *Tripartite*, pp. 39–40. Cf. Noonan, *Contraception*, pp. 162 (the earlier date given on p. 164 is an aberration).

fecerit, vel ad potandum dederit, ut non possit generare aut concipere, ut homicida teneatur.)[80]

This text, which was later to play a central role in the main collections of texts on avoidance of offspring, apppears for the first time shortly after 900,[81] in a work written and compiled by Regino, abbot of the Rhineland abbey of Prüm.

We can turn from these to Georges Duby's classic account of medieval rural economy, published in 1962, and his demographic analysis of ninth-century Carolingian estate surveys, while remembering these two texts from the Ardennes and the abbey of Prüm. Duby uses a polyptych of the abbey of Prüm, dated 892–93. This polyptych surveys the abbey's estates, which were very widely spread over the northern part of the kingdom of Lotharingia. The norm was for a manse to support one family. But the Prüm estates in the Ardennes (in today's Belgium and Luxembourg) contained, according to the polyptych, 116 families established on 35 manses, 88 of them on 22 manses. Duby also looks at eight villages near Paris, which in the demographically favourable conditions of the eighteenth century these villages were to number 5,700, and points to the extraordinary numbers of inhabitants they already had in the early ninth century, according to the earlier ninth-century polyptych of St Germain-des-Près: 4,100 people. The conclusion, according to Duby, was that at this late Carolingian period there were sporadic communities each of which was very densely populated. After citing the case of the abbey of Prüm's estate in the Ardennes, he writes of 'overpopulation'.[82] Noonan did not read polyptychs, and Duby did not read these penitentials. When brought together, however, these texts show a remarkable coincidence. While the Prüm polyptych shows overpopulation in the Ardennes, it is an abbot of Prüm who is the first person to record one remarkable text on avoiding offspring, *Si aliquis*, and it is a manuscript from the Ardennes which is the earliest of the two manuscripts of a penitential which, uniquely among such texts, describes the method of withdrawing to avoid conceiving.

When turning from John of Freiburg, William of Pagula and John Bromyard around 1300 and going back four centuries to Regino and the anonymous author of the St Hubert penitential, we are moving to authors who lived and wrote in a remote and very different tradition. Did the two groups of writers,

---

[80] Regino of Prüm, *Libri duo de synodalibus causis et disciplinis clesiasticis*, II.clxxxviii, ed. F. G. A. Wasserschleben (Leipzig, 1840), p. 248. See Noonan, *Contraception*, p. 168, for a felicitous but slightly different translation.

[81] Noonan, *Contraception*, p. 168.

[82] G. Duby, *Rural Economy and Country Life in the Medieval West* (London, 1968), pp. 12–14. Ch.-E. Perrin had usefully analysed the polyptych of Prüm in his 'Le manse dans le Polyptyque de l'abbaye de Prüm à la fin du IXe siècle', *Études historiques à la mémoire de Noël Didier* (Paris, 1960), pp. 245–58; he discussed the 'overpopulation' (*surpeuplement*) of the domains of the abbey of St Germain-des-Prés and the Ardennes estates of the abbey of Prüm, pp. 252–3, 258.

however, have one thing in common? Were both sets of pastoral experts reacting to a real increase in the committing of this sin by the women and men living in the straitened conditions of overpopulation?

The 1996 York Quodlibet Lecture

From the Ordeal to Confession:
In Search of Lay Religion in Early Thirteenth-Century France

John W. Baldwin

The two foci of this title converge at the Fourth Lateran Council which Pope Innocent III convoked at Rome in November of 1215. By removing the presence of the clergy, Canon 18 of the Council attempted to put an end to the ordeal. By mandating annual confession to a priest, Canon 21 sought to encourage and formalize the techniques of private penance.[1] This conjuncture was, of course, only emblematic; theologians and canonists had long prepared the groundwork throughout the twelfth century. The significance of the date is beyond question because the Council was the largest and most influential to its time. It drew more than 400 bishops and 800 other clergy; its enactments and reforms set the course of the Latin church in the thirteenth century. Although laymen were present, the clergy were entirely responsible for the legislation which they redacted in Latin. The official language of the clergy, this language had monopolized the articulation of religion since the early Middle Ages. To understand not only the clerical goals and institutions but also the beliefs and practices of the laity, therefore, historians have depended entirely on documents composed in a language exclusively written by and for the clergy.

Latin, however, was not the language of the laity whose vernacular voice was set into writing only during the course of the twelfth century by itinerant jongleurs and minstrels, who were perhaps clerics themselves, but who sought to entertain lay audiences composed largely of the lay aristocracy in their own tongue. Composed in verse, their repertory consisted of chansons de gestes, romances of antiquity, and Arthurian romances by the end of the century. These tales were set in times and places distant from their contemporary audiences – to the days of Charlemagne, to Alexander or the fall of Troy or to the mythical figure of Arthur and his legendary kingdom. It is from this vernacular literature that I would seek to identify an authentic voice of the

---

[1] The canons are edited in *Constitutiones concilii quarti Lateranensis una cum commentariis glossatorum*, ed. A. García y García, Monumenta iuris canonici, Series A: Corpus glossatorum 2 (Vatican, 1981), pp. 66–8 and Mansi, XXII, 1006–10. From an abundant literature the most comprehensive study of the Fourth Lateran Council remains Raymonde Foreville's, *Latran I, II, III et Latran IV*, Histoire de conciles oecuméniques 6 (Paris, 1965).

laity, but the spokesmen I have chosen adopted a different stance from their predecessors. My choice falls upon two authors each of whom wrote two verse romances at the opening decades of the thirteenth century. They are Jean Renart who wrote *L'Escoufle* between 1200 and 1202 and the *Roman de la rose* (often called *Guillaume de Dole*) around 1209, and Gerbert de Montreuil who composed the *Roman de la violette* around 1227–29 and a *Continuation* to the *Conte du graal* of Chrétien de Troyes about the same time, all composed in the Francien dialect.[2] Unfortunately, neither their names nor their works are as familiar to audiences today as Marie de France or Chrétien de Troyes. Beyond their names nothing is known about their biographies. (Jean Renart is obviously a nom de plume.) Time does not permit to narrate the plots of their romances except to say that Jean Renart's *Escoufle* is the story of a youthful couple, consisting of Guillaume, the son of a count, Aelis, the daughter of an emperor, their precocious love, separation, journeys, and final reunion. His *Roman de la rose*, often associated with the 'cycle de gageur', tells of the love of Conrad, emperor of the Germans, for la belle Liënor, daughter of a simple knight. When her reputation is calumniated by a wicked seneschal, she vindicates her virtue and becomes the emperor's wife. Gerbert de Montreuil's *Roman de la violette* is a tale of another calumny, this time by Lisïart, the malevolent count of Forez, against the virtue of Eurïaut, the *amie* of Gerart count of Nevers. Once again the couple regain their honor and are finally married. Gerbert's *Continuation*, like many other continuations, attempted to supply an ending to Chrétien's unfinished tale by recounting the purifying adventures of Perceval in search of the grail.

What draws me to these romances are not their principal stories, but the contexts in which they are set.[3] Rather than the distant or never-never-lands of

---

2   The principal texts employed in this study are Jean Renart, *L'Escoufle*, ed. F. Sweetser, Textes littéraires français (Paris and Geneva, 1974); *Roman de la rose ou de Guillaume de Dole*, ed. F. Lecoy, Les classiques français du moyen âge (Paris, 1979); Gerbert de Montreuil, *Le roman de la violette ou de Gerart de Nevers*, ed. D. L. Buffum, Société des anciens textes français (Paris, 1928); *La continuation de Perceval*, ed. M. Williams and M. Oswald, 3 vols., Les classiques français du moyen âge (Paris, 1922–75); Chrétien de Troyes, *Le roman de Perceval ou Le conte du graal*, ed. W. Roach, Textes litteraires français (Geneva and Lille, 1956); *Le chevalier de la charrete*, ed. M. Roques, Les classiques français du moyen âge (Paris, 1983); Béroul, *Le roman de Tristan*, ed. E. Muret and L. M. Dufourques, Les classiques français de moyen âge (Paris, 1982).

The principal studies on Jean Renart are R. Lejeune-Dehousse, *L'oeuvre de Jean Renart: contribution à l'étude du genre romanesque au moyen âge*, Bibliothèque de la Faculté de Philosophie et Lettres de l'Université de Liège 61 (Lille, 1935) and M. Zink, *Roman rose et rose rouge: Le roman de la rose ou de Guillaume de Dole de Jean Renart* (Paris, 1979). Gerbert de Montreuil has not received comparable attention. See *Dictionnaire de lettres françaises: Le moyen âge*, ed. G. Hasenohr and M. Zink (Paris, n.d.). For the dating of Jean Renart's *Roman de la rose* see my ' "Once there was an emperor . . .": A Political Reading of the Romances of Jean Renart', in *Jean Renart and the Art of Romance: Essays on Guillaume de Dole*, ed. N. V. Durling (Gainesville and Florida, 1997), pp. 45–82.

3   I have sought to exploit this particular character of Jean's romances in the following

preceding romance which were peopled by ancient or legendary characters, Jean and Gerbert framed their narratives with features of *hic et nunc*. Jean's geographical space was both precise and familiar to his audiences, citing, for example, Cologne, Liège, Saint-Trond, and Toul in the middle space between the kingdoms of France and Germany, generally known as Lotharingia. In addition to this area Gerbert set his story in lands to the south of the royal domain, for example, Château-Landon, Montargis, and Nevers. Except for the major characters who were patently fictive, all of the secondary figures were historical personages – for example, Richard Coeur de Lion, Michel de Harnes, and Dauphin d'Auvergne – whom contemporary audiences could immediately recognize. These specific details, which modern historians can still identify, served as 'effets de réel', to lend verisimilitude to the narrative.[4] Through the specific and historical character of their settings Jean's and Gerbert's romances formed an intertextual coherence which distinguished them from preceding writers.[5] To emphasize this novelty Gerbert asserted that he will not sing of the Round Table nor of the knights of Arthur, but tell a fine and pleasant story in which he speaks the truth (*Violette* vv. 34–8). This novelty, however, pertains only to Jean's two romances and to Gerbert's *Violette*, but not to his *Continuation* which, as a completion of Chrétien's tale, reverted to the characteristic features of Arthurian romance. (His *Continuation* is important to my concerns, however, because of Gerbert's particular preoccupation with religion.)

Although Jean and Gerbert rejected programmatically their forerunners, the preceding literature nonetheless formed the 'horizon of expectations' for their audiences.[6] Our romanciers composed their narratives in full awareness that their listeners and readers were profoundly steeped in the chansons de gestes, the legend of Tristan and Iseut, the lais of Marie de France, and the romances of Chrétien, including, of course, his *Graal*. This awareness must also guide our own reading of their texts. As Chrétien before them, Jean and Gerbert addressed their romances to the 'courts of kings and counts', or the high nobility (*L'Escoufle* v. 12, *Rose* v. 5646).[7] In particular Jean sent *L'Escoufle* to the noble count of Hainaut. He was Baudouin, who became the ninth count of

---

studies: 'Jean Renart et le tournoi de Saint-Trond: Une conjonction de l'histoire et de la littérature', *AESC* 45 (1990), 565–88; 'The Crisis of the Ordeal: Literature, Law and Religion around 1200', *JMRS* 24 (1994), 327–53; and ' "Once there was an emperor..." '.

4 The phrase, with modification, is that of Roland Barthes, 'L'effet de réel', *Communications* 11 (1968), 84–9.

5 Philippe Walter, 'Tout commence par des chansons . . . (Intertextualités lotharingiennes)', in *Styles et valeurs pour histoire de l'art littéraire au moyen âge*, ed. D. Poirion (Paris, 1990), pp. 185–209.

6 The phrase, with modification, is that of Hans Robert Jauss from 'Literary History as a Challenge to Literary Theory', in *Toward an Aesthetic of Reception*, trans. T. Bahti, Theory and History of Literature 2 (Minneapolis, 1982), pp. 3–45.

7 Chrétien de Troyes, *Erec et Enide*, ed. M. Roques, Les classiques français du moyen âge (Paris, 1970), v. 20.

Flanders in 1194 and the sixth count of Hainaut in 1195 (vv. 9060, 9079–90). The *Roman de la rose* was sent to Milon de Nanteuil in the territory of Rheims in Champagne (vv. 5–7). He was prévôt of the chapter of the cathedral of Rheims from 1207 before he was finally elected bishop of Beauvais in 1217. Gerbert designated the *Roman de la violette* for Marie, countess of Ponthieu, who held the county from 1225 to 1231 during the exile of her husband (vv. 58, 6643–4).[8] (Gerbert's *Continuation* was unaddressed.) Although the addressees were great barons, their courts were teeming with knights and ladies of the lower aristocracy, all of whom constituted the audience of Jean's and Gerbert's writings.

In addition to striving for verisimilitude another attraction of Jean's and Gerbert's romances to our search for lay religion is their chronology. Since Jean wrote clearly before and Gerbert after the Lateran Council, they provide testimony to the effects of the Council on the laity. Religion, however, remained the realm over which clerics claimed final authority as the Council continued to reiterate. To assess lay reactions to religion, therefore, we must always keep the vernacular of the laity in dialogue with the Latin pronouncements of the clergy. None could serve our purposes better than the contemporary theologian, Peter, Chanter of Notre-Dame at Paris, and his influential school which included the papal-legate and cardinal, Robert of Courson, who worked assiduously to prepare the Council, Thomas of Chobham, the author of a guide to confessors, and even Innocent III, who as pope was both the convener and the supreme authority behind the Council itself.[9]

Exterior Religiosity and the Ordeal

Jean Renart opens the *Roman de la rose* with the declaration that his romance sings of 'arms and love, and both together' (vv. 24–5). Like preceding romances the affairs of the laity preoccupy the narratives of *L'Escoufle*, the *Rose*, and the *Violette*. Even the *Rose* which was addressed to a cleric was perhaps the most secular of all. The clergy who do appear are limited to high prelates, and their roles are confined to performing the liturgy. Since these were romances of love, the liturgical duties consisted largely of marriages and blessing the nuptial chamber.[10] Because they treated imperial affairs, the clergy were also

---

8 For the biographies of these patrons, see Baldwin, ' "Once there was an emperor ..." ', pp. 49–51.

9 Baldwin, *Peter the Chanter*, I, 3–46. The principal works employed in this study are: Chanter, *Verbum*, short version in *PL* 205, 1–554 and long version in Vatican, MS Reg. Lat. 106; Chanter, *Summa*; Robert of Courson, *Summa*, in Paris, Bibliothèque Nationale, MS Lat. 14524; Courson, *Summa*, ed. Kennedy; and Chobham, *Summa*.

10 Marriages: *L'Escoufle* vv. 1704–38, 8329–33; *Rose* vv. 5284–396; *Violette* vv. 6597–633; *Continuation* vv. 6631–752. Blessing of the nuptial chamber: *L'Escoufle* vv. 1740–3; *Continuation* vv. 6773–802.

called upon to perform coronations. Thus the pope crowns Guillaume and Aelis at Rome (*Escoufle* vv. 8944–65) and the archbishop of Cologne, Lïenor at Mainz (*Rose* vv. 5374–85). Although the clergy were most visible at the great feasts of the liturgical calendar – notably Pentecost – glimpses of them can also be seen providing daily masses required by the royal routine. The religious obligations of the laity were chiefly restricted to participation on pilgrimages. Journeys were mentioned to the popular shrines of Santiago de Compostela (*Escoufle* vv. 6184–351, *Violette* vv. 1116–21) and Saint-Gilles du Gard (*Escoufle* vv. 6478–523). The supreme pilgrimage was, of course, the crusade. A decade after the celebrated Third Crusade of Frederick Barbarossa, Philip Augustus and Richard Coeur de Lion, Jean opened *L'Escoufle* with a Richard, count of Normandy, departing for the Holy Land, fighting the Saracens and winning a truce for three years (vv. 124–1329). This was a subject which befitted his addressee, Count Baudouin of Hainaut and Flanders, who was allied with Richard and about to depart on a crusade himself.

Although the clergy's duties are limited to the ceremonial, God is not absent in Jean's and Gerbert's romances. As in the chanson de geste, he is omnipresent and omnipotent. His ubiquity was expressed in the habit of romance writers to punctuate their verse with a torrent of oaths evoking the name of God and his saints: 'my God', 'in the name of God', 'if it pleases God', 'God help me', 'by the Virgin', 'by Saint Peter', 'by Saint Paul . . .'.[11] Often these phrases were introduced solely to fulfill stylistic needs of meter and rhyme (saint Pol, for example, rhymed with col [neck], *Rose* vv. 2561–2); nonetheless, their very banality recalled God's presence on every page.

Making the sign of the cross, evoking Christ's redemptive, death, was, of course, the most habitual gesture of Christianity. Jean and Gerbert employed it widely to protect against great misfortune, upon receiving terrifying news, even departing on ordinary journeys.[12] As Perceval and Gauvain encounter mounting adventures and dangers, they cross themselves with greater frequency in the *Continuation*. Perceval thereby protects himself from seduction (vv. 2572–86), but when the less pious Gauvain crawls into bed with a treacherous maiden, he only then remembers to cross himself. The gesture uncovers a dagger concealed beneath the bedclothes with which the maiden had intended to kill him (vv. 12598–609). The theologian Thomas of Chobham had recommended the practice before retiring to bed, doubtless thinking of less melodramatic circumstances.[13]

God is not only everywhere in Jean's and Gerbert's romances, but he also responds powerfully in answer to prayer. Count Richard's victory over the Saracens is in direct response to the prayers from the nuns at Montivilliers as

---

[11] For some examples: *Escoufle* vv. 319, 327, 4482, 5377; *Rose* vv. 291, 687, 1280, 1588, 3017, 4747, 4775; *Violette* vv. 972, 2057; *Continuation* vv. 4074, 7193.

[12] For some examples: *Escoufle* vv. 4560–61, 5084; *Rose* vv. 906–07, 3590, 4602–3; *Violette* 9760.

[13] Chobham, *Summa*, p. 261.

well as the count's own supplications before the altar of the church of the Holy Sepulchre in Jerusalem (*Escoufle* vv. 247–56, 616–39, 1330–1). At each turning point Gerart's search for Eurïaut is facilitated by prayer. When the heroine is bound to the stake to be burned for a murder of which she was innocent, she offers to God a long invocation which continues for a hundred-fifty verses and closes with the Lord's Prayer (*Violette* vv. 5177–331). Its very length, of course, allows the hero time to come to her aid in good romance fashion, but it nevertheless demonstrates God's willingness and ability to answer prayer.

A notable example of the belief in divine intervention into human affairs was the legal institution of the ordeal.[14] From the early Middle Ages ordeals were called 'judgments of God', because they affirmed that God could and did intervene in the judicial process to decide difficult cases through the hot iron or water, cold water or judicial battle. Essential to the operation of the procedure was the presence of the clergy who provided the relics on which the oaths were sworn and blessed the iron or water to ensure God's participation. Ordeals played central roles in narratives of the *Rose* and the *Violette*. In the *Rose* Jean Renart employed this device to expose two falsehoods and to restore justice. A seneschal who is jealous of the emperor's love for the lowly Lïenor learns from the girl's indiscreet mother that she has a birthmark shaped as a rose on her inner thigh. (Hence the name of the romance.) With this compromising information the seneschal is able to convince Conrad that he has seduced the maiden, thus rendering her unfit for marriage to the emperor. Not to be outmanoeuvred, Lïenor devises her own stratagem. Journeying to the imperial court at Mainz, she sends the seneschal a belt, purse, and jewels as a gage d'amour from a fictitious châtelaine de Dijon, who requests the seneschal to wear them next to his skin if he cares to enjoy her favors. Appearing before the emperor's court, Lïenor then accuses the seneschal of raping her and stealing her jewels. Having never seen the girl before, the seneschal quickly denies the charges, but his innocent plea collapses when he is required to reveal the belt and purse under his tunic. Confronted with this inculpating evidence, the seneschal requests an ordeal (*joïse*) of cold water. Taking an oath that he has not raped the girl, he enters the ordeal basin, sinks, and is straightway cleared. But so is Lïenor. If the seneschal has not raped the girl, neither has he had her maidenhood, because, as Lïenor proudly declares, 'je sui la pucele a la rose!' (vv. 4024–5101). Throughout the narrative Jean is scrupulous in observing current procedures for conducting the trial. He specifies the oath, the name of the church at Mainz where it took place, and identified the archbishop who administered it.

Equally important, Jean Renart fully integrated this ordeal into the belief in divine interventions. In accordance with the romance convention to invoke God and the saints Lïenor calls upon the Holy Spirit to counsel her as she devises her strategy. She expresses her confidence that Christ, who fed his entourage with five loaves of bread and two fishes in the Gospels, will now

---

14 For what follows on ordeals see Baldwin, 'The Crisis of the Ordeal', pp. 327–53.

produce an open miracle (*miracle aperte, Rose* v. 4268). As she enters the imperial court, she crosses herself and addresses her complaint interspersed with oaths now freighted with providential meaning: 'Noble and honored emperor in God's name, my dear lord, hear me, and God help me because I am in need. One day, not long ago, your seneschal came by chance . . .' (*Rose* vv. 4602–3, 4775–82). Jean's cold water ordeal did, in fact, effectively expose a double falsehood – Lïenor's fabricated accusation of rape against the seneschal and the seneschal's calumny against Lïenor.

Ordeals, however, had already come under suspicion in the romances of the late twelfth century which provided the 'horizon of expectations' of Jean's and Gerbert's audiences. The Tristan legend contained Iseut's equivocal oath which perverted the hot iron trial to exonerate the lovers' patent adultery (Béroul, vv. 4197–208), an oath that was repeated by Chrétien's Lancelot to conceal his adultery with Queen Guenièvre (*Charette* vv. 4971–84). The various branches of the *Roman de Renart*, from which Jean doubtlessly took his name, mercilessly parodied the false oaths which undermined the ordeal.[15] More important, ordeals came under blistering attack at Paris from Peter the Chanter who argued that they were profoundly immoral because they tempted God and that they did not always work as they should. Because they depended upon the clergy's blessing, he concluded that all ecclesiastics should be unconditionally excluded from involvement. After initial hesitation, Pope Innocent III accepted his teacher's arguments and prohibited the clergy henceforth from blessing iron or water in Canon 18 of the Lateran Council. In addition, he renewed the censures of previous councils to abolish trial by battle.[16]

The influence of the Council on judicial practice was mixed. The iron and water ordeals began to disappear, but judicial battle persisted more tenaciously. Similar results were obtained in literature as can be seen in Gerbert's *Violette* composed two decades later. Consciously replicating the *Rose*, the *Violette* contained two ordeals, but both substituted battle for the iron and water. As we have seen, Eurïaut was awaiting execution at the stake unjustly accused of murder. While the fire is being prepared, during which time the heroine offers her long prayer and declares her innocence, her lover Gerart arrives on the scene and proposes to defend her in battle. Eurïaut, however, offers to clear herself by ordeal (*juïse*), but Gerart rejects this alternative as long as he is prepared to fight. Needless to say, Gerart defeats her accuser in combat and forces him to admit Eurïaut's innocence (vv. 5332–643). Gerbert, like Jean, has been careful to follow the contemporary legal procedures, but this time the unilateral ordeal is explicitly rejected for the bilateral duel, and most significant, the clergy and their relics are conspicuously absent.

[15] Baldwin, 'Crisis of the Ordeal', pp. 336, 339 and 340.
[16] *Constitutiones*, p. 66; Mansi XXII, 1006–07. J. W. Baldwin, 'The Intellectual Preparation for the Cànon of 1215 against Ordeals', *Speculum* 36 (1961), 626–36.

The second example, however, reveals that the judicial scene was more complex. A second injustice remains to be righted. A second villain, Lisïart, count of Forez, has been able to calumniate the virtue of Eurïaut after spying on her in her bath. (He learns of the violet on her breast; hence, the romance's title.) Armed with this information, he wins a wager with Gerart, count of Nevers, who thereby forfeits his county. Gerart, citing new evidence, accuses Lisïart of falsehood in the court of King Louis at Montargis and challenges him to battle. Once again, the procedures of battle are meticulously respected, but this time the clergy reappear with their accoutrements. Mass is said, the testimony of Scripture is invoked, and relics are brought forth on which the two parties swear their oaths. 'By Saint Clement', Gerart protests, 'the liar does not tell the truth' (vv. 6368–70). For a final time God upholds justice by bringing the calumniator to defeat (vv. 6212–563). When this duel is compared with the first, however, the Lateran Council's influence on romances appears more equivocal. A dispute over the possession of land reintroduced the clergy and their instruments. Although iron and water were again omitted, battle remained an appropriate mode of proof in cases trying murder and disseizin.

A comparison between Jean Renart's romances and those of Gerbert de Montreuil's reveals some salient continuities of the religion of the laity before and after the Lateran Council. Since the narratives are preoccupied with secular affairs, the high clergy are relegated to the routinized performance of the liturgy on special occasions and high feasts. Abiding faith in God's intervention nonetheless remains strong. Despite attacks from some romance writers and clerics, the ordeal, as it was performed in the *Rose*, continued to embody the exercise of God's power up to the eve of the Council. Afterwards the specific devices of the iron and water were clearly discontinued. Throughout these romances lay religion was externalized and routinized in the liturgy of the clergy. The ordeals touched the body, not the soul. A personal sense of sin is absent. Divine justice intervenes to vindicate only Lïenor's good name; Eurïaut, about to die on the stake, has no thoughts about her own sins. In an emblematic scene at the opening of the *Rose*, Jean gaily introduced Conrad and his courtiers on a Spring hunt in amorous pursuit of ladies. After the assault – 'Chevaliers aux dames' – which is followed by post-orgasmic exhaustion, Jean commented: 'They did not think much about their souls. Relying on birds, they did not need bells, churches, or chaplains to arise them from their joys' (*Rose* vv. 222–7).

Interior Novelties: Hermits, Doctrine, Penance and Confession

These continuities may be found in all four of our romances, but Gerbert's *Continuation* composed after the Lateran Council in 1215 announced some startling novelties: a new clergy, a new interest in Christian doctrine, and a new preoccupation with a sacrament, that of penance. Although new to our four romances, these novelties first appeared in Chrétien's *Conte de graal*

composed before 1190, but Gerbert's *Continuation* fully elaborated their potential.

Alongside the high clergy in Gerbert's *Continuation* appeared a new figure, the religious hermit, who is isolated deep in the forest, lodged in a hermitage with a chapel close by, and lives alone except for an occasional cleric. Absent from the *L'Escoufle*, *Rose* and the *Violette*, this new figure may be found sporadically in the Tristan legend and Chrétien de Troyes's earlier romances, but he emerged as the sole clergyman in Chrétien's *Conte de Graal* and dominated Gerbert's *Continuation*. The phenomenon of the hermit who combined solitude, hospitality, friendship, prayer, and asceticism originated in late Antiquity and was revived at the end of the eleventh century in western France and England, the specific setting of the Arthurian legends.[17] In the romances the hermit's chief service was the daily celebration of mass, the *opus Dei* or the divine *mestier*.[18] Since the incessant journeys of the chevalier errant take him through vast stretches of forest, the hermit helps to satisfy his need not only for lodging but also for religion by celebrating the offices each morning. Chrétien's Perceval learns to practice daily observance only at the end of the *Conte du Graal*; thereafter and throughout Gerbert's *Continuation*, he attends divine services every day without fail.

In addition to saying masses the hermit's second function in Chrétien's *Graal* and Gerbert's *Continuation* was to instruct the laity in Christian doctrine. Those elements of faith appropriate for the laity were contained in the ancient creeds. The *Credo in Deum* (the so-called Apostles' Creed) was to be recited by the congregation during the mass after the reading of the Gospels, and priests were encouraged by contemporary synodical statutes to preach sermons which explained the different articles of belief.[19] Apparently Peter the Chanter was dissatisfied with this program for imparting theological instruction because he complained that in his day there was no virtue more lacking than that of faith. Thomas of Chobham noted that many are well versed in fatuous chansons and the vernacular deeds of Charlemagne but were totally ignorant of right faith.[20] These observations are confirmed by Jean Renart's romances

---

[17] On the historical phenomon of hermits see *L'eremitismo in occidente nei secoli XI e XII, Pubblicazioni dell'università Cattolica del Sacro Cuore, Contributi*, Serie terza, Miscellanea de Centro di Studi Medioevali 4 (Milan, 1965). On western France see Jean Becquet, 'L'érémitisme clérical et laïc dans l'Ouest de la France', pp. 182–211; on England, Hubert Dauphin, 'L'érémitisme en Angleterre aux XIe et XIIe siècles', pp. 271–310.

[18] For examples from the *Continuation*: vv. 7126–35, 7382–7, 8828–31, 10,252–4, 14,184–9, 15,746–801.

[19] Jean Beleth, *Summa de ecclesiasticis officiis*, ed. H. Douteil, CCCM 41a (1976), II, 73–5, 214, 218. C. 62, 84, Statutes of Paris (1197–1208) in *Les statuts synodaux français du XIIIe siècle*, vol. 1, *Les Statuts de Paris et le synodal de l'Ouest (XIIIe siécle)*, ed. O. Pontal, Collection de documents inédits sur l'histoire de France. Section de philologie et d'histoire jusqu'à 1610, 9 (Paris, 1971), pp. 74 and 84.

[20] Chanter, *Verbum*, PL 205, 268; Chobham, *Summa*, pp. 242–4.

which were completely devoid of doctrinal learning except for an occasional oath like 'God who was born without sin' (*Rose* v. 5308).

After Perceval is terrified by the knight-angels in the forest, the youth throws himself on the ground and recites the entire creed and all the prayers his mother had taught him (*Graal* vv. 155–8). This is less a profession of faith than the response of fear, comparable to crossing himself. After this opening scene, however, in the *Conte du graal*, Chrétien introduced an important innovation. The neophyte is instructed not only in the first tenants of chivalry, but also in the rudiments of faith by his mother, a number of others, and finally by his uncle, the hermit. Five years later on Good Friday Perceval is reproached for forgetting the Christian message: 'My dear friend, do you not believe in Jesus Christ who wrote the *novel loi* and gave it to Christians?' (vv. 6255–7). Throughout the subsequent continuations of Chrétien's *Graal* the 'new law' becomes the principal term for designating Christian doctrine.

Pressed by mounting heresy and theological controversy, Pope Innocent III and the Lateran Council were likewise dissatisfied with limiting doctrinal instruction to the articles of the ancient creeds. The opening canon of the Council offered a greatly expanded statement of Christian faith phrased in the most recent terminology fashioned in the French theological schools.[21] Diocesan church councils which convened in France and England shortly after the general council urged archdeacons to explain these new formulations of the faith to the priests in simple words so that they, in turn, could instruct their parishioners in the vernacular.[22] As if in response to this urging, Gerbert de Montreuil inserted into his *Roman de la violette* the most lengthy doctrinal statement in the vernacular to his day. We remember that to stall for time in this romance cliff-hanger the heroine Eurïaut offers a lengthy prayer. Her recitation outlines the principal tenets of Christian faith phrased according to the Biblical narrative of salvation (vv. 5182–334). Although the precise formulation is not that of the Council or of the theological schools, she is nonetheless performing simply (*simpliciter*) and in the vernacular the task which the diocesan statutes urged upon the clergy. Throughout the *Continuation* Gerbert assigns to his numerous hermits the duty of continuing Perceval's doctrinal instruction by elaborating the articles of faith, namely, the Creation, Fall, Incarnation, Atonement, and the Sacraments.

The sacrament to which Chrétien and Gerbert devoted most attention was undoubtedly that of private penance. The theologians had been working on this sacrament at Paris for nearly a century. The basic elements were formulated by Peter Abélard, systemized in the collections of Peter the Lombard, and their practical application was worked out by Peter the Chanter and his circle by the end of the century. The Lateran Council incorporated their

---

[21] *Constitutiones*, pp. 41–3; Mansi XXII, 982.
[22] C. 3, 4, Statutes of Salisbury (1217–19) in *Councils & Synods*, II(1), 61. C. 123, 124, 132, Statutes of Angers (1217–19) in *Statuts synodaux français*, ed. Pontal, I, 226–34.

results into the statutes of 1215.[23] Designed to treat sins committed after baptism, the new penance offered a radical alternative to the penitential system which had been in practice through the eleventh century. Rather than severe penalties and humiliations imposed publicly and ceremoniously on sinners, it was administered privately and secretly by confessors who adapted remedies according to the circumstances of the individual sinner. Setting a pattern, Abélard divided penance into three elements: *penitentia, confessio,* and *satisfactio.*[24] Although vernacular terminology varied slightly, Maurice de Sully, bishop of Paris, translated these as *repentance del corage, la confessions de la bouce,* and *la penitence.*[25]

The features of private penance were virtually absent in the early chansons de geste and romances.[26] In Béroul's *Tristan,* for example, the lovers feel little remorse for their adultery nor inclination to confess. Although the hermit Ogrin urges them to repent, he allows them to conceal their shame with deliberate lies (vv. 2353–4). We have seen that personal penance plays no role in Jean Renart's *Escoufle,* or *Rose* or in Gerbert's *Violette.* The contemporary Pierre de Blois complained that the laity can weep copiously over the tragedies of Arthur and Tristan, but are indifferent to God's love or true repentance.[27] Perceval's religious instruction omits penance at the opening of Chrétien's *Conte du graal,* but on Good Friday after five years of oblivious wanderings, Perceval meets a company of knights and ladies who have just confessed to a hermit. They not only remind him of the articles of faith, but also urge him to do penance on this day. This is the most important duty a Christian can perform who wishes to return to God. In distress for his sins Perceval locates the hermit, tearfully falls at his feet, seeks counsel, confesses his sins and receives the eucharist on Easter Day as a sign of forgiveness (vv. 6337–513). On at least eight major occasions throughout Gerbert's subsequent *Continuation* the numerous hermits and even Perceval himself exhort the practice of private penance to all who will listen.[28] What Chrétien and Gerbert called *repentance* was simply Abélard's *penitentia,* later called *contritio cordis* by the theologians.[29] Since Abélard's initial suggestion, the theologians agreed that contrition of the heart, or interior penance, was the most important element of

---

23 The comprehensive and authoritative study is Paul Anciaux, *La théologie du sacrement de pénitence au XIIe siècle,* Universitas catholica Lovaniensis, Dissertationes ad gradum magistri in Facultate theologica vel in Facultate Iuris Canonici consequendum conscriptae, Series II, 41 (Louvain, 1949). See also Bériou, 'Latran'.

24 *Peter Abelard's Ethics,* ed. D. E. Luscombe (Oxford, 1971), p. 76.

25 C. A. Robson, *Maurice of Sully and the Medieval Vernacular Homily* (Oxford, 1952), p. 98.

26 The principal study on penance in vernacular French is Jean-Charles Payen, *Le motif du repentir dans la littérature française médiévale (des origines à 1230)* (Geneva, 1967).

27 Pierre de Blois, *Liber de confessione,* PL 207, 1088–9.

28 *Continuation* vv. 29–33, 199–205, 2750–64, 5128–31, 9635–63, 9907–15, 9967–75, 14206–40, 14304–09, 15841–51.

29 Chanter, *Verbum,* PL 205, 339A; Courson, *Summa,* ed. Kennedy, p. 295; Chobham, *Summa,* p. 7.

penance. No sin could be forgiven without it; in extreme cases it was sufficient for complete remission. Robert of Courson understood the potential of this doctrine for the solitary knight errant of romance literature. What if one died in a forest where priests were unavailable? Confession, Robert replied, can also be performed with the interior lips of the heart as well as to a priest. If a sinner is contrite and confesses to God alone, he can be saved.[30]

At the end of the century the theologians' attention turned to the role of the second element, confession by the mouth, which, with satisfaction, belonged to the exterior forms of penance. Peter the Chanter defined confession as that act by which 'we confess to priests by mouth our sins nakedly (*nude*), openly (*aperte*), and stripped of skin (*excoriate*) with all their circumstances'. 'No circumstance should be hidden', he continued, 'that sin not be garbed in robes but revealed to the confessor as it was done.' Thomas of Chobham added that a priest cannot absolve sin which has not been confessed, because if a sin is hidden, there is no confession and no absolution.[31] Confession likewise stood at the center of Gerbert's attention. Approaching a hermit for confession, Perceval was urged to reveal all: 'In the name of penitence, my friend, I command you to say your sins without concealing any . . . You should know for a certainty that there is no hiding towards God. If, by chance, you receive seven mortal injuries and were healed of six, but left the seventh unattended without medicine, you would most surely die' (*Continuation* vv. 14206–20).

After confessing his sins on Good Friday, Perceval worthily partakes of communion on Easter Sunday in direct fulfillment of the hermit's command. After an extended discussion of the times when one should come to confession, Thomas of Chobham reported the custom that it sufficed to confess once a year. Although practice varied, in 1215 the Lateran Council mandated in the well-known Canon 21 that 'all believers of either sex after arriving at the age of discretion should each faithfully confess all of his or her sins to his or her priest at least once a year and strive to fulfill the enjoined penance so that he or she could reverently receive the sacrament of the eucharist at least at Easter'.[32]

Peter the Chanter elaborated the importance of the priest's role in confession. By recounting one's faults to an experienced priest the sinner can thereby receive instruction as to the gravity of his misdeeds so that he can better know how to do penance and how to avoid them in the future. Paying close attention to all of the accompanying circumstances, the priest would be able to distinguish between venial and mortal sins. This close attention to *circumstantia* became the hallmark of the Chanter's school and generated countless pages of casuistical discussion. Benefiting from this instruction, the priest is likened to a spiritual physician who has the skill of prescribing medicine to the sick. 'As a skilled doctor who pours wine and oil on the

---

[30] Courson, *Summa*, ed. Kennedy, pp. 300–1; Anciaux, *La théologie de pénitence*, pp. 427–8.

[31] Chanter, *Summa* II, 279, 306, 420; *Verbum*, PL 205, 343C; Chobham, *Summa*, pp. 264–5.

[32] Chobham, *Summa*, pp. 236–7. *Constitutiones*, pp. 67–8; Mansi XXII, 1007–10.

wounds of the sick', the Lateran Council continued, 'so the discerning and careful priest diligently inquires into the *circumstantia* of the sinner and the sin so that he may prudently understand what counsel he should offer and the appropriate remedies, since there are different means susceptible to healing the sick.' The *Summa confessorum* of Thomas of Chobham and other guides to confessors which originated in the school of Peter the Chanter were written to serve as medical handbooks for curing sin. Although the medical analogy was ancient, Gerbert continued in this tradition in having Perceval urge the Dragon Knight to seek divine healing. 'True confession is a doctor (*mire*) who heals without fire or iron those wounds for which one burns in hell' (*Continuation* vv. 9971–5).

In the decree stipulating annual confession the Lateran Council specified that each person should perform this duty to his or her priest (*proprio sacerdoti*). If, however, anyone claims just cause to confess his sins to another priest (*alieno sacerdoti*), he should first obtain permission from his own priest. This conciliar decree enacted the conclusions to which the Paris theologians had arrived after extensive discussions. Peter the Chanter argued that we are held to confess first to our own pastors to whom we are committed because they see us frequently, are able to warn us of dangers, and can also help against further occasions for sinning.[33] In Chrétien's *Graal* and Gerbert's *Continuation*, however it was scarcely feasible for knights-errant to return to their parish priests with any regularity. Those clergy most accessible were the hermits who were isolated in the forests and had never seen the penitent before. Throughout the wide-ranging debates of the Chanter's school as to whom one should confess, numerous possibilities were considered, including monks and hermits.[34] The synodical statutes after the Lateran Council likewise investigated the problem of monks and hermits hearing confessions.[35] After addressing the many possible objections, Thomas of Chobham arrived at an unequivocally negative conclusion.[36] Since cloistered monks and hermits have no parochial responsibilities, they should not hear confessions. Peter the Chanter, however, suggested a solution for the 'other priest' which his student Robert of Courson further developed. Robert distinguished three possibilities: (1) simply to offer advice, (2) to indicate penance, and (3) to enjoin penance as an obligation. Any knowledgeable person could perform the first two; 'the other priest', therefore, could legitimately perform the first two but only the last if he had the special permission of a superior.[37]

---

33 Chanter, *Summa* II, 429; III (2b), 693; Anciaux, *La théologie de pénitence*, pp. 591–2.
34 Chanter, *Summa* II, 312–31, 322–5, 425–6, 428–33, 439–40.
35 C. 45, Statutes of Cambrai (1238–48) in *Les statuts synodaux français du XIIIe siècle*, IV, *Les statuts synodaux de l'ancienne province de Reims (Cambrai, Arras, Noyon, Soissons et Tournai)*, ed. J. Avril, Collection de documents inédits sur l'histoire de France, Section d'histoire médiévale et de philologie 23 (Paris, 1995), p. 36. C. 34, Statutes of an English diocese (1222–25) in *Councils & Synods*, II(1), 145–6.
36 Chobham, *Summa*, p. 200.
37 Chanter, *Summa* II, 324 and 432. Courson, *Summa*, ed. Kennedy, p. 326.

Courson's solution thereby offered to hermits a legitimate role as confessors in romance literature. In Chrétien's *Graal* Perceval meets a lady on Good Friday who affirms that the hermit offered only *conseil* along with confession (vv. 6309–11). Perceval himself in great distress seizes the hermit's feet and pleads for *conseil* of which he has great need (vv. 6356–9). It is only after the hermit has revealed himself to be Perceval's uncle that he enjoins and gives (*enjoindre et doner*) penitence (vv. 6432–3). Once kinship was established between the confessor and the penitent, the hermit plausibly had the right to impose penitence as 'his own priest'. Throughout Gerbert's *Continuation*, however, none of the hermits who hears confessions was recorded as enjoining penitence. Apparently his ministrations were interpreted as merely offering advice as the theologians recommended.

Exterior penitence included both confession and the satisfactions of works. This was the 'penance imposed' (*injunctam penitentiam*) by the priest which the Lateran Council commanded the parishioner to perform between confession and the receiving of communion. Most often it was designated as *penitance* proper in the vernacular literatures and consisted of fasting, vigils, prayers and alms-giving which the priest might impose (*encarge*).[38] In the *Graal* Perceval's uncle enjoins him to attend church each day before setting off on the next leg of his journey, a duty which the young knight performs faithfully throughout the *Continuation*. In addition, Perceval is commanded to come to the aid of all ladies or orphans in need and to share the hermit's austere diet before communicating on Easter (vv. 6440–7).

In Gerbert's *Continuation*, however, not all confessions were followed by works of satisfaction. Peter the Chanter and Thomas of Chobham had argued that the first reason why confession by the mouth is necessary is because it produces shame (*erubescentia*). When anyone confesses odious wickedness to a priest, the shame that results becomes sufficient penitence. In fact, confession productive of shame is the greatest part of satisfaction or exterior penance.[39] In Béroul's *Tristan* the hermit had advised the lovers to disguise their shame (*honte*) with lies (vv. 2353–4), but the hermit who treated confession most fully in Gerbert's *Continuation* accepts the theologians' assessment. After warning Perceval against leaving any sin unconfessed, the hermit pleads with the knight not to allow shame (*vergoigne* = *verecundia*) to hinder him from confessing his sins. 'When God, our lord, sees a soul in distress over his sins, and when the soul avows its shame, God wipes its heart clean and remits the sins... Shame is the penitence (*la vergoigne est la penitence*) which greatly helps to alleviate (*alegier*) sin' (vv. 14228–39). As Thomas of Chobham concluded, shame (*erubescentia*) in confession is the sign of interior contrition of the heart, which, from the time of Abélard, had remained the one necessary element of all true penance. Accordingly, the wicked knights Lugarel and the Dragon

[38] Robson, *Maurice de Sully*, p. 98.
[39] Chanter, *Summa* II, 282; *Verbum*, PL 205, 342D–3A; 345B; Chobham, *Summa*, pp. 8–9, 203.

Knight in the *Continuation* are saved by the tears of their confessions, even though they are unable to perform works of satisfaction (vv. 10006–9, 14979–84). Although fear of eternal damnation remained a sanction, the new penance sought to encourage an acute sense of repentance which abhorred sins for their own sake.

The Ordeal *versus* Confession

Confession was confirmed in the Lateran Council at the same time that the ordeal was condemned. Although the one touched the soul and the other the body, both were in competition because both sought to deal with sinful or criminal behavior. Thomas of Chobham reported a depraved custom which permitted the friends of one who died suddenly to apply the cold water ordeal to ascertain whether the sinner had died in a state of penance and was thereby eligible for Christian burial. In Thomas's judgment the general prohibition of ordeals ruled out this practice altogether.[40] Robert of Courson considered interaction from the opposite direction. When a man accused of homicide was brought to the gallows, he was offered the choice of clearing himself by cold water or the hot iron. After the accused had made confession of the crime to a priest, what advice should the priest offer to the accused as part of penance? Courson did not consider the question of how the man's confession and absolution would affect the operation of the ordeal. His solution, like Chobham's, was simply to forbid the ordeal under all circumstances.[41]

The question which Courson neglected to consider – how did confession affect the ordeal? – was discussed extensively in collections of *exempla* compiled by Cistercians in the two decades surrounding the Lateran Council. The most notable was the *Dialogus miraculorum* of Caesar of Heisterbach from the Rhine valley.[42] A number of these *exempla* argued without equivocation that true confession was capable of saving a guilty defendant from the judgment of an ordeal. Among the cases cited was that of a certain man who was accused of disbelief in the sacraments. Under fear he agreed to submit to the hot iron, but before the appointed day he repented of his lack of faith, confessed it to a priest and received due penance. Carrying the iron without harm, he praised the power of confession to cleanse him from all disbelief.[43] Sincere confession was even able to efface the marks of the ordeal after it had

---

40 Chobham, *Summa*, pp. 260–1.
41 Courson, *Summa*, ed. Kennedy, p. 303.
42 Jacques Berlioz, 'Les ordalies dans les exempla de la confession (XIIIe–XIV siècles)', in *L'aveu*, pp. 315–40. In addition to the well-known *Dialogus miraculorum* (1224–26) of Caesar of Heisterbach is the collection from the Cistercian abbey of Beaupré (*c.* 1200). See Brian Patrick McGuire, 'The Cistercians and the Rise of the Exempla in Early Thirteenth-Century France: A Re-evaluation of Paris BN MS Lat. 15912', *Classica et mediaevalia* 34 (1983), 211–67.
43 Berlioz, 'Les ordalies', p. 323, note 20.

already been performed.[44] Those, however, who in contempt of confession relapsed into their wicked ways after having been cleared by the ordeal were punished more severely. An adulterous woman, for example, who made confession and then was exonerated by the iron, but who resumed her old habits later, was burned horribly by the same iron when she picked it up in jest.[45] In these Cistercian collections, therefore, confession openly challenged the ordeal and sought to obstruct its decisions. Caesar of Heisterbach acknowledged that these cases were exceptional – this was not the normal function of confession – but he raised them as *exempla* to demonstrate the confession's efficacy as medicine for the soul.[46] This was a possible meaning of Gerbert de Montreuil's assertion that true confession is a doctor who heals without fire and iron those wounds which consume endlessly in hell (vv. 9971–5).

In Caesar's terminology the ordeal was designated a marvel (*mirabile*) but in these *exempla* confession was termed a *miraculum*.[47] The Chanter called penance the greatest of miracles (*maximum miraculum*).[48] A marvel was against nature (*contra naturam*) – the Chanter could have added by the procuration of the devil and the permission of God[49] – but a miracle, although also against nature, occurred through God's direct intervention. In the *Rose* Lïenor had prayed to God for a *miracle aperte* (v. 4268) like those in the Bible. Except for the ordeal Jean Renart's romances and Gerbert's *Violette* were entirely free from the marvelous or the supernatural. Under the inspiration of the Breton lais, however, romances, such as those of Chrétien, contained numerous marvels (*merveilles, merveillos*) and prodigies.[50] Following Chrétien closely, Gerbert, unlike his *Violette*, likewise included numerous fantastic beasts, serpents, ointments, and other wonders.[51] The archetype of the *merveille* in romance literature, however, was undoubtedly the legend of the grail, which in Chrétien's initial version consisted of a vessel and a lance which bled – less spectacular when compared with later versions. Whether intentional or not, Chrétien's great stroke of genius was to have left his story unfinished, which generated a vast literature to supply the ending. In the verse continuations

---

44 Caesar, *Dialogus* III.xvi, I, 132.
45 Berlioz, 'Les ordalies', p. 325, note 26.
46 Caesar, *Dialogus* III.xix, I, 135.
47 Caesar's precise term is the comparative adverb *mirabilius contra naturam*, *Dialogus* X.xxxv, II, 243. This example occurs in a section devoted to *De miraculis*. Confession was specifically designated *miraculum*, as was to be expected in a collection of miracle stories. *Dialogus* III.xv, I, 131. Berlioz, 'Les ordalies', pp. 334–5.
48 Chanter, *Summa* II, 214.
49 An example of this frequently used phrase: *domino permittente propter peccata nostra vel diabolo procurante*. Chanter, *Verbum*, Long Version, f. 99va.
50 Lucienne Carasso-Bulow has studied them in *The Merveilleux in Chrétien de Troyes' Romances* (Geneva, 1976).
51 For some examples in Gerbert, *Continuation*: beasts, vv. 8379–406; serpents, vv. 573, 8674–728; ointments, vv. 4869–6154; perilous seat, vv. 1159–612; magic letter, vv. 899–1158; magic pillar, vv. 963–7; magic ointment, vv. 5075–8, 5601–25.

which were attached directly to Chrétien as well as in the prose versions, these sequels searched for the meaning (*senefiance*) of the grail vision which Chrétien's inept Perceval had neglected to ask of the Fisher King.

Gerbert attached his *Continuation* to the end of the Second continuation in verse (the so-called Wauchier de Denain or Perceval Continuation).[52] Perceval had just paid a second visit to the Grail Castle, witnessed the ceremony, and had mended the sword except for a tiny notch in the blade. Awaiting a response to his question over the meaning of what he saw, the Second Continuation breaks off before the Fisher King can answer. At this moment of high anticipation for the audience Gerbert took up his version, but he deflected a direct answer:

> 'I shall not speak about the grail, nor will you yet know the secret of the lance', the king replies. 'But listen – I shall tell you this: I know of no man in this world who can ever know about these things but you; but make sure that you do not lose that prize through sin. And if you do fall into sin and anger God, then confess and repent and abandon sin and do thorough penance. And know this too . . . that if you can return here, it could well be that you'll repair the notch, and then you can ask about the grail and the lance; and truly then, you may be sure, you would know the profound truth, the secrets and the divine mystery' (vv. 12–42).

Fully obedient, therefore, Perceval begins a long journey of adventures to purify himself of his sins and merit another grail vision. After 17,000 lines when the hero arrives at the Grail Castle for a third time at the end of the *Continuation*, he witnesses the ceremony, repairs the notch perfectly, and awaits a response to his question, but once again Gerbert breaks off like his predecessor, leaving his audience where he had first found them (vv. 17040–86). This may strike us as a pure tease, but Gerbert did consent to supply the meaning (*senefiance*) for other secondary marvels. Only the supreme quest of the grail lies without a direct response because the full answer is, in effect, the arduous process of penance itself, the central subject to which Gerbert devoted his entire romance. Confession has become the true miracle and has thereby displaced the grail as the supreme *merveille*.

In effect, Gerbert de Montreuil's transformation of the grail legend into an allegory of penance was comparable to Peter the Chanter's treatment of ordeals and modern miracles a generation earlier. When he refused to accept the ordeal as a modern miracle, Peter was thereby obliged to account for the difference between Old Testament days when miracles were permitted and modern times when they are to be avoided. In ancient times the Lord allowed miracles to be performed for the spreading of the faith; now that Christian belief is widespread God prefers from the faithful good works rather than

---

[52] Second Continuation vv. 32584–94 in *The Continuations of the Old French Perceval of Chrétien de Troyes*, ed. W. Roach (Philadelphia, 1971), IV, 512. Gerbert, *Continuation*, ed. Williams, I, 1.

wonders. Exorcists, for example, no longer cast out demons as they did in the primitive church.[53] When the Devil suggested to Christ that he change stones into bread, Jesus replied: 'It is written that man does not live by bread alone but by every word that proceeds from the mouth of God' (Matthew 4.3–4). The *Gloss* elaborated that Scripture teaches us to fight more with doctrine than with miracles. The Devil is overcome not through swords or miracles but by faith and good works.[54] Just as Peter the Chanter taught that modern miracles and the ordeal should now give way to faith and good works, so Gerbert likewise sought to replace the marvellous grail of Arthurian legend with the penitential duties of contrition and confession now enjoined by the Lateran council on all Christians.

Jean Renart's two romances and Gerbert de Montreuil's *Violette* presented to their lay audiences a religion which consisted chiefly of routinized liturgy performed by the high clergy on the great liturgical feasts. It was driven by a firm belief in an omnipresent and omnipotent God who was moved to respond to prayer, holy gestures, and pilgrimages. Supremely emblematised by the ordeal, this was a god whose power was focussed on the human body. A generation after Jean, Gerbert de Montreuil's *Continuation* and to a lesser extent his *Violette* presented to later audiences a new clergy, the hermits, who celebrated the daily offices, preached the *novel loi* of doctrine, and urged the purging of penance with emphasis on contrition and confession – all made available to the solitary and wandering knight of romance. As an interiorized religion of the soul, it competed with but did not entirely replace the exteriorized forms of the previous generation. Nor was the chronological divide between the two generations abrupt despite Jean's preceding and Gerbert's following the Lateran Council. The chief features which Gerbert developed in his *Continuation* had already appeared in Chrétien's *Conte du graal* before the Council at a time when the Chanter's circle had begun their discussions of the new penance. Although relinquishing the iron and water, judicial practices nonetheless clung to judicial battle. The thrust towards interiority, however, was so strong that Gerbert was prepared to relegate the grail, the supreme *merveille* of romance, to the status of the ordeal, and to subsume both of them to the nearly miraculous power of contrition and confession. Gerbert's *Continuation*, we know, was not the end of the quest for the grail. The answers he neglected to provide were finally supplied by the near-contemporary Manessier at the same point in the narrative and by the prose *Queste del saint graal*.[55] Nor did theological discussion subside with the Chanter's school. Subsequent theologians shifted their emphasis on contrition

---

[53] Chanter, *Verbum*, PL 205, 227CD and 228CD.
[54] Chanter, *Verbum*, PL 205, 226D and 228B.
[55] The Third Continuation by Manessier in *The Continuations of the Old French Perceval of Chrétien de Troyes*, ed. W. Roach (Philadelphia, 1983), V, and *La queste del saint graal*, ed. A. Pauphilet, Les classiques français du moyen âge (Paris, 1984).

of the heart and confession of the mouth to the works of satisfaction, now motivated less by abhorrence of sin than by fear of judgment.[56] Gerbert de Montreuil nonetheless enregisters an important moment in the history of lay Christianity when audiences began to be receptive to the teaching of the Paris theologians on the interior workings of contrition and confession.

[56] For the later development, see Nicole Bériou, 'La confession dans les écrits théologiques et pastoraux du XIIIe siècle: Médication de l'âme ou démarche judiciaire?', in *L'aveu*, pp. 261–82.

INDEX

The following index lists names and works of medieval writers, names only of post-medieval writers, and place-names. The list under the heading 'Manuscripts' excludes the lists of manuscripts of the Tripartite Penitentials (pp. 55–61) and William of Auvergne's *De poenitentia* (part of *De sacramentis*) and *Tractatus novus de poenitentia* (pp. 98–9 n. 8). Medieval names and titles of works have not been standardised to one language.

Lightning Source UK Ltd.
Milton Keynes UK
UKOW051246081112

201878UK00001B/40/A